HOW CAN EUROPE SURVIVE

HANS F. SENNHOLZ

D. VAN NOSTRAND COMPANY, INC.

Toronto   New York   London

NEW YORK

D. Van Nostrand Company, Inc., 250 Fourth Avenue, New York 3

TORONTO

D. Van Nostrand Company (Canada), Ltd., 25 Hollinger Road, Toronto

LONDON

Macmillan & Company, Ltd., St. Martin's Street, London, W.C. 2

309.24
.S97

PRINTED IN THE UNITED STATES OF AMERICA

Contents

Acknowledgment

I am grateful to the Earhart Foundation, Ann Arbor, Michigan and Mr. J. H. Pew, whose generous assistance have made this work possible. I am greatly indebted to Dr. Ludwig von Mises for having read the manuscript and having made many valuable suggestions. I thank Miss Vernelia Crawford for the preparation of the index and acknowledge with gratitude the assistance given me by my wife in all stages of this book.

H. F. S.

Introduction

LET us suppose that I were to maintain that import restrictions gain us the friendship of neighboring countries, exchange controls enhance the freedom of citizens, and the nationalization and blocking of foreigners' property make for close international cooperation and integration. Thus stated these propositions might indeed seem startling for an economist to advance. And yet contemporary economic thought as advocated by numerous famous economists and accepted by many governments consists precisely of such propositions. They urge us to adopt policies of welfare planning which depend for their effectiveness on import and export prohibitions, tariffs, exchange controls, and many other government measures of enforcement. But simultaneously the governments whom they urge to impose discriminatory restrictions are to cooperate with each other in the elimination of the very effects which restrictions bring about.

Policies of government planning and welfare and the disintegration of the world economy into heterogeneous national units are two aspects of the same phenomenon. Like a coin on whose two sides two different symbols are impressed, government planning and the disintegration of the world market are two aspects of a single problem. The upper side of the coin, visible and familiar to everybody, shows the fascinating picture of a welfare state designed by our welfare economists and put into effect by progressive governments. The other side of the coin reveals a picture that indicates the price, expressed in terms of economic nationalism and international conflict, which must be paid for the realization of the welfare state. That is to say, every welfare measure by a national government bears inescapable effects on foreign relations and the international exchange of goods.

1

Long before our age of world wars and welfare states, men dreamed of a united Europe. Plans of unification always emerged when the system of political organization resulted in disintegration and separation. During the age of mercantilism, Europe was always fighting or preparing to fight. Throughout this period numerous writers and statesmen devised plans for states to pool part of their sovereign powers or to create systems of collective security and permanent international arbitration. Men were dreaming and praying for perpetual peace and international cooperation.[1]

During the nineteenth century the idea of European unity receded into the background. It was a century of individual freedom and decreasing international restrictions upon the movement of men, goods, and capital. The world economy was an interdependent system, on the way to economic unification which makes political unification irrelevant. It was an era of unprecedented progress.

The liberal century was followed by the age of economic and social planning. And, again, ready plans for international unification and government cooperation followed the early symptoms of disintegration and international conflict. In order to stem the inescapable effects of prevailing political and social ideologies, modern writers and statesmen began to design ready solutions. "Europe must unite," said Winston Churchill. "The Western nations must unite," said others. And these admonitions have been echoed again and again by such people as Paul van Zeeland, Léon Blum, General de Gaulle, Count Sforza, Konrad Adenauer, Robert Schuman and many other European and American statesmen and politicians. Scarcely a dissenting voice is heard. Everybody concerned agrees and nobody objects. Every sort of association for unification is formed, and an immense literature is written about the last choice open to the Western nations: unite or perish.

To prevent the inescapable effects of our economic and social policies, we are urged to unite. But can we counteract the effects through unification and continue to adhere to the causes of disintegration? Our contemporary adherents of unification assure us we can. You are free to continue your social and economic policies, they say, provided you unite.

A selection of famous doctrines and plans of unification is analyzed in Part Two of this treatise. As will be shown, most of the ready plans and schemes offer government cooperation as the panacea for present deplorable world conditions. Scarcely an author has

---

[1] For a historical presentation of the United Europe idea, see Edouard Bonnefous, *L'Europe face à son destin*, Presses Universitaires de France, Paris, 1952.

ever dealt with the causes of disintegration and disunity. But as long as the causes of conflict are not recognized and removed, there cannot be cooperation. A plan that neglects to go to the root of the evil must, therefore, be found wanting and superficial.

The several institutions for the promotion of unity set up by Western European governments are analyzed in Part Three. They are examined in the light of the compatibility of their functions with the true principles of unification. Where the objectives and means applied by the several institutions are found to be incompatible with the principles of unification, failure is believed to be inevitable.

In Part Four, the author is searching for a world economy of peaceful cooperation, a world without trade barriers and restrictions upon the liberty of man, a world without incentives for war and aggression. He commends his conclusions to all men working and praying for peace and the advancement of mankind.

On Peace
and Present-day Ideologies

THE friends of socialism and interventionism maintain that the free market economy has failed in this age of atomic power and giant cities, and that it hurts the vital interests of the public. They condemn the market economy for having brought about war and depression, slavery, oppression and exploitation of the immense majority of the people by greedy businessmen and capitalists. Having blamed the market economy for every conceivable vice, past and present, they proceed to offer as a ready panacea their various plans of government authority as a substitute for the plans of free individuals. Thus, they maintain, order and stability, welfare and prosperity, would replace the "anarchy of production." The socialists advocate complete and immediate abolition of the market economy and its freedoms for individuals, and the setting up of one central agency to plan and regulate all economic activity. The interventionists differ from the socialists in that they recommend a third system which is said to retain the advantages of socialism and the market economy, and avoid the shortcomings of both. This system of "the middle-of-the road" concurs with socialism in its critique and rejection of the unhampered market economy and, if not abandoned in time, will also lead to socialism.

THE CASE FOR INTERVENTIONISM

The case for government planning and middle-of-the-road policies is most fervently presented by Alvin H. Hansen in his book *Eco-*

6

nomic Policy and Full Employment.[1] "The plain fact is," says Alvin
H. Hansen, "that all advanced individual nations have moved very
far away from the atomistic individualism of the mid-nineteenth century. Then economic opportunity meant essentially a chance to
operate your own farm or small business. Today economic opportunity means largely a chance to get a job. Then the bulk of the
population lived in the country—on farms or in small villages. Today they live in great urban centers. Industrialization and urbanization have come upon us with a speed that no one could have
imagined in 1850. Torn from the old individualist pattern of work
and living into a society characterized by great factories and giant
cities, modern man must erect a new social structure adapted to the
changed conditions."[2] The *new social structure* differs from that of
the nineteenth century inasmuch as it not only must keep open the
door for new enterprise and the acquisition of a farm, but also it
makes it a primary responsibility for modern society to maintain
at all times *adequate employment opportunities.* "In all modern
countries," says Hansen, "the trend of technology, whether in industry, transportation, or distribution, restricts economic opportunity, for the overwhelming majority, to the getting of a job—not
to establishing a business of their own."[3] A hundred years ago the
right to free land meant economic opportunity; today it is the right
to useful, remunerative, and regular employment. To maintain a
high and stable level of employment should, therefore, be the primary aim and *responsibility of government.* This is the new responsibility which the political democracies of our time must
undertake.

Hansen anticipates innumerable difficulties in the government
pursuit of a full-employment policy. But the fact that this experiment will prove difficult should not permit us to evade it. The
full-employment experiment will command the ingenuity and re-

sourcefulness of government officials and government economists for many decades to come. In Hansen's concept of a free society, personal liberty will be preserved by a government guarantee of the citizen's right to choose between numerous employers, including private entrepreneurs, cooperatives, and governments. "Thus the great goal of full employment, if it is to be achieved in a free society, involves planning to make the market economy function in a workable manner so as to provide adequate employment opportunities together with the privilege of choice between different employers." [4]

Democratic Planning. Hansen rejoices in the active role present-day government must take in economic life. "If the democratic countries were not now planning and developing new institutional arrangements designed to make the market economy function more effectively than it did in the past," he states, "the future would be black indeed." [5] Conditions have changed and, therefore, our institutions must change to meet the problems of today. New plans, domestic and international, should be devised, for "the old market economy has broken down. It failed us utterly in the two decades between the two world wars. In England unemployment, never falling below 10 per cent, reached in some years 22 per cent of the labor force and averaged 14 to 15 per cent for the entire decades. In the United States, taking account of the whole interwar period, the spotty twenties and the depressed thirties, unemployment averaged about 12 per cent, and in the worst years, 1932-1933, reached 24 to 25 per cent of the labor force." [6] The prewar market economy cannot be restored, for "the great depression which shook the entire world and fanned the flames of the ensuing world conflagration" has shattered all hopes for its restoration. International economic cooperation and division of labor were destroyed and economic warfare was substituted. Thus the old order collapsed.

Modern government should rely upon three measures for a policy of stability and full employment: (1) Government spending for public investments should supplement private spending, acting as a balance wheel to the private sector; (2) a broad and comprehensive social security system should be introduced to sustain and advance the level of income and spending; (3) variations in the basic income-tax rate should counteract the fluctuations of the business cycle.

International Planning. National planning for stability and wel-

4 *Ibid.*, p. 17.
5 *Ibid.*, p. 17.
6 *Ibid.*, pp. 17, 18.

fare must not stop short at the national boundaries but must be supplemented by government planning on an international level to achieve international stability and expansion. Hansen expresses his satisfaction regarding the numerous international conferences held by the leading governments during and after World War II. He expressly mentions the world conference on Relief and Rehabilitation in Atlantic City, on Food and Agriculture in Hot Springs, on international monetary problems in Bretton Woods, and the conference on the United Nations Charter in Dumbarton Oaks and San Francisco. He praises the United Nations Social and Economic Council through which the member nations endeavor to solve the common economic problems of stability and full employment. Only nations that succeed in the realization of domestic stability can contribute to international stability and be good neighbors in the family of nations. To contribute to international stability the United States government must, above all, achieve a high and stable level of prosperity. But also new international institutions are needed if we are to escape the disastrous effects of policies of confusion and planlessness. "We have become convinced, at long last," Hansen proclaims, "that the old machinery will not work. In all the advanced countries we are reaching some degree of agreement about what we need to do to reshape our world in order to make it again a functioning and manageable system." [7]

Progressive Programs Adopted. The programs of government planning and development designed by our numerous progressive economists are busily put into effect by governments all over the world. During the last thirty years the local, state, and federal governments in the *United States* have assumed an ever-increasing responsibility and authority for the control of the entire economic system. Government indeed has not taken over every farm, business, and factory, but it has assumed complete control over the basic functions of credit, electric power, transportation, and insurance, including the so-called welfare activities. The rest of the economic system has remained in private hands which are carefully controlled and supervised by numerous government bureaus. The "record of progress," as our progressive economists like to call it, is indeed very impressive. It includes progressive principles of taxation, expenditure, and borrowing, monetary depreciation and devaluation, progressive banking and security exchange legislation, an ever-expanding system of social security, government home financing and guaranteeing, public housing and public works, etc. Finally,

[7] *Ibid.*, p. 25.

the Employment Act of 1946 declared it the continuing policy and responsibility of government to secure maximum employment, production, and purchasing power.

In *England* the Churchill government follows a program which it issued in May, 1944, under the title "White Paper on Employment Policy" which was supplemented by Sir William Beveridge's report on "Full Employment in a Free Society," published in June, 1944. The main elements in contemporary British government planning are based on these two documents and can be described as follows: (1) financial control; (2) control over raw materials; and (3) price control.

The most important financial control for the sake of British economic stability and full employment is government control over foreign exchange transactions the principles of which are laid down in the Exchange Control Act of 1947. This act confers on the Treasury the power to regulate the buying and selling and the lending and borrowing of foreign exchange and gold, the making of payments to foreigners, the issue or transfer of securities to foreigners, the import and export of securities, and the transfer and settlement of property outside the United Kingdom. The Borrowing Act of July 1946 imposed government controls on borrowing and issuing new securities. It set up a Capital Issues Committee to regulate new issues according to the general government program of capital investment.

The British government also imposed controls on the purchase and sale of raw materials. As most raw materials have to be imported from abroad, this control is largely exercised through foreign exchange control, import licenses, and systems of allocation of raw materials to the consuming industries. These controls, finally, are supplemented by a system of government price control. Maximum prices are fixed for a large number of commodities and services and a purchase tax is levied to supplement price controls. Also a broad system of social security and national health insurance serves the general purpose of sustaining and advancing the national level of spending and employment.

The *Canadian* government is committed to a policy of stability and full employment. The levels of employment and income are planned to be greatly above those ruling before the war which, according to Hansen, will call for government expenditures at higher than prewar levels. The Canadian government also embarked upon policies "to stabilize markets and purchasing power through export credits, floor prices, public investment, and extended social serv-

ices." [8] For periods of declining business the Canadian government
has pledged itself to expand expenditures boldly and deliberately
plan for large deficits.

In *Australia* the government has issued two documents declaring
its responsibility to stimulate spending to the extent necessary to
maintain full employment. According to these official papers, a
minimum program of public investment is believed to be vital for a
high standard of living, and a compensatory program of public
spending is prepared to attain a full-employment economy. In addition, the Australian government is committed to a high level of
spending for social services, such as invalid and old-age pensions,
child endowment and widows' pensions, education, health and medical services, kindergartens and libraries. Numerous other government controls are imposed to stabilize the private sector of economy
and eliminate fluctuations as far as possible.

Another government which is frequently applauded by progressive economists for its extensive economic planning is the *Swedish*
government. It is owner of the public utilities, the telephone and
telegraph system, the railroads, large parts of the forests, and it
holds liquor and tobacco monopolies. Furthermore, numerous pulp
and sawmills, iron works, and other enterprises are owned by the
Swedish government. This extensive government ownership in
diversified fields of production, says Hansen, puts Sweden "in a
peculiarly favorable position to implement effectively public investment in its over-all employment program." [9] That is to say,
widespread government ownership of the means of production
greatly facilitates a policy of full employment and a high standard of
living.

For purposes of full employment and economic stability the Swedish government has introduced a system of subsidies to agriculture
and forestry. To direct private investment various taxes have been
levied or exemption from such taxes has been granted. A special
agency has been created that is charged with stockpiling during a
period of recession. Through the device of stockpiling it is hoped
that each branch of production will be kept fully employed, which
would avoid the shifting of labor and capital to public works and
other fields of government spending. Furthermore, several other
measures have been adopted to sustain and stimulate spending and
consumption.

This system of planned economy as advocated by numerous pro-

[8] *Ibid.*, p. 82.
[9] *Ibid.*, p. 100.

gressive economists has gradually spread *all over the world* and has been accepted by all nations that are not outright socialist or communist. It is the system called interventionism which is preparatory to socialism. It is a system of continuous government interference and transformation of the market economy into socialism.

THE FALLACIES

The Condemnation of the Market Economy. Progressive economists unanimously base their clamor for government planning and control over the economic system on the assertion that the market economy no longer works, that it is identical with a state of confusion and planlessness, and that economic freedom leads to depression, exploitation, and war. Hansen declares the old machinery, i.e., the market economy, does not work. It has broken down and has lead to decades of depression, unemployment, and world conflagration. We must reshape the world "in order to make it again a functioning and manageable system."

This most popular interpretation of recent history reveals a tragic distortion of the causal relations of historic phenomena. It flagrantly contradicts elementary rules of causal explanation based on simple economic reasoning and rejects all rules of scientific relevance. Serious and obvious mistakes in political and economic reasoning and historical understanding render the entire system of "progressive thought" hollow and empty. However, it derives its eminent importance from the fact that it is accepted by public opinion and applied by numerous governments all over the world. Ideas find their realization in human action and the results of such action, no matter whether they are derived from correct or faulty reasoning, from established facts or mere superstitions.

The assertion that it was the market economy and its individual freedoms which inaugurated this age of economic turmoil and international conflict is unsupported by facts or reasoning. It is true, during the two decades between the two world wars, that the market economies of the Western nations broke down or failed to function effectively. But why? Why did they fail to work effectively in our century after having made the nineteenth century the great century of Western civilization? Our progressive economists either entirely fail to answer this important question, or they take refuge behind explanations that defy all scientific thought. Hansen, for example, points to great factories, giant cities, technology, industrialization, and urbanization as the deciding factors of changed conditions requiring a new social structure. That is to say, the market economy, which is the very system that created the great factories, giant cities, etc., is said to have collapsed because of its most beneficial effects. This is absurd! Because our cities are larger than they were some time ago, we are urged to resort to central planning! Because our factories have increased in size and productivity, we are urged to adopt a new social structure. Because our technological knowledge has advanced during the last decades, we are to resort to government control. Because our means of transportation are more efficient and comfortable, we are urged to relinquish the freedoms of our forebears. Such an explanation lacks any basis in reason or fact.

There is only one reason for an unsatisfactory operation of the market economy: it is government intervention. A market economy that is crippled and mutilated, modified and hampered by a host of government regulators and planners can no longer operate as smoothly as a free market economy. Government interference is intended to have certain effects and, indeed, always has. But as far as its actual effects are concerned, whether intended or unforeseen and undesirable, the market economy must be acquitted from all responsibility. Human principles of justice and fairness forbid us to condemn someone for a crime which not he but someone else committed. And justice and fairness also forbid us to condemn the market economy for undesirable conditions which someone else brought about. How, for example, can the market economy be declared responsible for inflation and its concomitant effects? It is the government that regulates the money supply. How can we blame a butcher or baker for a crime, in this case inflation and its effects upon prices, which the Secretary of the Treasury and the governors of the Reserve Banks committed? How can we possibly blame the market economy for periods of depression and unemployment if our economic planners and regulators conduct policies resulting in depression and unemployment? But this is precisely what our progressive economists are trying to do. They blame the market economy for the interwar period with all its deficiencies, its wounds and mutilations, which, in fact, the planners themselves inflicted upon it.

TWENTY YEARS OF GOVERNMENT PLANNING

Let us pause here for a moment to review the economic history of the two decades between the two world wars. Throughout World War I the governments of the belligerents of Continental Europe imposed socialist controls upon their economies and inflated their currencies at an unprecedented rate. During the postwar period of "reconstruction" the monetary depreciation in Europe moved forward rapidly. Europe was buying enormous quantities of goods on credit from the United States and other parts of the world, which created a fictitious prosperity. The funds which Europe needed for the purchase of materials were largely financed by the United States government which, in the two years following the Armistice, spent practically as much money as it had spent during the war itself. The United States, to which the world was heavily indebted, rather preferred to grant loans than to allow foreign countries to pay their debts with goods imported. Reaction and collapse were inevitable and, in 1920, the first postwar crisis appeared.

In 1921 and 1922 the *United States* government under President Harding continued to raise the tariffs, first by an agricultural tariff bill that had relatively little significance because American agriculture is an export industry and, second, by the Fordney Tariff Act of 1922 that raised rates sharply on many manufactured goods. This tariff imposed a grave barrier against European industrial revival and severely hurt the export trade of the American farmer who primarily sold his products to Europe. Europeans who could not sell their industrial goods on American markets obviously could not buy from America, unless the U. S. government was willing to continue to finance these purchases. The American tariff legislation granting protection to domestic industries thus cut the American farmer from his export markets which amounted to 60% of the cotton produced, 40% of the lard, more than 20% of the wheat, 40% of the tobacco. It created a serious agricultural problem in the United States which plagues us to this very day.[10]

In *Japan* conditions were worse. Early in 1920, the progressive economists and government officials got together and destroyed the market economy. The decline in commodity prices was arrested and the Japanese government held the prices above the receding world prices for seven years. During these years Japan suffered from chronic industrial stagnation and at the end, in 1927, many great branch bank systems as well as many export industries broke down. "It was a stupid policy," said Anderson. "In the effort to avert losses on inventory representing one year's production, Japan lost seven years, only to incur greatly exaggerated losses at the end. The New Deal philosophy began in Japan in early 1920—a planned economy under government direction designed to prevent natural

[10] Benjamin M. Anderson, *Economics and the Public Welfare*, D. Van Nostrand, Co., Inc., New York, 1949, p. 90.

market forces from operating and, above all, designed to protect
the general price level." [11]

In *Germany* the government embarked upon a policy of inflation
at an unprecedented rate. The central bank printed paper money
to supply the government with funds with which to bring about full
employment and prosperity. From the summer of 1919 to the time
of the Dawes Plan in 1924 the price for German marks in foreign
exchange markets dropped from 8 cents per mark to about 16 trillion
marks to the dollar. Vast quantities of newly created marks were
sold by the German government in the speculative foreign exchange
markets at whatever price they would bring. This money sold
abroad brought in, year after year, the foreign exchange with which
foreign goods could be purchased. The German people thus could
consume more than it produced at the expense of the buyers of
marks in foreign countries. The incredible depreciation of German
marks naturally had an utterly demoralizing effect upon the economic life of this industrial nation. The German economic middle
class was pretty well wiped out in this process. Working capital of
German enterprises largely disappeared and the standard of life of
the people sank steadily.

In *France* weak and short-lived governments ran up enormous
deficits, which progressive economists like to glorify and call "government investment," to secure full employment and prosperity. In
1919 the government deficits amounted to 46.7 billion francs; in
1920, 42 billions; in 1921, 27.9 billions; in 1922, 18.9 billions; in 1923,
16.6 billions; and in 1924, 14.1 billions.[12] In the foreign exchange
market the franc dropped continuously and prices for commodities
rose. Throughout this period French and foreign liquid capital left
France and went into foreign values. French private holdings of
gold, dollars, sterling, Swiss francs, Dutch guilders, and securities of
foreign countries increased considerably while the French economy
lacked funds for expansion and improvements. French conditions
only improved when, in July 1926, Poincaré began cutting government expenditures and government pensions, dismissing needless
government officials, and creating a fiscal surplus.

The *British* government brought economic distress and turmoil to
its people through an entirely different set of interventionist measures. At the end of World War I Britain began to straighten out her
public finances, balanced her budget, and even reduced her public
debt. The pound, which had depreciated from the par of $4.8668 to

[11] *Ibid.*, pp. 75, 76.
[12] *Ibid.*, p. 100.

a low of $3.18 in February of 1920, recovered quickly and sold at approximately 10% below parity in early 1925. Under the leadership of Winston Churchill as Chancellor of the Exchequer the British government then embarked upon an extremely harmful policy of *deflation* in order to bring the pound back to par. While a parity of 90% of the old par had been suitable for monetary stabilization, Churchill, motivated by pride in the British monetary tradition and Britain's position as leading banker of the world, but with an utter ignorance of the economic consequences of a policy of deflation, preferred to go all the way back to the prewar par. Consequently a downward readjustment of British prices and costs of about 10% was effected.

A country with an unhampered market economy can take such a readjustment in its stride. But England had lost her economic flexibility. The wages of organized labor were rigid. The prevailing progressive ideology supported union leaders in their outright re-fusal of wage cuts in accordance with reductions in the cost of living. Furthermore, large price-fixing combines in British industries were considered desirable and were encouraged by the government which granted efficient protection through tariffs and other import restrictions. Therefore the downward readjustment in prices and wages was slow and painful. It was accompanied by heavy chronic unemployment which lasted to the eve of World War II. But this institutional unemployment did not result from the nature of the market economy, but from the lack of it. The British *government* endeavored to increase the purchasing power of the pound, which necessitated a downward readjustment of wages. The labor unions, having received power, favors, and reputation by government legis-lation, counteracted the readjustment policy and held wages above the height which the supply and demand would have dictated. The inevitable effect was unemployment.

These were the economic conditions in the major countries prior to the great depression of 1929-1940. The paper currencies outside the United States were depreciated or fluctuated violently in value. Until about 1925, through the operation of Gresham's Law the banks in the United States gained gold steadily from the outside world, although most of the important countries had restricted gold payments or had ceased to make them. Gresham's Law (the princi-ple that bad money drives out good money) asserts that a man does not sell his gold or foreign exchange to his central bank which short-changes him by giving depreciated domestic money in ex-change. He rather sends his gold to a country where he is not shortchanged in an exchange transaction but where he receives a price in accordance with the true purchasing power of gold.

The American Prelude to the Great Depression. The fact that foreign gold continued to flow into the United States, however, does not mean that the American monetary authorities refrained from policies of inflation and credit expansion. It merely indicates that the United States dollar was better than other important currencies and that the rate of inflation and credit expansion proceeded more slowly than abroad. Indeed, the United States government flooded the money and credit market in three great moves. The first of these came in 1922 when the Federal Reserve Banks made heavy open market purchases of government securities in order to acquire earning assets. In 1924 the Federal Reserve banks bought large amounts of government securities for the deliberate purpose of flooding the money and credit market. These transactions may be considered the first government measures of New-Deal type of planning and regulating the money supply to attain prosperity and full employment. Then again in the latter part of 1927 the Federal Reserve System for the third time purchased government securities to bring about easy money and expansion of credit. Simultaneously the Federal Reserve banks lowered their discount rates. When the Chicago Federal Reserve Bank refused to fall in line with this policy, it was overruled by the Federal Reserve Board in Washington, by whose action the Chicago rate was reduced in line with the others.

The newly created credit went rapidly into security loans and bank investments in securities. Business conditions at home and abroad did not warrant a productive expansion; therefore, business in general refrained from making use of the newly created funds. Commercial loans only increased moderately during this predepression period. Tempted by low interest rates, the stock market took the money. Stocks went rapidly higher, generating a psychological boom atmosphere. Supplied with abundant money the stock market rose by leaps and bounds. According to the *Dow-Jones Industrial Index*, stock prices moved as follows:

Date	Closing Price
November 15, 1922	95.11
January 10, 1924	97.23
November 10, 1924	105.91
November 15, 1927	195.37
February 15, 1928	197.59
November 15, 1928	269.42
August 29, 1929	376.18

The huge amount of money and credit created by the Federal Reserve banks also caused the volume of new securities, domestic as well as foreign, to grow at an enormous rate. Many of them did not survive the big crash of 1929 and the following years of depression. The excessive supply of Federal Reserve money created speculation in every field, especially in the field of real estate. Mortgage bonds were issued at a tremendous pace and real estate values soared. Bank and business consolidations increased with great rapidity. The easier the financing and floating of all kinds of securities became, the greater grew the number of holding companies, investment trusts, and other combinations.

Finally, the Federal Reserve authorities became alarmed about these undesirable effects of their own policy. They began to reverse it. They raised rediscount rates and sold government securities on the open market. But the boom went on. It had caught the public imagination. And so much new money had been created in the period from 1922 to 1929 that the problem of reabsorbing it was extremely difficult—indeed too difficult for the monetary planners to control the situation of their own creation.

Reaction Sets In. On October 24, 1929 the stock market prices began to break initiating a readjustment which was long overdue.

The forthcoming period of readjustment could have been a period of orderly liquidation and adjustment followed by a normal revival. The financial structure of business was very strong. Fixed costs were low, as business had refunded a good many bond issues and had reduced debts to banks with the proceeds of the sale of stock. In the following months earning power of almost any business continued to make a reasonable showing. But there were weak points in the banking system. Many small banks that had participated in the boom were loaded with illiquid bonds and mortgages based on very exaggerated real estate prices. A fall in price would hit them hard. Also, the international credit picture looked very dark. High American tariffs interfered with the movement of goods and prevented the European debtors from paying their debts with goods or services. Recognition of this fact and of the disastrous effects of a policy of cheap money and credit expansion would have eased the situation and led to orderly readjustment. But the American government was dead set against any readjustment. Instead it turned to government planning to bring about continuous boom, prosperity, and full employment.

President Hoover, in an address to the business leaders, urged them not to cut prices, not to cut wages, but to increase capital out-

lay and other expenditures. He advised them to spend to keep purchasing power high. This was the "progressive" way of dealing with
periods of readjustment. Hoover put the government into the wheat
business in a strenuous effort to hold prices up. But though government storages were being filled, prices of wheat here and abroad
continued to decline. Early in 1930 the Federal Reserve policy of
artificially cheap money was renewed, but production continued to
decline. As B. Anderson put it: "The jaded economic organism
could no longer respond to financial stimulus." [13]

Congress Legislates Depression. Then came the crowning folly of
government planning and intervention. In June 1930, Congress
passed the Hawley-Smoot Tariff Bill which gave high tariff protection to American industries. The consequences of this Act were
tragic. The world was staggering under a load of international debt
which could be carried only if the debtor nations were allowed to
pay by exporting goods to the creditor nations. But the United
States, the great creditor nation of the world, raised its tariffs again.
"Once we raised our tariffs," wrote Benjamin Anderson, "an irresistible movement all over the world to raise tariffs and to erect other
trade barriers, including quotas, began. Protectionism ran wild over
the world. Markets were cut off. Trade lines were narrowed. Unemployment in the export industries all over the world grew with
great rapidity, and the prices of export commodities, notably farm
commodities in the United States, dropped with ominous rapidity.
Farm prices in the United States dropped sharply through the whole
of 1930, but the most rapid rate of decline came following the passage of the tariff bill." [14] When President Hoover signed the bill the
industrial stocks broke 20 points in one day. Now, the world was
really heading towards its severest depression.

The economic situation further deteriorated when, in 1931, first
Austria and Germany and later Great Britain went off the gold
standard. Their banks had been employing short-term acceptance
credits in long-term transactions and with government encourage-
ment had expanded credit to the limit of their ability. When Austria
and Germany ceased to make foreign payments, large British and
American funds were frozen. When also Great Britain suspended
gold exports, additional American funds were tied up in England.
While Austria and Germany each made a strenuous fight to stay
solvent, the Bank of England continued its easy money policy and
went off the gold standard at the modest rate of 4½%. The princi-

13 B. Anderson, *Ibid.*, p. 224.
14 *Ibid.*, p. 225.

ples of "progressive" banking had gotten hold of the British monetary authorities.

The freezing of foreign credits affected only a few large New York institutions and the holders of foreign securities. But another consequence was much more serious. The fall in foreign bond values set off a collapse of the general bond market which hit the American banks at their weakest point—their investment portfolios. By scores and by hundreds, over-invested banks closed their doors.

When Roosevelt became President the policy of internal regimentation triumphed. By Presidential decree it became unlawful to own or hold gold coins, gold bullion, or gold certificates. Gold exports and foreign exchange transactions were controlled, and it ceased to be lawful to export gold in making payments to foreigners except under license from the Secretary of the Treasury. Of course, the President pretended that these measures were temporary. But up to this very day they are in effect and the monetary authorities continue their policies of internal regimentation.

Business Upturn Averted. After production had dropped to unprecedentedly low levels in 1932 and early 1933, an extraordinary rally in American business took place. It was the inevitable upswing from extreme panic and depression. But the upturn was nipped in the bud by a new government act: the National Industrial Recovery Act of 1933 which imposed new internal regimentation and contained new provisions for restrictions on imports. The purpose of the Act was to raise prices of manufactured goods through restraint of trade and production. Industries of all kinds were called upon to prepare codes concerned with shorter hours, minimum wages, and price fixing disguised as prohibitions of sales below costs. The Act was a naïve attempt at "increasing purchasing power" by increasing payrolls. But, naturally, the immense increase in business costs through shorter hours and higher wage costs worked as a most successful *anti-revival* measure. The South, especially, suffered a great deal of unemployment caused by the minimum wage provisions under NRA. Southern wages were greatly increased above the height of the free market, which forced about 500,000 Negroes out of work. Some industries were even diverted from the South to the North and Pacific Northwest.[15]

The first real revival came in the summer of 1935 when the Supreme Court declared the NRA unconstitutional. Business again began to pick up. But after a short period of growing activity and

[15] Roose, Charles, NRA *Economic Planning*, Principia Press, Bloomington, Indiana, 1937, p. 166 *et seq.;* see also B. Anderson, *Ibid.*, p. 327 *et. seq.*

sinking unemployment, effected through successful business readjustment under fearful handicaps, President Roosevelt and his progressive planners in Congress dealt the American economy another
series of painful blows. In July, 1935, Congress passed the Wagner
Act. At first it did not effect great changes in labor relations. But
following the election of 1936, the labor unions began active union-
ization and forced wage raises. Ugly labor conditions developed, in-
flicting heavy losses on business. In Detroit laborers occupied the
plants but refused to work, while the State of Michigan looked on,
refusing legal remedies. Such conditions resulted in a startling increase in labor costs with a simultaneous decrease in the productivity of labor. All this occurred while unemployment stood well
over six millions.

But the New Deal was not content. Through the Undistributed
Profits Tax of 1936 it struck a heavy blow at corporate savings.
Corporations were taxed on their savings in order to prevent them
from expanding through putting profits back into the business. Re-
tained profits are the major basis for a country's growth. But the
New Deal planners did not want industrial capacity to grow; they
were thinking in terms of spending and consumption.

Other major factors working towards the violent collapse in industrial activity in the fall of 1937 were continuous government
deficits, Roosevelt's shocking attempt to subdue the Supreme Court
by packing it with his own appointees, and the government policy
directed at destroying the stock market.

The violent collapse in industrial activity was finally set off by a
sudden break in the stock market followed by the most violent
break in economic activity in American history. Within the short
period of eight months, unemployment climbed to over 10 millions.
The winter of 1937-1938 became a period of gloom and fear both
for the country and the progressive planners in Washington.

But this was not all. In 1938 the President forced his last New
Deal law through Congress: the Wage and Hour Act. "It was a very
dangerous piece of legislation," said B. Anderson, "and, coming on
top of all the other measures which had made complications to business, it had very ominous possibilities." [16] It provided that increases
in minimum wages should be speeded up and working hours should
be limited to 44 hours a week during the first year, 42 hours for the
second year, and 40 hours a week thereafter. Overtime had to be
paid for at not less than 1½ times the regular wage. This law had
relatively little significance in those industries, mostly located in the

[16] *Ibid.*, p. 468.

North, in which the productivity of labor was already higher than the costs imposed by the law as minimum. But it affected severely the South and, above all, Puerto Rico, where capital was scarce and labor productivity low. Immense unemployment resulted. Only the war, through substituting a catastrophe for the economic disaster, brought relief to a suffering country and its progressive planners in Washington. The American nation had experienced its severest and longest depression in history. If it had not been for the war and the unprecedented monetary depreciation, the depression would have continued indefinitely until Washington had been purged of its planners.

According to the Conference Board Economic Record, unemployment in the United States moved as follows:

Year	Unemployment (in millions)	Unemployment as per cent of labor force
1929	429	0.9
1930	3,809	7.8
1931	8,113	16.3
1932	12,478	24.9
1933	12,744	25.1
1934	10,400	20.2
1935	9,522	18.4
1936	7,599	14.5
1937	6,372	12.0
1938	10,099	18.8
1939	9,080	16.7

Source: *Conference Board Economic Record,* March 20, 1940, quoted by B. Anderson, *Ibid.,* p. 488.

A World of Government Planning and Economic Nationalism. Similar conditions existed throughout the world. Government planning became paramount, and the world economy disintegrated rapidly. Some nations finally decided to do something about it. Instead of freeing the individual and restoring the market economy, which offered the only solution to their problems, they chose to shoot their way out of the planned chaos. To the immense suffering of the whole world, they continued on the road to disaster.

Throughout this period the international situation offered a comfortless picture. With the spread of socialist and welfare ideas, whose international aspect is tantamount to economic nationalism, the world community disintegrated into numerous strictly controlled and greatly self-sufficient areas. Through differential tariffs, import and export licenses and quotas, exchange controls and clearing agreements, barter treaties, government import and export monopolies, socialist and welfare governments succeeded in destroying the world economy. The system of bilateralism, i.e., the principle "we buy where we sell," enforced by nearly all governments, replaced the free system of multilateralism, thus creating as many more or less independent "national economies" as there were national governments. Because of inevitable divergencies in national and social planning, foreign trade decreased materially and the cleavage between the national price and cost systems grew. Under such conditions the greater economic units enjoyed a relative advantage over the smaller ones since they were less dependent on foreign trade. Smaller nations had to tie themselves economically to larger units whose bilateral bargaining position endangered the economic independence of the smaller units. To the same extent, the political independence of the smaller nations was endangered by the disintegration of the political world and by their loss of economic independence. Thus economic and political blocs developed which, although themselves divided into numerous national units, meant further disintegration of the world economy. Out of the ruins of a free world community a world of socialist and interventionist planning emerged, bringing in its wake chaos and war.

The "planned world" was a world of fluctuation and irregularity. We could observe abrupt closing or opening of foreign trade markets caused by changing political conditions and domestic positions of pressure groups. Foreign trade was increasingly politicalized. The world market became a vast dumping ground where governments or their subsidized monopolies dumped whatever their foreign or domestic policies prescribed. Agricultural and industrial protectionism prevailed. The destruction of the gold standard by central banks and national treasuries and its substitution by monetary planning, which always means inflation and depreciation, resulted in domestic instability and chronic international chaos. Thus the doctrines of full employment, monetary and credit management, fair and social taxation, government protection for farmers, workers, and many other groups led to progressive disparities of prices and wages and to a constantly growing separation of economies and nations.

The Nature of Business Cycles. Socialist or welfare planning means chaos internally as well as internationally. An economic crisis is inevitable as soon as a government or pressure group empowered by government interferes with the smooth operation of the market

economy in order to realize ambitious schemes of progressive planning. On the other hand, there are full employment and prosperity
when business is allowed to operate profitably. When profits are
improving, business expands. When profits decline or when a decline is anticipated because of unfavorable political, monetary, labor,
marketing and other conditions, business contracts. Profits, according to business terminology, are the excess of gross income over
costs of which labor costs are overwhelmingly important. It is obvious that business must decline when labor costs are forcedly increased either by government or labor unions in utter disregard of
profits. Also, the government policy of inflation and credit expansion
always results in a cycle of boom and depression. In the beginning
everything looks fine. Prices rise and profits increase because of the
rise in prices and the low business costs. Business begins to expand.
The demand for the several factors of production—land, capital, and
labor—increases. We have full employment, even labor shortages.
The increased demand for the production factors naturally raises
their prices, which are business costs. Costs are climbing. They
climb until they reach the point where business is no longer profitable. At this point the downfall begins. We enter a period of recession and readjustment. It lasts until the costs have come down and
business becomes profitable again.

The only inference to be drawn from this knowledge is that government should refrain from interfering with the operation of the
market economy and refrain from policies of inflation and credit
expansion. Booms and busts do not lie in the nature of human
economy. They are imposed upon us by "omniscient" government
economists and public officials who like to do the planning for the
citizens. Hansen, for example, would step up public capital outlays
if the citizens' outlays decline. "Thus," he says, "the public sector
can act as a balance wheel to the private sector. With adequate
planning, much could be done to stabilize the construction industry
as a whole, taking account of both the public and the private sectors.
Public projects should be built in the usual case under private contract. Thus contractors would switch from private to public projects
as private capital outlays declined and public outlays took up the
slack. But the construction industry, privately owned and operated,
would find a stabilized volume of outlays, public and private combined." [17] Indeed, very easy! If the citizens do not spend, government should spend. We need no science of economics, no economic
reasoning, indeed no further questions! The all-important question

[17] A. H. Hansen, *Ibid.*, pp. 21, 22.

as to why there is a business slack, for example, need not bother us. This is precisely what progressive "economists" want us to believe. "Let government watch the business indices," they say, "and spend accordingly."

It is almost too superficial to require further refutation. As illustrated previously, the business downfall begins when business is no longer profitable because of climbing costs. And the following period of recession and readjustment lasts until the costs have come down and business becomes profitable again. Now, if government really acts as a balance wheel to the private sector and maintains the aggregate volume of demand through stepping up public demand, it necessarily will stabilize the prices of the factors of production. That is to say, government keeps wages and other factor costs up. But high business costs are the very reason for the downtrend! If government perpetuates this reason, how can business recover? It cannot. The depression is perpetuated because government fights against the revival. President Roosevelt did it for many years and how successful he was!

We may illustrate our contention with a short example. Let us assume that building costs have soared to a point where a downtrend in the industry develops; costs are just too high. But immediately government intervenes. It begins to spend vast amounts on public projects and, through its demand for the factors of production, keeps wages and other building costs skyhigh. The labor unions may even persuade the government to raise wages. What are the consequences? The cause for the business slack, i.e., high costs, is perpetuated or even intensified. And the economy will continue to recede.

Government Spending Means Inflation. But still another aspect of the policy of government spending must here be mentioned. According to our progressive economists and politicians, government outlays should vary according to the requirements of stability and full employment. "If private capital outlays decline," says Hansen, "public outlays can be stepped up." Yes, but where does our government get the money? When business declines, government revenues decline. In all likelihood, our government is running deficits even without progressive investment programs. Well, it may raise taxes. But taxes mostly constitute a factor in business costs a raise of which would only intensify the depression. Taxes taken from consumers would only decrease private demand and substitute government demand. Or our government may borrow from its citizens. But a government loan, like taxes, is merely a shift of demand from private hands to government hands. Finally, and this is what our planners have in mind, our government may *create* money and credit and embark upon a policy of inflation and credit expansion. How does inflation work? Does it tend to make business profitable by lowering business costs? Except for a small decrease in the cost of money and credit, it does not. It rather leads to further increases in the costs of labor and material. Thus the depression continues.

Tax Relief Does Not Remedy the Evil. "But public spending alone is not enough," say our progressive economists. "Also variations in the basic income tax should counteract the fluctuations of the business cycle. That is to say, in periods of business recession taxes should be lowered and be increased again in periods of full employment." But such a measure does not remedy the evil. It is true the lowering of taxes on business lowers costs, which makes business more profitable. We may experience an economic revival and comeback. But at the same time our government is running deficits which are financed through inflation and credit expansion. Finally, business costs begin to soar again until the point of unprofitability is again reached. It is even conceivable that government would refrain from imposing any business taxes whatever and, yet, we may have depression and unemployment because high union wage rates and other costs make business unprofitable.

Our government also may lower taxes on consumers while it finances its own spending through inflation. In this case the prices of consumers' goods tend to rise which gives relief to business. But then the inflationary spending of government causes the prices for producers' goods, i.e., business costs, to rise until another downfall begins.

These are the inevitable effects of policies of government planning. If history could offer proof for knowledge won through reasoning, the history of the recent decades would offer cogent proof for these contentions. Government intervention leads to boom and bust. There is no remedy but to refrain from intervention and establish the unhampered market economy.

Progressive Taxes Destroy Capital. "Public spending alone cannot be depended upon as a stabilizing factor of the economy as a whole," say our planners. According to Hansen, "a broad and comprehensive system of social security and social welfare, combined with a progressive tax structure, acts steadily and continuously as a powerful stabilizing factor." [18] The progressive tax structure of which Hansen is speaking refers to confiscatory tax rates in higher

[18] *Ibid.*, p. 22.

income brackets. His objective is to avoid saving and the accumulation of capital and to stimulate spending. That is to say, progress is spending, no longer saving, as it used to be throughout the ages. The truth is that labor productivity, the standard of living and, in general, the wealth of a nation mainly depend on the accumulation of capital and investment per head of population. And the bulk of capital is accumulated by people in the higher and middle income brackets. If our government confiscates most of their income, capital formation is rendered impossible. The savings of well-to-do people are employed in production, i.e., in stocks, bonds, factories, apartment houses, etc. If we consume their capital, we impede production and thus lower everybody's standard of living. A consistent policy of spending and capital destruction may even lower our living conditions to a level of an underdeveloped country.

Social Security Based on Government Debt. We also disagree with the progressive planners on their contention that social security and social welfare are powerful stabilizing factors. What is social security and how does it work? Social security is a compulsory exchange of present contributions against claims for future benefits. While employed, a man pays in to the social security fund. The federal government receives the money and spends it. In return, it deposits investment bonds, which are claims against the federal government, with the Social Security Administration. Now let us assume business begins to taper off and we head towards a depression. Immediately contributions decline while claims for benefits tend to increase. The social security administration needs money. It turns towards the government to cash the bonds. But government is running deficits, for also government revenues decline in depression. The final solution is inflation. But inflation is the cause of evil, it cannot be remedy.

Planning and the Cumulative Depression. Our progressive economists have a lot to say about the cumulative feature of the business cycle. If governments would follow his designs of planning, Hansen maintains, "the cumulative features that have characterized the cycle for a hundred years would tend to disappear. Under the automatic forces that controlled the cycle in the past, once the downward movement got started, the cumulative process fed on itself. Unemployment spread fear among consumers and reduced the volume of expenditures. Falling prices and falling markets induced pessimism among businessmen and cut off new capital outlays." [19] We readily admit that there is a cumulative feature in the business

[19] *Ibid.*, p. 22.

cycle. But we emphatically disagree as to the nature of this cumulative feature. We believe that there is a psychological tendency in government, once it has brought about the cycle through a policy of inflation and credit expansion, to "correct" the undesirable effects of the cycle through additional measures of government intervention. Nobody, least of all public officials, likes to admit the mistakes made and be responsible for the consequences. They rather blame the market economy, businessmen, speculators, etc., than admit failure. They sooner speak about loopholes and embark upon additional intervention. And this additional intervention has cumulative effects. Throughout the nineteenth century falling prices did not induce pessimism among businessmen and did not cut off new outlays. It was a century of continuously sinking prices which meant rising standards of living, a century of huge capital accumulations and outlays. It was a century of unprecedented progress. But we readily admit that under prevailing progressive ideological conditions falling prices may indeed induce pessimism among businessmen because falling prices in the eyes of our planners are evil and provide occasion to encroach upon our liberties and the market economy. This thought fills us with fear.

Controls versus Progress. "Social and economic planning is a new and great experiment," say the progressive planners. To stabilize the construction industry they urge our governments to develop the national resources and to modernize our roads and railroads, airlines, and waterways. They urge us to "rebuild America on lines commensurate with the potentialities of modern science and modern technology." [20] The physical conditions of our great cities are deplorable, they say. Urban and rural housing is substandard, transportation facilities are congested, and natural resources are wasted.

Though we are in utter disagreement as to the deplorable conditions of this great country, we may yield this argument, for there is no way to determine exactly through reasoning the deplorable state of conditions. We merely raise the question as to why conditions are so deplorable. Why is urban and rural housing substandard? [21] Why are our transportation facilities congested? Why are our roads, railroads, and waterways in need of modernization? The answer is simple. In all the fields mentioned government intervention and control are hampering business activity most severely. Urban and rural housing is subject to numerous government controls. For many

[20] *Ibid.*, p. 23.
[21] For the sake of argument let us assume we know what the "standard" is.

years rigid rent controls by all levels of government restricted building activity. Our transportation facilities are bound to be congested because there is hardly an industry that is more intensively regulated as to rates and operation than the transportation industry. Our railroads are literally controlled and taxed to death. Other transportation facilities are even owned and operated by the states or municipalities. Is it a surprise that they are congested?

Government as Entrepreneur. Hansen's remark that we should rebuild America on lines commensurate with the potentialities of modern science and modern technology obviously is addressed to our governments. They are to rebuild America. He expressly states that governments should thoroughly modernize our transportation facilities, develop natural resources, rebuild cities, etc. In other words, they are to modernize and rebuild America. This is the most presumptuous statement a government planner can make. What makes government so suited to build and rebuild, to produce and to create? For over 150 years the U. S. government had an excellent opportunity to prove its entrepreneurial ability. For over 150 years it has been owner and manager of the postal service. Inferring from the statements of our government planners, we may assume that the U. S. Post Office is our most efficient industry, being constantly rebuilt and modernized commensurable with the potentialities of modern science and modern technology. However, such an assumption would be an outright contradiction of fact. Our post offices are most pitiful and deplorable. They constitute the greatest waste of the American economy.

Let us pause for a moment to inspect this government enterprise. The operations of the United States Post Office in its latest audited year cost every man, woman, and child in the country $4.50 more than each paid in ordinary postal charges. [22] That is to say, the American public paid a total of $727,000,000 in taxes to the government in addition to charges for its postal services. The Post Office spent $4 for every $3 it received, paid no taxes, and enjoyed a formidable monopolistic position. These figures are provided us by government accountants. Reality looks even worse. In all fairness, Mr. Hansen's suggestion to entrust the modernization and reconstruction of America to the owner of the U. S. Post Office must be rejected.

The Planner, Education, and Welfare. The progressives' critique of the market economy even extends to education, health and nutrition, recreational facilities, and cultural activities. "Forty per

[22] *New York Times,* February 13, 1954, p. 9.

cent of our children grow up in areas deplorably deficient in educational facilities," says Hansen. "A disquieting percentage of the young men drafted into the service were adjudged 'functional illiterates' or were physically unfit for military duty." [23] It is obvious that there is hardly a vice for which the free economy is not blamed and for which the planned economy is not offered as ready panacea. Wild accusations and arbitrary assertions are made for which no proof is offered, nor can be offered. What, for instance, does "deplorably deficient in educational facilities" mean? What standard do we use? It cannot be the world average as standard, which itself is rather ambiguous, for the world's education is much more deficient than the American. How does Hansen arrive at the figure of 40 per cent? Why is it not 60 or 90 per cent? According to assertions of those who oppose the public school system, 95 per cent of the educational facilities are deplorably deficient. They at least offer the fact as proof that 95 per cent of our educational facilities are publicly owned and operated. Another arbitrary judgment of Hansen's is contained in the assertion that "a disquieting percentage of the young men drafted into the service were adjudged 'functional illiterates' or were physically unfit for military duty." What is functional illiteracy and who determines it? It is obvious that these concepts are based on expediency and depend on the judgment of the person who determines the standard. In the final days of World War II, 99 per cent of the German male population between 14 and 70 years of age were adjudged functional literates and physically fit for military duty. Was the Nazi state so successful?

National Planning and International Cooperation. According to our progressive economists, national planning for stability and welfare must be supplemented by planning on an international level to achieve domestic as well as international stability and economic expansion. New international institutions are needed, says Hansen, "to reshape our world in order to make it again a functioning and manageable system."

This contention that nations should conduct policies of economic and social planning in order to contribute to international stability reveals a lack of economic knowledge and reasoning. Government planning always means interference with the market economy and the international division of labor. It is planning for international disparities of prices, wages, and production structures. In its domestic effectiveness it depends on tariffs, import and export licenses and quotas, exchange controls, and a multiplicity of other controls which

[23] A. H. Hansen, *Ibid.*, p. 24.

protect the domestic economy from competition of the world market. Government planning is identical with economic nationalism. A government that guarantees its farmers a cotton price above that of the world market must inevitably prohibit imports of cotton or risk the whole world production being shipped to its country. But prohibition of imports causes international conflict. And this conflict is constantly fed by the multiplicity of sovereign states and planners. Each national plan is constantly changed according to the politicians, parties, and pressure groups in power. Thus the world economy is in a continuous maladjustment.

Ideologies of Conflict. The present age of war and conflict is testimony to the fact that ideologies accepted by the majority of the world's population are those of aggressive nationalism, communism, socialism, Fair-Dealism, and other systems of intervention which cause international conflicts. The numerous adherents of these ideologies deny this contention. They maintain that unrestrained individuals do not cooperate and thus cause the world turmoil. Their remedy is a social system of coerced cooperation. If all the world were communistic, socialist, or interventionist, they maintain, no cause for world conflict and war could exist.

A glance at the nature of these ideologies and their systems of social organization reveals the fallacies of this assertion. If the entire world were communistic, for example, the problem of leadership could not be solved. Also, central planning in the "interest of the world" would necessarily create additional serious problems because certain parts of the world would be favored to the detriment of others. Discrimination through world planning, like national planning, would take the form of regulating prices and costs, fixing production and export quotas, allocating raw materials and capital goods, and many other means of world government planning and regulation. The richer nations would probably take the view that the instruments of production invested in their areas are their property and no other nation should be entitled to benefit from them. On the other hand, the poorer nations would insist upon sharing the benefits from the capital and favorable production conditions enjoyed by the richer nations. They would undoubtedly insist upon the right to migrate in vast numbers to places with more favorable conditions of production. How could a world board for economic planning solve all these problems without deciding in favor of one side against the other? Even a "fair" compromise would constitute a decision that benefits or harms someone. Last but not least, the absence of a market economy under communism would render the calculation of capital and costs of production impossible, which means communist planners would be deprived of any way of ascertaining whether or not a certain production or method of production were economically worth while. Thus, if the entire world were communist, numerous conflicts would arise and turn the world into an arena of war and planned chaos.

If all the world were interventionist, peaceful coexistence of sovereign nations would also be impossible. Government interference with the operation of the market economy favors certain producers to the detriment of other producers and consumers. This "favor" and "protection" usually takes the form of influencing and regulating prices, which in turn is based upon the restriction of imports and exports. Import and export restrictions, however, are measures of economic nationalism and cause international economic conflict. Inflationary policies together with arbitrary parity regulations bring about foreign exchange shortages, which in turn lead to further government restrictions on foreign trade. Numerous other forms of government intervention and protection—restriction of competition and investment, control of quantity and quality of goods produced, supervision of the methods of production employed, taxation that consumes capital and drives liquid capital elsewhere, and protection of numerous trade and professional organizations—are either direct acts of economic nationalism or depend upon supplementary acts of economic nationalism. No matter how we may analyze the system of interventionism, its inherent international aspect is the disintegration of the division of labor. Each act of economic nationalism requires painful adjustments on the part of those countries that deal with the offending country. In the final analysis, the structure of production in all countries, interdependent through foreign trade, is forced to make adjustments because of a single act of economic nationalism. Only the system of individual liberty and the unhampered world economy can provide the enormous advantages of the international division of labor and provide the milieu for nations to live in peace.

Doctrines and Plans
of Unification

WITH the spread of socialist and
welfare ideas and their adoption in the political world, the impedi-
ments to the free movement of men, goods, and capital grew. With
each new obstacle created for the benefit of domestic pressure
groups mutual advantages of international cooperation and division
of labor were sacrificed. Central planning and government welfare
finally became identical with economic nationalism and disintegration of the world economy. The detrimental international effects of
the "progressive" policies became apparent almost immediately upon
the adoption of each welfare and protection measure. And with the
first symptoms of disintegration, plans for cooperation and unification always emerged. Able minds of various nations holding various
political beliefs began to reflect on the abolition of economic barriers
and the creation of economic and political union. Some plans were
even put into effect. The League of Nations, the United Nations,
and the several organizations described in Part Three of this book
must here be mentioned.

It is impossible to examine thoroughly all doctrines and plans of
unification ever devised. They are as abundant as the detrimental
effects of disintegration are numerous and diverse. In general they
deal with the inescapable effects of our socialist and welfare policies
and offer ready plans for government cooperation as the panacea
for the deplorable state of international affairs. "You are free to
continue your socialist and welfare policies," they proclaim, "provided your governments unite." But scarcely a scheme of government cooperation and unification deals with the causes of
disintegration and disunity. Such a plan would merely earn derision

33

and hostility, for it inevitably would unmask and indict the prevailing ideologies of government planning and welfare upheld and cherished by public opinion. It would demand that governments henceforth refrain from interference with the liberty of the individual.

The following part on the "Doctrines and Plans of Unification" offers an analysis of a selection of unification plans. They are selected from the abundance of material on grounds of two principles: (1) their success and popularity as indicated by public acceptance and approval, and (2) their material relevance for the critic.

I

Clarence K. Streit and the Federal Union of Democracies

The Author. In 1938, one year before the outbreak of World War II, the American writer, Clarence K. Streit, summoned the free democracies of the world to unite against the rising threat of the totalitarian states in Europe and Asia. His book, *Union Now,*[1] gave life to a Federal Union movement, which today has thousands of followers in all states of the United States and in many parts of the world. The success and popularity of the "Freedom and Union Movement," as it was named by its founder, can be recognized by the fact that his book was translated into several foreign languages and sold more than 300,000 copies as of 1949. The movement works through the association "Federal Union, Inc." in Washington, D.C., with local branches all over the United States; its president is Clarence K. Streit. Its monthly magazine, *Freedom and Union,* promotes the stated objective of the association: "the education in the basic principles of federal union as exemplified in the Constitution of the United States, with a view to attaining world order by a Federal Union of Democratic Peoples."

The Objectives of Federal Union. The supreme objective of Streit's Union proposal is "individual freedom," and the individual's protection from "the dangers with which depression, dictatorship, false recovery and war are hemming us in."[2] "To provide effective common government in our democratic world in those fields where

---

[1] The following quotes are taken from the last edition of *Union Now,* A Proposal for an Atlantic Federal Union of the Free, Harper & Brothers, New York, 1949. See also his *Union Now with Great Britain,* Harper & Brothers, New York, 1941, which was written in accordance with the special war-time conditions and does not differ essentially from *Union Now.*

[2] *Ibid.,* p. 3.

such government will clearly serve man's freedom better than separate government," a Union of the free democracies of the world should be formed. Independent national governments are to be maintained "in all other fields where such government will serve man's freedom." Finally, the Union is so designed as "to create by its constitution a nucleus world government capable of growing into universal world government peacefully and as rapidly as such growth will best serve man's freedom." [3]

An effective common government is to be provided in five different fields in which the states' functions are to be transferred to the Union. The five functions of the government of the Union are:

a. Citizenship, the granting of which should be the exclusive right of the Union.
b. A Union defense force, having the right to declare war and make peace, and to employ force or to conclude treaties.
c. Regulation of foreign trade and interstate commerce in a customs-free economy of the Union.
d. Control of the value of money, which is to be uniform throughout the territory of the Union.
e. Control of the Union postal and communication system.

The Union government would guarantee "against all enemies, foreign and domestic, not only those rights of man that are common to all democracies, but every existing national or local right that is not clearly incompatible with effective Union government in the five named fields. The Union would guarantee the right of each democracy in it to govern independently all home affairs and practice democracy at home in its own tongue, according to its own customs and in its own way, whether by republic or kingdom, presidential, cabinet or other form of government, capitalist, socialist or other economic system. The Union, furthermore, shall be so constituted by "founder democracies" as to "encourage the nations outside it and the colonies inside it to seek to unite with it instead of against it. Admission to the Union and to all its tremendous advantages for the individual man and woman would from the outset be open equally to every democracy, now or to come, that guarantees its citizens the Union's Bill of Rights." [4]

Federal Union and Liberty Are Identical. The liberty of the individual and the Union of individuals are inseparable concepts. "We cannot be for liberty and against Union," says Streit. "We cannot

[3] *Ibid.,* p. 3.
[4] *Ibid.,* pp. 4, 5.

be both for and against liberty and Union now. We must choose." [5]
By transferring the states' rights in the aforementioned fields of
government to the Union, state interference with the freedom of the
individual is reduced, and the rights of the individual are extended
over the narrow boundaries of the national state to the vast territory
of the Union. Streit contrasts a Union, which is a Union of men,
free and equal, with unification of states in leagues or alliances, in
which the states are the equal units.

The Fifteen Founder Nations. The world-wide Union of democratic peoples, as envisaged by Streit, should be founded by the
fifteen oldest democracies, the people of which have proven their
ability to self-government under all conceivable conditions. Their
people are most advanced and experienced politically. They belong
to the same civilization, enjoy close economic relations, and were not
at war with each other for over 120 years. The common concept of
state, government, and freedom unites them ideologically as their
geographic location around the oceans of the world unites them in
matters of communication. Streit names the U.S.A., United Kingdom, Canada, Australia, New Zealand, Union of South Africa, Ireland, France, Belgium, the Netherlands, the Swiss Confederation,
Denmark, Norway, Sweden, and Finland. In these countries five
languages are spoken by more than 300 million people, of which
about half are living in Europe. The countries combined occupy
more than half the earth's surface, produce half the world's output
of raw materials, and even more of the world's total production.
Their large capital accumulation, together with the aforementioned
factors, lend the fifteen democracies overwhelming economic as well
as political and military strength and power.

The Advantages of Federal Union. Such a Union of democracies
would by far outbalance any eventual single aggressor or alliances of
nondemocratic aggressors, says Streit. The defense of the democracies and their way of life would be secured permanently by the
superior strength of the Union, which, without fear of aggression,
could even afford to disarm. The saving of huge armament expenditures would immediately reduce the burden of taxation and thus
raise the standard of living of the Union citizens. The common
money of the Union would "solve most of today's insoluble monetary
problems" and would bring about a monetary stability based on "a
single responsible government overwhelmingly powerful in the economic world, a single budget, and a single gold reserve." [6] No other

[5] *Ibid.,* p. 7.
[6] *Ibid.,* p. 122.

combination, according to Streit, is strong enough to achieve such monetary stabilization. The common money in a customs-free economy of the Union would induce interstate trade to increase considerably and thus improve living conditions. Control of the Union over the system of communications would bring about a unification and standardization of all means of transit and communication, the regulations of which could be simplified. A saving of costs would lower prices and raise income correspondingly. A uniform government, furthermore, would eliminate excessive government and needless bureaucracy. It would abolish passports, visas, quotas, permits, etc.; it would end duplication and dangerous wasteful competition among various government departments and agencies, and thus would allow reduction of taxation and governmental debt.[7] A Union government, finally, "overwhelmingly powerful in the economic world," could meet the threat of depression and fight unemployment by opening "vast new enterprises" and by many other available means.[8]

Member States Are Free to Experiment Politically, Economically, and Socially. The Union would not only mean freedom and prosperity to the individual, but would also guarantee existence of many national autonomies in the Union in which the states would be free "to experiment politically, economically, and socially."[9] The member states would be free to choose their own system of social organization, capitalistic or socialistic. "It is a profound mistake," says Streit, "to identify democracy necessarily or entirely with either capitalist or socialist society, with either the method of individual or of collective enterprise. There is room for both methods in democracy."[10] Democracy, and logically the Union of democratic peoples, may even include "Marxist governments, parties and press as well as *laissez faire* governments, parties, and press."[11] Nazi political theory, however, "is incompatible with democracy." Yet, "basic Marxist political theory may easily be compatible with democracy however much it . . . may be made to serve the ends of absolutism."[12] Inclusion of member states organized according to the capitalist system of society, which often is accused of constituting the major cause of war, is defended by Streit with the following argument: "Whether or not the capitalist system is one of the causes

[7] *Ibid.*, pp. 14, 125.
[8] *Ibid.*, p. 124.
[9] *Ibid.*, p. 16.
[10] *Ibid.*, p. 81.
[11] *Ibid.*, p. 81.
[12] *Ibid.*, p. 81.

of war, it is true that the problem of organizing peaceful relations among the nations was not solved when all the world was capitalistic. It may possibly be that if all the world were communistic the problem would be solved. No one can say." [13]

The Union Constitution. To bring such a Union of democracies to life only a constitution is needed, which would include the Union Bill of Rights and set up and organize the governmental machinery, its legislative, executive and judicial departments and, finally, the mechanism for amending the constitution. Streit suggests a Bill of Rights which, in its essence, is identical with that of the American Constitution. But "I would favor adding to this bill," says Streit in a note on page 215 of *Union Now with Great Britain*, "the following sweeping 'economic rights': Freedom from both overwork and unemployment as defined by law." [14] Regarding the organization of government, Streit suggests a two-house Union legislature. Every half or one million citizens should be represented by one deputy in the House, while two senators should be elected by the people of each state. A slight modification of this principle of equal representation of the population of each state in the Senate is favored by Streit inasmuch as states having over 25 million inhabitants should have the right to be represented by two additional senators. The United States of America, with a population of almost 50 per cent of the Union, should be allowed to delegate eight senators. The executive authority of the Union should be vested in a Board of five persons. Each year there should be an election for only one member of the Executive Board, which thus would enjoy permanency and consistency.

No Period of Transition. Having agreed on the constitution of the Union, the founders of the Union need not bother about additional agreements on the problem of transition to the Union. When the United States of America was created, says Streit, its founders, in 1787, "abolished each State's rights to levy tariffs, issue money, make treaties, and keep an army, and they gave these rights to the Union without waiting for a plan to meet the difficulties of changing from protection to free trade, etc. They did not even bother trying to work out plans to meet all these difficulties of transition." [15]

Leagues and Alliances Are Rejected. Streit then proceeds to compare his scheme of unification of democratic unions with other alternatives of unification. He unhesitatingly rejects leagues and

[13] *Ibid.*, p. 41.
[14] Published by Harper & Brothers, New York, 1941.
[15] *Ibid.*, p. 28.

alliances because they are mere associations of states and governments. Leagues of nations, according to Streit, "never worked, are undemocratic, untrustworthy, unsound, and unable either to make or enforce its law in time." Alliances are "primitive forms of leagues" and usually lack the machinery for reaching and executing international agreements in the economic, financial and monetary fields.[16] Even worse than these forms of unification is the policy of pure nationalism and isolationism which rejects every type of interstate organization and which is the opposite of world government, law, and order. American isolationism, Streit complains, refuses to judge even in the most flagrant cases of international aggression.

A Union of democracies, however, would remedy our evils and ills. A Union can act swiftly; it can enforce law and prosecute law breakers without assistance of the states' apparatus or without causing major interstate incidents. A Union would protect its citizens from invasion by foreign aggressors and would bring about military as well as "economic disarmament." It can act swiftly on a mere majority vote, whereas leagues and alliances need unanimous decisions in order to be able to act. The Union would be the initial step towards universality of mankind.

Streit denonunces the former "League of Nations" and the present "United Nations" organizations as suffering from the shortcomings inherent in all leagues of government and states. As loose associations of sovereign states they could not and cannot overcome the existing anarchy which arises just "from the refusal of the democracies to renounce enough of their national sovereignty to let effective world law and order be set up."[17] However, Streit deems it advisable for the Union of democratic peoples to join the United Nations as a member state.

European Unification Rejected. Finally, Clarence K. Streit opposes the existing plans for European unification. Such a union, according to Streit, is a halfway measure which leaves the democracies divided. Because it would not outbalance in military and economic strength any combination of eventual aggressors, it could not prevent wars but would lead instead to isolationism and chaos. Once the European nations embark upon a unification of their own, other nations would follow their example and form similar unions in all parts of the world. Their equality of military and economic strength, says Streit, would invite aggressor states to attack. Each union of states would lack the vast superiority in military and eco-

16 *Ibid.*, p. 26.
17 *Ibid.*, p. 11.

nomic strength which a union of all democracies would enjoy. Only superiority in strength avoids war and not a balance of power! The limited economic strength of a European union furthermore would not be sufficient to prevent depressions. Only a union of all democracies with its vast resources and reserves could achieve such an objective.

Unification Is Our Immense Opportunity and Obligation. In the last ten years, according to Streit, considerable progress has been made towards union.[18] The prerequisites for a unification of democracies were never as favorable as they are now. The threat of Soviet Russian aggression gives the unification problem urgency and utmost importance; it makes it a question of survival. The mounting economic pressure, caused by the necessity of reconstruction and rearmament and an increasing burden of national debts, also directs the democratic nations towards unification. The Marshall Plan and the Atlantic Pact are intermediary steps of mutual assistance among the free nations of the world on the way to Union now.

CRITIQUE

Things Are Not What They Seem. The scheme of unification, as designed by Clarence K. Streit, at first glance, gives the reader a pleasant picture of unification which seems to rest on the solid foundation of individual freedom and points to the creation of the United States of America as the ideal example. The freedom which the United States has given and continues to give to its citizens, the security stemming from its economic and military strength, and the prosperity of its individuals of all walks of life are the points of departure from which Streit endeavors to proceed to a Union of all democracies. He projects the gratifying picture of American history. to a modern unification towards which—as he believes—the democracies are now moving.

On second glance, however, the unification, as designed by Streit, unfortunately reveals certain errors and fallacies in his fundamental conception and logical reasoning that render his scheme of Union unrealizable and which would bring about effects contrary to his own intention. We maintain—and will endeavor to prove our conviction in the following—that certain features of Streit's plan of unification do not permit its realization under present-day ideological conditions. Other fundamental shortcomings of his plan for Union render its realization unfeasible under any conditions conceivable.

[18] *Ibid.*, p. 256.

And, finally, certain characteristics of Streit's projected Union would adversely affect the very objective of his planning for Union—man's liberty.

An Inquiry into Free Migration. One of the features of unification that makes Streit's plans unworkable, under present-day ideological conditions, is the function of the Union to grant common citizenship. The Union citizenship, according to Streit, would open up "the Union's tremendous advantages for the individual man and woman." The individual would gain in his liberty by belonging to a vast Union of democracies which would abolish passports, visas, quotas, permits, etc. The individual would be free to migrate from one part of the Union to another without having to encounter the numerous difficulties and discriminations that face him today. The barriers of migration would be abolished immediately and the individual would be free to seek home and employment wherever the conditions of life and employment would suit him best. Indeed, Streit draws a picture of a wonderful world!

However, can we expect and hope for the realization of such a world under present-day ideological conditions? Is the majority of people ready and willing to bear the essential effects of free migration within the Union? Do the notions and ideas prevailing in man's mind warrant the hope for an early realization of the Union? All three questions must be answered in the negative. In order to come to a conclusion on this problem, we must draw inferences from the point of departure—the freedom of migration within the Union—to the *effects* which such freedom must bring about for all or part of its citizens. Then, having gained knowledge of the effects, we may easily conclude whether or not people will approve the effects as well as the point of departure.

It is an undeniable fact that standards of living in the founder democracies comprising the Union-to-be vary essentially. The population of the United States enjoys by far the highest standard of living. The average income of the United States citizen amounts to at least triple the income of the citizens of the other democracies, Canada excluded. Compared with the poorest parts of the Union, the American income per head of population is more than fivefold. The people of the United States and Canada produce and consume much more than the citizens of the remaining thirteen democracies combined. American production, due to larger accumulation of capital per head of population, is superior to that in other parts of the Union. It is the unfailing effect of such conditions of production that millions of American workers enjoy an income and living conditions that are the envy of millions of foreign workers who even work longer and harder and under inferior working conditions. While the American worker is assisted by thousands of horse power of machinery of production and transportation, the non-American worker often toils by hand or with the assistance of machinery which his American colleague would reject as outmoded, inefficient, and "unfair to labor."

Free Migration Means Mass Migration to the United States. It is a fundamental law of human action that man seeks to remove the burden of labor. If man can improve his living conditions, he will attempt to do so. If the European, African, or Australian citizen of the Union is free to double or triple his real income and improve his living conditions by mere migration to another state, he will not hesitate to do so. A stream of migrants would flow from places where productivity and wages are low to places with higher productivity and better wages. And the larger the difference, the stronger would be the stream towards more favorable production places. We may therefore assume, without exaggeration, that millions from all parts of the Union would emigrate to America and endeavor to raise their standards of living just by offering their services on the American labor market.[19]

The mass migration to America necessarily would continue until the individual could no longer reap an advantage by migrating. That is to say, as soon as the living and working conditions throughout the Union were equal, the migration movement would cease. The fact that a large part of the population naturally does not take part in the migration movement, because of age, sickness, wealth, position in life, and other factors, would retard the movement but

[19] This assertion presumes freedom of migration which logically means the freedom to enter a country and choose an occupation of one's liking and for which one is trained. The mere freedom to enter a country, while being excluded from taking part in its economic life because of closed professional organizations and closed shop agreements protected by the state, is not the freedom of migration which either Streit or this discussion implies. A judge from Sweden, England, Germany, or France will scarcely consider it freedom of migration if, upon entering the United States, he is barred from working in his profession. A judge who finally may earn his livelihood as a window cleaner at the courthouse and a medical doctor who is hired as a hospital worker, provided both are accepted by the respective labor unions, very rarely have the incentive to immigrate. The obstacles of "legal requirements" (as, for example, citizenship which can be obtained by staying and waiting for five years in the country, repetition of long and costly studies, passing of state examinations, obtaining of numerous licenses, memberships of professional organizations which also have their "minimum requirements," etc.) are too great and the time needed for their acquiring too long. It is even conceivable that there is freedom to enter a country, but that immigrants, because of professional organizations and controls, must live on welfare and charity. It is obvious that this is not freedom of migration.

would *not* affect the outcome. If everyone were motivated by the advantages which migration would give him, the migration movement would proceed in one vast trek and be completed within a few weeks after the removal of migration barriers.

Migration Equalizes Income. Richer Nations Reject Free Migration. The essential economic effect of the vast migration movement would be an equalization of the rates of income in all parts of the Union. American living conditions would be lowered essentially, while non-American conditions would tend to improve. Lowering of American rates of income would be brought about by the smaller amount of capital invested per head of the increased population. Although the population would increase considerably, the amount of capital goods employed in the process of production would remain constant.[20] That means the amount of capital goods with which each worker can be provided decreases with every increase in the number of workers. Thus the undeniable effect of a Union as ardently advocated by Streit with its influx of millions of immigrants would be a considerable reduction in American wage rates. For the American citizen the problem of a Union of democratic peoples thus is synonymous with the problem of voluntary reduction in his standard of living. The crucial question now arising is: "Will American and Canadian citizens acquiesce in a Union which brings about these effects?" Emphatically, no! "Will American and Canadian citizens vote in favor of a realization of a Union that brings about these conditions?" Certainly not!

Streit's scheme of Union falls by the first problem which we put to a test. And, yet, our assumptions were moderate. Only the effects of a migration within a Union of a few homogeneous democracies were tested. Streit goes much further. In the event other countries would accept the "Union Bill of Rights," they, too, would qualify for admittance to the Union. If China and India and other underdeveloped countries, for example, were admitted to the Union, the extent of the migration movement would be scarcely imaginable. The income per head of population in the underdeveloped countries, in which more than half of the world's population lives in extreme poverty and hardship, amounts to $25 to $50 per year. A unification according to the plans of Streit would bring about a migration such

---

[20] The assumption that the capital invested per head of population in the United States would continue to increase, no matter how many millions of foreigners would immigrate, is an assumption as fallacious and superficial as the belief that the people of the United States can feed the population of the world, no matter how fast their number increases.

as the world has never seen. [21] The American average income of over $1500 per head of population would simply collapse and sink to a level of an underdeveloped country. Whether the American citizen would vote in favor of a Union having these effects, we neither need nor dare to ask.

Free Migration Permits Invasion of Undemocratic Ideologies. But the picture of a realization of Streit's Union is even darker than we have indicated. Immigrants like natives embrace certain political and economic ideas and religious principles which find expression in their way of life—in their notions regarding state and government, society and individual, religion and faith, etc. Since it is man's mind, his values, ideas, and notions that govern his daily actions, man creates his surroundings and way of life in accordance therewith. The political, economic, and religious ideas prevailing in those countries from which the millions of American immigrants would come have created ways of life and standards of living which we may easily evaluate. While the citizens of the thirteen other "founder democracies" enjoy relatively fair living conditions, most of the world's population, which would eventually qualify for admittance to Streit's Union, lives in extreme poverty. Their political and economic ideologies and religious principles, which are the sole factors bringing about their living conditions, are, for most of the world's population, ideas that lead to poverty, starvation, war, chaos, etc. There is no other logical explanation conceivable for poverty and chaos, but that man's ideas governing his actions have brought them about. Indeed, if we look at countries with the poorest living conditions, we will perceive that their ideologies and principles of life are most hostile to individual freedom and to capital accumulation and production. They may be ideas of collectivism with regard to state and government, society and man, ideas of nationalism and socialism or communism, racism and class struggle, or a combination of these. The religious principles may prohibit the equality or collaboration of women in economic life or even command the worship

21 The fact that two or three European countries have national quotas of immigration to the United States which, in some years, are not even filled does not refute the contention. The institutional barriers erected by labor unions, professional organizations, and professional codes and requirements by the states are as efficient checks on immigration for skilled and professional persons as are restrictive immigration laws. Around 1890, Mark Twain in *The American Claimant* brilliantly described the life of a young immigrant from England who came to the United States "to try equality and work for a living." He could not get work because he did not belong to a union and could not gain admission to one. If these barriers existed already at the time when Mark Twain wrote his stories, they are many times greater today after more than twenty years of government favors to labor unions and professional organizations.

of fires and cows. In their effects all these ideas are identical. They bring about, sooner or later, the loss of individual freedom and the deterioration of living conditions.

The common explanation that natural resources, climate, or other factors of man's surroundings determine man's standard of living is as superficial as it is fallacious. The governments of the underdeveloped countries often boast about their "vast supplies of national resources," about "the favorable conditions of production," etc. And, yet, what they need and plead for are *only capital* and *machinery* from the United States. If it were true that natural conditions determine man's living conditions, then the American Indians, who occupied the North American continent, should have had a high, or even the highest, standard of living of their time.

Having elucidated the common principle that man's ideas govern his actions, which in turn determine his social and political organization, his relation between individual and society, and his state and government, we may infer that the millions of emigrants from all parts of Streit's Union would enter the United States with ideas that are not only alien to American ideas, but that are ideas conducive to poverty, starvation, chaos, and war. The millions of new citizens, to whom Streit's Union would give equal rights of Union citizenship, would begin to influence American policies and determine the future course of America. And darkness would overcome mankind!

An Inquiry into Free Migration of Capital. We think it worthy of pausing to inquire whether this migration problem cannot be solved through other means of unification. We inquire into this question which Streit does not think worthy of mention, in order to conclude whether Streit's scheme of unification can be spared our unconditional rejection. We are raising the question: Can a common Union citizenship and the freedom of the Union citizen to migrate be attained in ways other than advocated by Streit?

The only conceivable substitution for actual mass migration is the freedom of migration of *capital* within the Union. Under the condition of equal security for capital in the Union, capital will migrate to those parts where the natural conditions for production are most favorable. It will continue to migrate until no further advantage can be obtained by moving to other places. Since wages are the main cost factor for many industries, many enterprises would find it advantageous to migrate to countries with lower labor costs. The effect of migration of capital from one country to another would be a reduction of the amount of capital invested per head of population in the country from which capital emigrates, and an increase of capital investments in the country of its new location. Wage rates in the former country necessarily would decrease, while the rates in the latter would increase. Thus a tendency towards equalization of wage rates throughout the Union would result. After a few decades of such an equalization process through freedom of migration of capital, which necessarily lowers the migration pressure of individuals, common citizenship and freedom of migration probably could be granted by the Union without causing a hurricane of migration of individuals.

Capital Is Consumed by Governments. But these deliberations on migration of capital within the Union are purely theoretical and academic, for the foregoing assumption of "equal security for capital in the Union" is neither fulfilled under present-day economic conditions, nor would it be fulfilled in Streit's Union. Capital invested in land, factories, machinery, and other fixed assets obviously cannot be transferred from one part of the Union to another. Transfer of certain forms of liquid capital to other states where conditions are more favorable to capital is identical with a liquidation of the enterprise at home. But a businessman who does not want to or cannot emigrate to follow his liquid capital abroad will scarcely want to liquidate his own enterprise which is his very existence.

Today, throughout the world, the capital of individuals is decimated by nationalization, outright confiscation, confiscatory taxation, controls and limitations, devaluation and inflation, sequestration, etc. Even in the country that is relatively safest for capital—the United States—income taxes, government controls and licenses, devaluations, and even government seizures of whole industries have been and, in some instances, still are in effect. To invest capital outside the United States and Canada without a special permit and guarantee by foreign parliaments, and for more than a few surveyable weeks, usually results in a total or partial loss of the capital, not to mention its interest. In Streit's Union, where capitalist, socialist, and Marxian communist countries are to exist side by side, capital would be subject to a multiplicity of government means of expropriation.[22] We may thus draw our final conclusion: neither under present-day economic conditions nor under the conditions as given in Streit's Union can capital migrate and bring about the equalizing effect which would reduce the pressure of migration of

[22] For a detailed analysis of the world's conditions regarding the safety of capital investments, see Franz Pick, *Black Market Year Book*, New York, 1951, 1953.

the individual. Even this roundabout way towards Union citizenship is impossible.

Migration of Capital Hindered by Governments and Labor Unions. Even if we assume equal security conditions for capital throughout the Union and agree with Streit on excellent Union conditions, we arrive at the same result because the nations from which liquid capital would emigrate are neither willing nor prepared to submit to a concomitant reduction in wage rates. They would rather vote against any scheme of unification having these effects.

We can presently observe this very problem of migration of capital from less favorable to more favorable production places in the United States of America. In recent years, numerous businesses in the Northern sections, and especially in the New England states, migrated to Southern states where production conditions are more favorable. Wages and taxes are lower; strikes and other union troubles are less frequent. The inevitable affect of this migration is some unemployment and lowering of wage rates in the North, while wage rates in the South tend to rise. Furthermore, the whole territory of the South is rapidly developed. The New England states and their local unions, having brought about this migration of business either through heavy taxation on the part of the former or forced increases in wage costs on the part of the latter, then vigorously protest against emigration of business. They attempt everything in their power (i.e., through inquiries, controls, new taxation, slow-downs, strikes, etc.) to keep business in the state. Naturally, they do not consider reducing business costs, taxes, and wages. That their own countrymen in the South gain by this migration does not soften the anger and indignation of the population in the North.

In Streit's Union of democratic peoples migration of liquid capital would occur on a much greater scale since the differences of production conditions are more distinct. The wage rates in countries from which capital would emigrate would drop considerably. Having arrived at this conclusion, we must raise again the crucial question: "Will people whose wage rates are lowered by an emigration of capital acquiesce in and vote in favor of a Union bringing about these results?" Definitely not! "Will people who even object against a migration that is harmful to them though it benefits their own countrymen acquiesce in a migration that hurts them considerably, though it benefits 'foreigners' at the other end of the world?" There cannot be any doubt that they would neither consent to the migration nor assent to the Union. From whatever aspect we may analyze Streit's contention that his Union would guarantee common citizenship and freedom of migration of the individual, we arrive at conclusions that are contrary to his contention and that deny the realizability of his Union.

An Inquiry into a Customs-Free Economy. The next problem we would like to analyze is the feasibility of a "customs-free economy of the Union." It is one of the important functions of Streit's Union to create a large free-trade area without barriers of national tariffs. However, it is maintained here that the hope for a realization of a "customs-free economy" is unrealistic, under present-day ideological conditions, and that a Union that attempts to bring it about would unhesitatingly be rejected by our contemporaries. The proof of this contention shall be presented in the following.[23]

The main function of modern government is to guarantee to its citizens economic and social security and protection. Under the pressure of public opinion, governments are firmly committed to a policy of interventionism and, especially, protectionism with regard to competition by foreigners. National tariffs, import and export restrictions, licenses and foreign exchange controls are the modern tools with which the policies of protection from foreign competition are executed. They are the tools by which the blessings of modern government are "fairly" administered and apportioned to the constituents. "Fair prices" are guaranteed and "fair wages" and incomes are decreed. If and when, for some reason or another, prices sink below the government parity plan, production is restricted by government order or goods in vast quantities are bought up by agencies and dumped or burned or shipped out of the country. If wage rates do not move as labor unions and government would like them to move, pressure is exerted to raise wage rates to a "fairer level." Unemployment inevitably results. If and when, for some reason or other, the price of a commodity that is partially supplied by foreign producers falls below the government parity price, steps are immediately taken by domestic producers and their representatives in Congress to limit the supply on the market by restricting foreign imports and competition. No consideration is given to the fact that millions of consumers are hurt by the resulting rise in prices and that the producers' gain is only temporary. Furthermore, there is no regard for the fact that the whole market structure is disarranged

---

[23] The problem of abolishing national trade barriers and realizing a customs-free economy of the Union is dealt with in detail in the chapter on "Coudenhove-Kalergi," p. 69 *et seq.* To avoid repitition we will confine ourselves to a short theoretical exposition of the problem and some elucidations mainly in the light of contemporary American ideologies and policies.

because of the establishment of trade and production obstacles. The fact that foreign producers and a host of foreign workers will be hurt by necessary curtailments of their production finds only deaf ears among adherents of government protection. That the domestic *export* industries, too, will be curtailed accordingly, because the foreigners no longer earn the means with which to purchase their imports, is beyond the recognition of protectionists.

Public Opinion Favors Protective Trade Barriers. If we now assume with Streit that national trade barriers will be abolished in the Union, we must be willing and prepared to bear the effects brought about by such an abolition. If we remove government protection from industries, they will temporarily be hurt by an increased supply of goods, increased competition, and lower prices. This will be true no matter how beneficial the abolition may be for the whole economy. Streit assumes that the democratic nations of the world are prepared to bear the effects of an abolition of protective trade barriers for the sake of his Union, but such preparedness is to be doubted. To illustrate our contention we may refer to a country in which the policy of government protection and intervention is least pronounced as compared with the other "founder democracies," and in which the prerequisites for a Union are most favorable. We are referring to the present-day United States. The final question on which we are willing to build the whole defense of our skepticism is: "Are the people of the United States prepared to bear the economic effects of an abolition of protection for certain groups of producers?" If even the people of the United States should be found unprepared, we need not bother raising the same question regarding the other peoples of the Union since their ideas on protectionism and interventionism are more radical and of longer standing.

Agricultural Policies Versus Union. One of the most striking examples of American protectionist policies is the attitude of public opinion and of Congress towards the protection of the American farmer. The agricultural protection program of the Federal Government has reached a place in the minds of the public and of Congress where it is almost as secure and self-evident as social security. It is a foregone conclusion, indeed, that the agricultural market is a supported market and that farm income is protected by government intervention. A permanent farm program is enacted to prevent any considerable shrinkage of net income through governmental price supports, income supplements, cultivation quotas, credit policies, import restrictions, etc. A whole series of governmental agencies and bureaus is set up to carry out a policy of "maintaining farm purchasing power" which is to "affect the distribution of the national income in a direction favorable to the maintenance of high consumption." This is the accepted ideology in present-day America—in Congress and the Administration, in the Democratic as well as the Republican party. Since we do not have to enter into a discussion of who put the government into the wheat and potato business or what the ultimate effects of this governmental policy necessarily will be, we may confine ourselves to a discussion of the effects of similar farm policies on the prospect of Streit's Union.

Governmental efforts to uphold farm prices at a fixed "parity level" are made only if and when the free market prices sink below the parity level. The free market price is the world market price as determined by demand and supply on the international market. It is a matter of evident fact that a Federal support policy that would endeavor to uphold free market prices would have to support and uphold world market prices. As such an undertaking is scarcely within the intention or the strength of the Federal government, the national market for farm products must be protected from adverse price fluctuations on the world market. This protection is achieved by high tariffs, import restrictions, and so forth. Only when the American farm market is protected and excluded from the international market can Federal agricultural policies of protection and parity be conducted.

Indeed, if we look at contemporary Federal agricultural policies, we find that government price support is inevitably connected with import restrictions. When the government embarked upon the support of butter prices, for example, it prohibited foreign butter imports immediately. American borders were closed to butter imports in spite of numerous angry diplomatic protests and economic retaliations from injured butter-exporting countries like Denmark, Holland, and others. The same holds true of Federal import restrictions on other supported farm products like cheese, eggs, potatoes, grain, cattle, meat, and sugar. The Federal policy of farm protection in recent years was conducted in disregard of the damage done to foreign producers who used to supply the American market. Even the neighbors of the United States, Canada and the Central American countries, were given numerous reasons to complain about American farm policies. Wherever the Federal government was confronted with the alternative between agricultural protection and friendly relations with neighboring countries, it preferred farm protection. This preference for protection over an international ex-

change of goods was, and still is, made not only in the case of basic
food commodities like potatoes and grain, which are produced by
millions of American farmers, but also of products grown by only a
few thousand American farmers. Cuba, Puerto Rico, Jamaica, and
other Central American territories, for example, grow sugar cane
and largely depend on the export of sugar and related products for
their livelihood. In the United States only a few thousand farmers
in a few states produce cane and beet; and yet, their clamor, led by
a few large concerns, is sufficient to induce the Administration and
Congress to grant tariff and quota protection. Central Americans
suffer from U. S. import restrictions. We rather see them ship their
sugar to Soviet Russia than to allow the American price of sugar to
sink a few pennies below the parity level. The same holds true in
our relations with Canada, South America, and other parts of the
world.

Americans Choose Farm Protection, Not Union. According to
Clarence Streit, a Union of the democratic peoples of the world
would do away with all interstate trade barriers. Goods could be
freely imported and exported without any national obstacles against
trade. This means that butter, cheese, eggs, potatoes, grain, cattle,
meat, sugar, and so on, could be freely imported to the United States.
And immediately the domestic market prices of these supported
commodities would sink below the parity level. The whole farm
program of protection would have to be abandoned instantly or it
would collapse. The crucial questions regarding the possibility of
a realization of Streit's Union must here be raised again. Are the
people of the United States prepared to abandon agricultural protection for the sake of Union? Are the American farmers, who
constitute a large part of the American constituency, prepared to
vote in favor of a Union that wrecks their protection? Does the
farmer vote for a Union that "floods" his market? Undoubtedly
not!

Industrial Protection Versus Union. We reach the same conclusion if we analyze the prevailing policies of protection for industrial
commodities. A small American industry producing goods that are
partially supplied by foreign producers may find its foreign competitors quite bothersome. And immediately we may hear demands
by Senators and Congressmen for prompt action and protection; [24]

[24] Of course, nobody lays blame on Senators and Congressmen for conducting those
policies of trade restrictions since they merely execute the ideologies prevailing in
public opinion. Personal moral guilt only sets in where the legislator acts in bad
faith, i.e., where he is fully aware of the effects of his policies, but finds it convenient

or we may observe probes and hearings before Tariff Committees and Commissions. Does Streit really assume that the American legislators who just may have voted for protection of some watch producers will, perhaps minutes later, rise in favor of a Union which would "flood" the market with watches and put American producers out of the watch business? To assume that legislators would not realize the alternative is thoughtless and superficial.

Regulation of Foreign Trade or Union: An Alternative. Another function of Streit's Union renders its realization impossible. This is the regulation of foreign trade by the government of the Union. The problem of agreeing on foreign trade protection and on a common tariff would raise insoluble problems. Where the tariff is used to assist and protect a particular industry, it subsidizes certain producers and imposes sacrifices on all other producers and consumers. While it is relatively easy in a national state to persuade the countrymen to pay higher prices for the product of a particular group which they favor for some "national" or "social" reason, it would be extremely difficult to persuade the population of the Union to endure sacrifices for some small group of producers in another part of the world. English and French consumers, for example, would scarcely be ready to pay more for their tuna fish to assist 500 tuna fishers in California. On the other hand, would Americans be ready to pay more for their cup of coffee to help some French plantings in Central Africa, or the Dutch to pay more for their beef to benefit cattle growers in Texas? Definitely not! Protection by tariff becomes clearly impossible in a Union where a national group of producers lacks the legislative majority to impose sacrifices on others. There cannot be government regulation of foreign trade, where there is a Union; and a Union cannot exist where there is government regulation of foreign trade.[25]

FUNDAMENTAL FALLACIES

Another serious objection against Streit's scheme of Union is that certain shortcomings of his plan render its realization unfeasible under any conceivable conditions. Fallacious conceptions and grave errors in his reasoning have led Streit to statements on essence and features of his Union that are contradictory and incompatible with each other.

not to resign and continues to conduct restrictive policies. This case, however, is undoubtedly an exception. The vast majority of legislators are exculpated because they fully concur with the prevailing public opinion.

[25] For a detailed analysis of problems connected with a Union tariff, see the chapter on "Coudenhove-Kalergi," p. 69 *et seq.*

The Scope of State Governments Severely Limited. Streit assures us that the Union could and would allow its states the freedom to experiment politically, economically, and socially, and that the member states would be free to choose their own system of social organization, whether capitalist or socialist.[26] But what economic liberty does the member state enjoy in a customs-free economy of a Union in which goods, men, and capital can move freely from state to state? In order to assist a particular industry, contemporary government usually influences prices. By way of compulsory organization, government control, quotas, and other restrictions, the supply of goods is limited and thus prices are raised. But the success of such policies depends on and presumes exclusion of foreign competition. In a Union a member state would be incapable of raising prices materially because it cannot exclude the competition of businessmen from other member states. Any burden placed on a particular industry would be a boon for the neighboring industry, which would undersell the former and cause it to suffer from unemployment.[27]

With respect to financial policies the member states would be equally severely limited in their operation. Any discriminatory taxation would drive liquid capital and labor elsewhere. Even indirect taxation could not be freely employed by the member states since many commodities could easily be imported from neighboring states. A severe check on the member states of the Union, finally, would be the check on national borrowing as the national central banks would no longer be free to lend limitlessly by resorting to the printing press.

The freedom to indulge in social experiments by the state would be equally limited in a Union. Although Streit fails to elucidate what he means by "social experiment," we may assume from other remarks of his works that he means "pro-labor policies." Such policies consist in government-decreed and -enforced increases in production costs in favor of the workers. They include social security, limitation of working time and business hours, holiday pay, vacations, pensions, sanitary statutes, minimum wage laws, and so on. But all these national policies would be severely limited in a Union, for they raise production costs and place the domestic industry at a serious disadvantage as to other industries in the Union. National-

26 *Ibid.*, p. 16.
27 F. A. Hayek, "The Economic Conditions of Interstate Federalism," in *New Commonwealth Quarterly* Vol. V, No. 2, (September 1939), pp. 131-149, reprinted in *Individualism and Economic Order*, London, 1948.

ization of industries, which Streit may also have in mind, would be rendered more difficult if they have to compete with foreign industries in the Union. Under such conditions nationalized industries could scarcely constitute basic tools for social and economic planning by the national state.

A *Socialist Society Cannot Be Part of a Union.* Streit's contention that the member states are free to choose a system of social organization of their liking is the most fallacious statement in his book. The assertion that not only capitalist but socialist and even Marxian communist nations can be members of the Union is a profound mistake revealing erroneous conceptions and faulty reasoning as well as lack of economic and political insight. It is contended here, and it is almost too apparent and evident to require a detailed analysis, that a socialist society cannot be part of a Union.

In a socialist system private enterprise and private ownership of the means of production are abolished. Government ownership or control is substituted for the market economy. The individual is no longer free to determine by his buying and abstention from buying what is to be produced and in what quantity and quality. A government plan by economic commissioners and stabilizers alone settles all these matters. Imports from and exports to other countries are governed by the general plan. "Unplanned" and "selfish" individual actions, imports and exports on the individual's initiative, are prohibited insofar as they run counter to the master plan. All these features of a socialist economy can be derived by way of simple reasoning from the basic conception of government ownership in or control over the means of production.[28]

We may illustrate the necessity of strict export and import controls in a socialist economy by using a brief example. Let us assume that the central planner, Mr. Stabilizer, has decreed, for certain national economic reasons, that the price of a motor car is 1000 thalers, and that the price of a similar car produced by a neighboring industry amounts to only 900. Now, if the socialist economy is part of a customs-free economy of a Union, the citizens of the socialist country will not hesitate to import the equally good but cheaper car from the neighboring country. The plan of Mr. Stabilizer thus could not be executed because his cars would be left unsold, and his nationalized industry would soon be idle and unemployed. To execute his purpose, which, in the belief of Mr.

---

[28] For an excellent study on socialism, see L. v. Mises, *Socialism,* Yale University Press, 1951.

Stabilizer, can be attained only at a price of 1000 thalers, imports would have to be prohibited.

The same necessity for restrictions exists with respect to all other goods. It is obvious that import controls and restrictions by member states are incompatible with the nature of a Union.

Capitalism or Socialism: There Is No Other Alternative. A socialist economy deviates in price and wage structure from the market economy. To differ materially from the market economy is not only its purpose and objective, but such is the inevitable outcome of the substitution of one "national economic planner" for millions of individuals who used to do the economic planning by buying or refraining from buying. Differences in the structure of prices and wages, however, are equalized in a market economy in which individuals and groups of individuals compete and seek to profit from differences. The Union economy without national trade barriers would constitute a market economy with the tendency towards general price equalization. Only slight differences would continue to exist because of different costs of transportation for different places in the Union. The price and wage structure of a socialist member economy, which extends over only a part of the Union, would be quickly equalized to the structure of the Union economy at the time of its exposure to the market economy and its market prices. That is to say, the socialist organization would collapse.

In any organization of human society, in any federation of states or Union of democratic peoples, there is room for only one system of social organization. Either the system is socialist, and then it must be consistently so throughout the Union, or the system is capitalist. There is no other alternative.

That reality concurs with our theoretical contention may easily be illustrated by the existence of a small free trade area surrounded by a socialist economy. We are referring to Free West Berlin in the Russian occupation zone in Germany, some 120 miles behind the Iron Curtain. West Berlin is part of the Western German market economy. Although tens of thousands of Russian soldiers and Peoples' policemen are guarding the borders of West Berlin, and although trade between East and West Berlin is conducted with great risk of life, not to mention property, an exchange of goods continuously takes place, causing daily embarrassment to the socialist planners. If the borders of West Berlin were open to free exchange—and such an assumption concurs with Streit's contention on his Union—socialist planning in Eastern Germany not only would experience difficulties, but would clearly become impossible because of "unplanned" movements of goods. Even Soviet Russia, in the long run, would not be able, in our belief, to resist the radiation of the capitalist economy via the small island of West Berlin. For the socialist planners in Russia there is only one alternative: Either they guard their borders against market economies with hundreds of thousands of soldiers, tanks, guns, and ammunition—or they abandon socialism.

Streit's Union Makes Inroads on Man's Liberty. The final point and reason for our rejection of Streit's projected Union is the fact that it would affect adversely man's liberty which is the very central point and objective of Streit's Union. The following features of Streit's scheme of Union make inroads on man's liberty:

1. Controls and regulations by the Union government over the foreign trade relations of Union citizens.
2. Controls and regulations by the Union government over the value of money and media of foreign exchange.
3. Legislation and enforcement of "sweeping economic rights" by the government of the Union.

Controls and regulations by the Union government over the foreign trade relations of Union citizens necessarily infringe upon the rights of the individual by giving authority over man's actions to government officials and civil servants. Where the state controls foreign trade, the individual is no longer free to make his own decisions. He has to plead for licenses and permissions, inquire where he may buy, what he can buy, from whom he may buy; what, where, and to whom he can sell; at what price he may buy or sell, etc. That is what is meant by foreign trade control and state supervision. The individual may entreat, but only the government plans and decides.

Control and regulation by the Union government over the value of money and media of foreign exchange mean that the individual must settle debts and payments with a media of exchange the value of which is determined by government law. The individual is deprived of his freedom since he is forced to settle interpersonal debts and payments not under the terms of mutual choice and agreement, but under terms fixed by law. Such an infringement upon the liberty of man, to which most contemporaries are fully accustomed, is connected with immoral imputation and severe injustice if the value of money has been decreased by government credit expansion, outright inflation, or devaluation. An individual may have loaned a sum of $10,000 to another individual at a time when it was worth a certain amount of other goods—let us say, two houses. When the loan is due for repayment he expects to be paid an equal amount of money that will buy the same quantity of goods. But then government interferes and depreciates the value of money and says: "In repayment for your loan of $10,000 originally worth two houses you must accept these $10,000 of my latest issue that are only worth one house. If you do not abide by my order, I will take appropriate measures of coercion that will induce you to accept." No matter how immoral such a demand may be, this government, under present-day world conditions, is still considered to be fair in that the money lender receives a "fair deal" by losing only half of his loan. In all these interpersonal transactions the individual is defenseless against the authority of the state. Where, in all fairness, is his liberty to manage his own affairs?

Finally, Streit's "sweeping economic rights" curtail the liberty of the individual to use and employ his own labor. "Freedom from both overwork and unemployment as defined by law," which Streit favors adding to the Union Bill of Rights, can only mean, according to all rules of understanding, government legislation and enforcement of laws regarding "overwork and unemployment." The underlying notion of Streit's demand is based on the thought that the individual would overwork himself or be unemployed without government intervention. According to this notion, the individual endures both evils because of his own ignorance of what is good for him, or because some fellowman may impose overwork or unemployment upon him. In the first case, government intervention is clearly an infringement upon the individual's rights over himself, no matter how "foolish" his actions may be in the eyes of the legislator. In the second case, "protection from overwork or unemployment by fault of a second party" is apparently based on the Marxian doctrine that the worker in the capitalist economy can be exploited or left unemployed in the process of production. Such a thought is as superficial as it is fallacious. How can a worker, who is free to offer his services to a vast number of competing employers, and who may offer them to an employer of his own choice and liking, be compelled to overwork or to be unemployed? Unemployment does not lie in the nature of a market economy. Unemployment is a phenomenon brought into existence by governments impeding the mobility of capital and labor, and labor unions eager to raise wage rates above the height determined by the market. Only when wage costs are higher than the market rate can unemployment arise. But this unemployment is government- or union-created, and as such is a grave infringement upon the freedom of the individual and his opportunity for employment. However, could Streit have meant the protection of the individual from both evils in a socialist economy? Where the individual is confronted by one huge employer who determines where he shall work and under what conditions, and where the individual is no longer free to sever his work relation because of grievances, there he may be exploited and may suffer from overwork. But, as we can infer from other places in his writing, this is not the protection that Streit is suggesting for inclusion in the Union Bill of Rights.

The Socialization of the Communication System. A few other minor fallacies of Streit's proposed Union cause us also to reject it. According to Streit, one of the five basic functions of the government of the Union is to control a postal and communication system. Streit neither explains explicitly the reasons for his demand nor does he say exactly what he means by "communication system." We may assume that he probably includes all means of communication like interstate telephone, telegraph, and radio. Mr. Streit feels there is need for unification and standardization of all means of communication. He assumes that this can best be accomplished under Union government control. Thus costs could be saved and taxes reduced.

Why does Streit advocate Union controls over the communication system and the postal service, but not over other even more important services of human economy? We expect Streit to answer this question. What distinguishes human communication from other features of human action that justifies its government control? What distinguishes the individual's postal service from other services in his daily life? It cannot be the importance of postal service to the individual that induces Streit to ask for government control. For, other services are many times more important to the individual, such as the baking of his daily bread or the churning of his butter. Both services are rendered to him by fellow individuals in voluntary distribution of labor. Why should the interstate telephone and telegraph industry be controlled by the government of the Union? Private industries in the United States of America work very well and stand any comparison with the U. S. postal service. The unification and standardization of American private communication industries, which are constantly improving and expanding their services, are by far superior to the unification and standardization of the U. S. postal system, which is progressively cutting its service. The former are profitable and growing industries and are paying large sums into national and local treasuries; the U. S. postal system is an annual

burden on the Federal budget. Many billions in taxes have been
spent to subsidize the governmental postal system.

If Streit's Union of democracies would assume control over the
communication system and postal service, it would acquire an annual deficit that would surpass the civil budget of the United States.
In all fourteen democracies, the postal service as well as other communication services are presently controlled or owned by the state.
All these government systems have annual deficits that often constitute the total deficit of the national budgets. If the Union would
assume these obligations and, in addition, new deficit obligations
from extended Union ownership and controls, the total Union deficit
would probably amount to more than the total present deficits of
all member states. A Union that would be burdened with such a
load right from its beginning could scarcely fare well on its road
towards prosperity.

Contra-cyclical Policies Perpetuate Depression. The last objection which we raise against Streit's scheme of Union is the contra-
cyclical economic function of the Union government which, according to Streit, must be "overwhelmingly powerful in the economic
world." Only the combined strength of all democratic peoples of
the world is sufficient to achieve monetary stabilization and meet
periods of depression and unemployment.[29] No other governmental
combination, not even a United States of Europe, could achieve stability.

We find one correct line of thought in Streit's contentions. This
is the relationship that exists between the "power of government
in the economic world" and the occurrence of periods of depression
and unemployment. But although Streit asserts that "overwhelming
economic strength" can avoid a depression, we are convinced that
only under complete *absence* of government intervention in the economic world can a depression be avoided. Our explanation of cause
and effect of economic cycles is diametrically opposed to that of Mr.
Streit. If his assertion were correct, history and reality would have
to show that world-wide depressions are least severe where the economic power of state is greatest. Reality would have to show that
depressions are slightest where and when governments employ their
vast economic power. The depression of the 1930's, for example,
had to be least severe in the United States where the economic
power of the President was almost complete—with the exception
of a few Constitutional checks by the Supreme Court. And the year
1937 had to be a year of prosperity, since the administration was at

[29] *Ibid.*, p. 124.

the height of its economic power. The government enforced its numerous economic reconstruction acts, especially the Wagner Act, and even tried to subdue the Supreme Court. But reality reveals that the depression of the 1930's was most severe and extended in the United States, and that the year 1937 experienced the most violent economic decline in American history. Other "powerful" European states saw a similar depression. But it is a matter of fact that weaker nations, whose governments lacked that economic power, suffered least from depression and unemployment.

But history is a complex phenomenon. Therefore, we shall analyze Streit's contentions and reveal his fallacies by way of reasoning. Monetary inflation and expansionist credit policies of the government bring about a boom in which everybody is buying as much as he can buy because a continuous rise in price is anticipated. There is full employment and governments demand credit for periods of prosperity during the time of their administration. Rising prices induce the businessman in his economic calculations to anticipate future rises in prices. He combines the factors of production—land, labor, and capital—and employs them toward future production goals as long as the production process appears profitable. And, indeed, it appears profitable under the assumption of further rises in prices. While the boom is in progress, he embarks upon production processes that will yield their final products in the remote future. And the more remote in the future the product will be completed, the greater appears its profitability. The demand for factors of production increases sharply as numerous production processes are begun. This additional demand inevitably causes the prices of factors of production, i.e., business costs, to rise. The boom thus continues until business, in spite of the rise in prices, is no longer profitable because of the soaring costs. At this moment the decline begins. Costs, i.e., the price of land, labor, and capital, must come down before business becomes profitable again.

If the government of Streit's Union of democratic peoples would embark upon large expenditures for public works and public enterprise and would open up "vast new enterprises," as Mr. Streit advocates, the necessary adjustment would only be delayed and the stagnation prolonged. The demand for the factors of production by the Union government, which naturally would be financed by inflation, would only tend to keep their prices high and business unprofitable. If, in addition, the government would decree raises in wage costs or give labor unions a hand in forcing such raises, like the Roosevelt Administration did in 1936, business activity would come to a halt. If the government of Streit's Union would conduct such policies and make use of its "overwhelming strength in the economic world," Streit's Union would be a Union of lasting depression which it would be a grave risk to join.

Streit's Critique of Capitalism Unfounded. Streit's critique of capitalism for not having solved "the problem of organizing peaceful relation among the nations" at the time "when all the world was capitalistic," [30] is the customary critique of the advocates of interventionism or socialism. Capitalism is the system of social organization in which the means of production are owned by the individual who is free to employ them for his own purpose. Capitalism excludes government intervention. Where there is capitalism, there cannot be socialism or interventionism; and where there is state intervention or central control, there cannot be capitalism. If we agree on this conception of capitalism—and scarcely anybody will disagree—we must conclude that never in human history has capitalism been fully realized. Even during the "capitalist" nineteenth century, government interventions in the form of national tariffs, credit expansion, and government suspension of the gold standard and many other forms were commonplace.

But even if we assume that capitalism in the nineteenth century was paramount, it cannot be blamed for having failed to organize peaceful relations among the nations. It is an undeniable fact of history that the "capitalist" nineteenth century was the most peaceful period in human history. The few wars that were fought during this period were fought by non-capitalist nations. Scarcely anybody will maintain that the three wars fought between 1864 and 1871 by Prussia were those of a "capitalist" state or that the wars of Russia and Japan were wars of capitalist nations. But the nineteenth century was not only the most peaceful century in human history, it also allowed mankind to multiply to an unprecedented rate and improve its standard of living enormously. It proved to be a social system unrivaled in its beneficial effects. The standard of living of the American nation, the last nation to abandon the road of capitalism, speaks for itself.

The reason for continuous poverty, chaos, and starvation in many parts of the world lies in the fact that the people in those parts never have understood or embraced the doctrines of capitalism. Never in their history has the individual been free to save and to produce or to accumulate productive capital. The nations of the poverty-stricken Orient have always despised Western capitalism

---

[30] *Ibid.,* p. 41.

and are still sneering at it. It is inevitable that they must pay the price in the form of chaos, poverty, and starvation. Although the Western nations have reaped the ample reward and blessing of capitalism during the nineteenth century and the first decade of the twentieth, they have now abandoned the capitalist system and have chosen the road of interventionism and socialism. For each new step on this road a toll must be paid.

Summary. Clarence K. Streit's design of a Union unfortunately reveals certain basic errors and fallacies in conception and reasoning that make its realization impractical. His contention that free market economies as well as planned economies can live side by side in a Union is a fundamental shortcoming that obscures his eyes to the real difficulties and problems of unification. Numerous other assertions disclose a lack of sense of reality.

Streit's comparison with the history of the United States is ill-founded since the Americans who created this great nation were liberals, in the classical sense of the word. They abandoned restrictions, controls, protection, tariffs, and inflation with a stroke of a pen. They were disciples of the great English and French philosophers and economists who believed that the freedom of the individual shall be paramount. But their teachings are dead in the minds of our contemporaries. The significance of the difference between today and the past can clearly be recognized by the fact that the great opposition in the parliaments of the democratic nations today are constituted by parties that advocate expropriation or government seizure of private property, more and stricter controls, higher taxation and protection. The American opposition in Congress is comprised of Fair-Dealers and liberals in the modern sense of the word. How can these men be for unification and national economic protection at the same time? A divided world is further away from unification than ever; and alienation is still growing.

As it is the task of a critic of the plans of unification to reveal and refute the errors and fallacies of a proposal, it unfortunately does not lie within the scope of his task to elaborate the numerous points of mutual concurrence and agreement. Streit's basic approach to the problem of unification is sound and admirable. It is the individual who is the point of departure of Streit's planning for Union. His supreme objectives are individual freedom and prosperity and the individual's protection from dictatorship and war. These, indeed, are laudable objectives.

II

R. N. Coudenhove-Kalergi and the
European Parliamentary Union

The Author. An important role in the creation and development of a European Movement after World War I was played by Count Coudenhove-Kalergi whose book *Pan-Europe* was first published in Vienna, in 1923. The son of an Austrian diplomat and a Japanese mother, the author became a citizen of the new republic of Czechoslovakia by reason of the "Peace of Paris." He had written on philosophical and other political subjects, but he attained world-wide fame and reputation only when he, with much effort and skill, began to muster public support for his plan of European union. Coudenhove was a socialist, nationalist, ardent Catholic, humanitarian, and a keen advocate of European unification.[1] His Pan-European movement gained considerable public support from numerous prominent European statesmen and intellectual leaders. After World War II, in 1947, Count Coudenhove-Kalergi initiated a private organization, the "European Parliamentary Union," to facilitate contacts among the adherents of his Pan-European idea and to influence key individuals. This organization exercises great influence through its members in present-day political circles. The national legislatures of Western Europe contain numerous adherents of the "European Parliamentary Union." The French Parliament, for example, has more than two hundred and fifty deputies and senators who are members of the French section of the movement.[2]

---

[1] "My sympathies," says Coudenhove while speaking on his political outlook, "were definitely with Austrian Socialism, thanks to its broadminded social policies." See his *Crusade for Europe*, Putnam's Sons, New York, 1943, p. 86.

[2] John Goormaghtigh, *European Integration*, Carnegie Endowment for International Peace, New York, 1953, p. 69.

Objectives of Unification. The main objective of his plan for European federal union is to maintain peace and European independence with respect to the growing world powers of America and Soviet Russia. A federation, according to Coudenhove, would prevent every European state from being at the mercy, politically and economically, of the world powers. It would give Europe the strength to repel any military invasion and to meet any economic competition.[3] A united Europe also, "thanks to its intermediate position between England and Amercia on the one side, and between Russia and East Asia on the other, and thanks also to the tradition and native gifts of its inhabitants, would be both able and fitted to be the cultural center of the world for a long time to come." [4]

The Scope of Union. All the free nations of continental Europe, including Iceland, and their colonies are to be the members of the Pan-European federation. England should be excluded from Pan-Europe because she "would always sacrifice the interests of Europe to English imperial interests." [5] A union with England, according to Coudenhove, is possible after the British World Empire has disintegrated.

Pan-Europe and Economic Competition. "The basis of Pan-Europe is economic," says Coudenhove.[6] "The economic model for Pan-Europe is provided by the United States of America." A United States of Europe would also constitute a world power which could easily be defended from the economic competition of the other world powers. Europe must repel the economic competition of the other powers to safeguard its political and economic independence. And this end can be accomplished, according to Coudenhove, by "unifying its organization and rationally opening its African colonial empire, which is very nearly equal to Asiatic Russia in its extent." Under these circumstances, "Europe could itself produce all the raw materials and foodstuffs it requires, and thus also become independent in a material way." [7]

Pan-Europe and America. Coudenhove-Kalergi fears the competition of American producers and businessmen. He believes European economic independence is endangered by their competition. Therefore, in order to safeguard continental independence from America, Europe must unite. Coudenhove shows us the way. He

[3] R. N. Coudenhove-Kalergi, *Pan-Europe*, A. A. Knopf, New York, 1926, p. 34.
[4] *Ibid.*, p. 34.
[5] *Ibid.*, p. 40.
[6] *Ibid.*, p. 102.
[7] *Ibid.*, p. 34.

calls for abolition of the inter-European customs barriers and for
European autarky. Only a Europe, thus united and autark, "could
in the future maintain its economic independence with respect to
the United States of America and avoid bankruptcy and economic
servitude." [8] The inter-European custom barriers which now throttle industry, commerce, and transportation and split Europe into
economic fragments, must be abolished gradually, and the economic
national regions must be fused into one "Pan-European" region
"which alone would be successfully able to keep pace with American industry." [9]

The Inter-European Competitive Struggle. Not only is American
economic competition the object of Coudenhove's serious concern,
but he is also worried about the present "competitive struggle"
among the European nations. The economic consequences of the
"Peace Treaties of Paris," in 1919, and all their harmful effects on
postwar economic conditions in Europe are explained by Coudenhove in the existence of inter-European economic competition. On
page 128, he states: "Once economic cooperation in Europe has
taken the place of the present competitive struggle, all economic
presuppositions of the Peace Treaties will be automatically changed
and will press forward for amicable settlement."

The Advantages of Unification. The advantages of acceptance
and realization of his "Pan-Europe" idea are listed in summary by
Coudenhove as the following:

1. security from an inter-European war;
2. neutralization of Europe in world conflicts;
3. protection against Russia;
4. possibility of disarmament;
5. ability to compete with the American and British industries and
   avoid bankruptcy and economic servitude;
6. national minorities are insured against persecution, oppression, and
   denationalization;
7. nations which "did not receive fair treatment at the time the extra-
   European world was divided up, such as Germans, Poles, Czechs,
   Scandinavians, and Balkan peoples, would find in the great African
   colonial empires a field for the release of their economic energies." [10]

Such release of the economic energies of the European nations
would also serve his objective of making Europe autark and economically independent. Africa would be converted "into the future

[8] *Ibid.*, p. 179.
[9] *Ibid.*, pp. 127, 128.
[10] *Ibid.*, p. 179.

granary and source of raw materials for Europe," and thus free Europe from imports from other continents. But two main tasks would have to be accomplished: First, the Sahara Desert would have to be transformed partially into agricultural land; and second, the sleeping-sickness, which renders cattle-breeding and colonization impossible in the most fertile districts, would have to be extirpated from Central Africa.[11] These tasks, according to Coudenhove, would have to be accomplished by the combined forces of Europe.

Agrarian Reforms and Social Reforms. Speaking about the intermediate consequences of the abolition of inter-European tariff barriers, Coudenhove points out two means for their alleviation. "In Europe," says Coudenhove, "a sufficient amount of land is still available for allotment; agrarian reforms could in most countries provide sufficient land to absorb the workers thrown out of employment by the abolition of customs frontiers and of the national industries."[12] Thus, "through the progressive abolition of the inter-European tariff walls, proceeding hand-in-hand with the accomplishment of social reforms, especially land reforms, neither the nations nor the workers would suffer injury; no one, indeed, would suffer, save that group of industrialists who are unequal to a free competitive struggle in large inter-European industry."[13]

A Consolidation of Industries. The dangers that threaten the economic development and realization of Pan-Europe from the "outgrowths of the trust system" may be overcome by socialist controls which, according to Coudenhove, can be carried out in Europe more easily than in America, since socialism in Europe has a greater power. "In order to effectually combat that most dangerous and powerful enemy of Pan-Europeanism, there is a necessity for consolidation of all those industries which have no foreign competition to fear, and which would gain new markets only as a result of inter-European free trade." These industries are European agriculture and the European monopolist industries which are equal to any conceivable competition. It is imperative to separate these Pan-European monopolist industries from those industries that require tariff protection and consolidate them into the service of the Pan-Europe idea. In that way, according to Coudenhove, the capitalist resistance to the "United States of Europe" might be broken by capitalism itself.[14]

[11] *Ibid.*, p. 180.
[12] *Ibid.*, p. 189.
[13] *Ibid.*, p. 189.
[14] *Ibid.*, p. 190.

Stages of Unification. Coudenhove envisages the following stages of Pan-European development:

1. a Pan-European Conference should be called;
2. compulsory treaties of arbitration and of security pacts among all the democratic states of Europe should be concluded, and a compulsory Court of Arbitration should be set up;
3. a Pan-European customs union should be formed and Europe be federated into a coherent economic sphere—possibly, a monetary union should also be created;
4. a Constitution of the "United States of Europe" which would make provisions for two Pan-European chambers of legislature should be designed and accepted; a "House of Peoples" should represent the peoples of Europe, and the "House of States" should represent the European national governments.[15]

A Pan-Europe thus created would be a unit consisting of member states that would enjoy a maximum amount of freedom.

Bourgeois Parties Reprimanded. In discussing the support of his Pan-Europe idea by the European parties, Coudenhove praises the socialist parties for their keen political perception on the question of European federation and finds harsh words of criticism for the attitude of the bourgeois parties. "The leaders of European socialism," says Coudenhove, "more clearly recognize the necessity of Pan-European unity than do the leaders of the middle class."[16] He adds, "The attitude of the European bourgeois parties toward the question of federation is less clear; nevertheless, it will be decisive as regards their own fate. History once more gives them an opportunity to perform a great creative act. If they fail to pass this test, allowing petty interests to triumph over world-historical necessities, they will be proving the bankruptcy of their class and their inability to guide the destinies of Europe in the future. Strong arms will take up their heritage and complete the task which proved too great for them."[17]

His Socialist Support. Coudenhove contrasts the hesitating attitude of the bourgeois parties regarding his Pan-Europe idea with the positive reaction of the far-sighted socialist leaders. He quotes Georg Ledebour, a German Socialist leader and a member of the Reichstag, as a representative of full-hearted Pan-European support. "Capital, like Proletariat," says Ledebour, "instinctively presses forward toward an economic world system. But the monop-

15 *Ibid.*, p. 175.
16 *Ibid.*, p. 183.
17 *Ibid.*, p. 185.

olistic urge to exploit which characterizes Capital drives the capitalists of a country to resort, in the first place, always to the annexation or at least the economic subordination of the countries adjoining their own state once the need has shown itself by economically and politically fusing their own productive regions with those of that neighboring country. But such a capitalist propensity toward an extension of power invariably threatens to grow into a 'national' war, with drawn sword in hand." [18]

Coudenhove then proceeds to quote from Ledebour's discussion of the French occupation of the Ruhr district in Germany, in 1923, as an example of such capitalistic propensity. He quotes: "to find an escape from that fateful conflict is the most pressing task of the French and German proletariats. Having recognized the need (already apparent within the capitalistic framework) of an amalgamation of the French and German economic spheres, we must draw the inevitable conclusion, which is: the unification of Europe as a coherent economic system. Even as it is now, that need would be realized without difficulty once socialism came to the helm. Socialism, which will regulate the entire world economy, must immediately free mankind from the bonds of exploitation, no less than from the inter-state customs barriers which impede it. But even now, while we contend for power within our own capitalist state organism, we are justified in addressing to the capitalistically organized states of Europe the demand for economic federation. For such a federation is in no way incompatible with the capitalist economic system. On the contrary, already a general need in that direction is making itself felt across the narrow national boundaries." [19]

His Followers versus "Anti-Europeans." In conclusion, Coudenhove makes a fundamental distinction between his fellowmen. He distinguishes between adherents of his scheme of unification in a Pan-European federation and "Anti-Europeans." "A clear distinction must be made," says Coudenhove, "between Pan-Europeans and Anti-Europeans." A "decisive struggle will arise between the Anti-Europeans and the Pan-Europeans for the fate of Europe." [20]

CRITICISM

It is as easy to agree on the ultimate goal of Coudenhove's plan and movement for the integration of Europe as it is with all similar

[18] *Ibid.,* p. 183.
[19] Georg Ledebour, European Union, in "The Class War," 1923, as quoted by R. N. Coudenhove-Kalergi, *Pan-Europe,* pp. 183-84.
[20] *Pan-Europe,* pp. 191, 192, 193.

plans for unification. The objectives are desirable and the advantages of their eventual realization are entirely praiseworthy. Who would object to a plan designed to bring about security from an inter-European war or protection from a military attack by Soviet Russia? Who does not wish the national minorities in Europe to be insured against persecution, oppression, and denationalization, or the burden of armament to be decreased? However, as shall be proved in the following, the Pan-Europe plan by Coudenhove-Kalergi does not and, by its very nature, cannot bring about the effects its author claims for it. A Pan-Europe as envisaged by Coudenhove is *unrealizable* and cannot be brought about without force, the very avoidance of which is its objective.

The second fundamental objection against Coudenhove's Pan-Europe idea and the European Parliamentary Union movement is the fact that his plan is *a scheme for the attainment of wholesale socialism in Europe.* A socialist Europe, however, will bring about inter-European wars and invite Russia to an immediate attack. A socialist Europe cannot be a Europe of peaceful nations. Nor will it be able to compete economically with the other powers of the world, especially America. It will be of necessity a continent of poverty and starvation, of constant wars and unfree individuals who depend on omnipotent government officials and continuous aid and contributions from the free nations of the world.

European Autarky Leads to Chaos and Poverty. "The basis of Pan-Europe is economic," says Coudenhove. The inter-European customs barriers are the main obstacles to European unification. They split Europe into economic fragments and throttle industry, commerce, and transportation. Customs barriers therefore should be abolished gradually and the economic national regions should be fused into one Pan-European region.

The *extra*-European customs barriers, however, are to be maintained. Europe is to become independent in a material way; it is to produce all the raw materials and foodstuffs it requires. For only a Europe united and autark can "maintain its economic independence with respect to the United States of America" and avoid bankruptcy and economic servitude.

Coudenhove does not enter into a detailed discussion of the extra-European customs barriers, but we may infer from his objective of European autarky and economic independence that the European customs barriers towards the rest of the world are to be sufficiently high in order to bring about autarky. The raising of a European customs wall must necessarily be uniform to avoid an inflow of goods at the boundary with the lowest custom obstacle. A tariff, for instance, which endeavors to prohibit the importation of American automobiles but leaves the custom duties of one European country at a lower level is no longer prohibitive, but merely makes the latter country a road of importation for the whole of Europe.

A uniform European tariff must be sufficiently high to be protective. *Its minimum level must be identical with the highest present-day national tariff*, or it would no longer be protective for the national economy having the highest tariff. This, in fact, is another aspect of Coudenhove's plan of unification. To illustrate, let us look at the following example. We may assume that country A, which will be a member state of the United States of Europe, presently has a tariff on the importation of American typewriters that is absolutely protective. Behind this wall of tariff the domestic industry is enabled to produce typewriters of its own. Let us furthermore assume that the other European member states have lower customs barriers or none at all. A European tariff that is identical with the tariff of member state A would continue to protect the typewriter industry of A; a lower European tariff would be less protective and would increase American competition with the industry of A. To the other member states with present-day lower typewriter tariffs, the European customs necessarily would raise their trade barriers to the protective level of A, which would render the importation of American typewriters impossible. People in these countries would now solely depend on European production, especially on the production of the industry in A. Until the European tariff was established they preferred American typewriters to their domestic typewriters and those of A, for they had not raised their customs to the level of A, but had allowed American typewriters to be imported.

The European tariff would mean an unexpected *boon for the protected European industries*. In our foregoing example, the typewriter industry of A, which was inferior to its American competition, now would have to fill the demand for typewriters from all over Europe. And new and additional industries would have to be developed to replace the American industries which used to produce for the European market.

In conclusion, we may state the following inferences:

1. A European tariff must be uniform.
2. It must be as high as the highest national tariff.

These requirements of a European tariff of necessity have the following effects:

1. Those industries which presently are most protected from extra-European competition are favored; they will obtain those European markets for their products which previously were supplied by extra-European industries now cut off by the European tariff.
2. People who formerly imported goods from other continents and who preferred those goods to European goods because they were better or cheaper now depend solely on European production, and especially on the production in those European states which had the highest national tariff.

But still two other concomitant effects of a European tariff as envisaged by Coudenhove-Kalergi must be mentioned;

1. The European customs barriers that cut off American export industries from their European markets inevitably *bring about depression and unemployment in American export industries*. Without the European market they are overextended and have to contract. The depression will be most severe in the industries that depend greatly on European orders. These extra-European effects, however, may be disregarded by the European statesmen as being outside their field of interest.

2. The depression in the American industries which formerly earned European media of exchange and European credit balances with which European goods were purchased and imported, automatically spreads to the European export industries which now cease to receive American orders. Where foreign exchange cannot be earned, it cannot be spent. *The European export industries will suffer from the same unemployment of capital and labor* as the American industries will suffer by being cut off from European markets. Since the European export industries were only located in those countries where low tariffs had permitted an intercontinental exchange of goods, the depression in export industries must of necessity hit these countries.

With regard to the effects of a uniform protective tariff of Europe upon its different member states, we may now make the following statements.

1. The European tariff does not directly affect those countries whose tariffs were as high and protective as the European tariff.

2. The European tariff most severely affects the countries which had imported from and exported to other continents. It brings about unemployment in their export industries and, furthermore,

forces their population against their choice and will to depend solely on inferior European production, especially on the production in those European states with the highest national tariffs. The standard of living of the people in member states, adversely effected by the raising of European trade barriers, is lowered by the very advantage which the importation of goods from other continents had given them. European countries which have had the largest foreign trade per capita of population have always had the highest standard of living. Switzerland, Belgium, Holland, and the Scandinavian countries enjoy a relatively high standard of living on account of their foreign trade and international division of labor and production. How low their standard of living would drop in case of inter-European autarky, can only be imagined.

Public Opinion Against the Effects of European Autarky. Having arrived at the foregoing conclusions, we now may raise the fundamental question of the unification of Europe as designed by Coudenhove-Kalergi. It is the following: *"Will the people of those countries that enjoy the advantages of trading with other continents and correspondingly high standards of living voluntarily yield and submit to a lowering of their living conditions because of and for the sake of the unification of Europe?"* This question must be answered in the negative. There cannot be any doubt that scarcely anyone, however European-minded he may be, will vote for a united Europe if it involves a lowering of his living conditions, or even heavy losses and unemployment, as in the case of those export industries that formerly worked for outer-European markets. All may be convinced that Europe should unite, but they undoubtedly would vote against a scheme of unification that would bring about a deterioration of their living conditions. No statesman or politician could support a plan that would obviously lower living conditions and reduce wages.

Public Opinion Polls Are Misleading. After World War II, various public opinion polls and tests were taken in Holland, Belgium, France, and Germany. People from all walks of life were asked whether they would support a "United States of Europe" which would bring about peace, but which would involve a certain limitation of national sovereignty. Such a question, however, is superficial and misleading. It is like a public opinion poll on people's preference between war or peace, sin or righteousness. It cannot be surprising, then, that often eighty or ninety per cent or more of those questioned voted in the affirmative. A more truthful and elucidating question for public opinion polls and tests would have been: "Are you willing and prepared to suffer heavy losses, unemployment, and a lowering of your living conditions for the sake of economic readjustment necessitated by a unification of Europe?" One hundred per cent of those questioned would have answered in the negative.

Abolition of the Inter-European Tariffs Unrealizable Under Contemporary Ideological Conditions. The reader who may not yet be convinced that a Pan-Europe as envisaged by Coudenhove-Kalergi is unrealizable may also consider the following argumentation on the effects of the abolition of *inter*-European trade barriers on national economies. We maintain that, under present-day ideological conditions, people in Europe are not ready to bear the short-run consequences of such abolition, however favorable the long-run effects may appear to be.

Under the pressure of public opinion modern government is firmly committed to a policy of interventionism, and especially protectionism with regard to competition by foreigners. As soon as a particular domestic industry encounters difficulties because of sinking prices or rising costs, or lack of sales at a certain price, or on account of the appearance of new and competing products which the consumers prefer, groups of producers with the support of the respective labor unions ask for government measures of protection. The alleged reasons usually stated by the advocates of government protection differ widely; they are very old, some are even handed down to us from the time of early mercantilism. They were refuted and exploded innumerable times, but they are repeated again and again. The reason for such illogical tenaciousness of life is the fact that *protective measures temporarily improve some people's position.* By imposing a duty on the importation of a good, the competitive position of domestic producers is strengthened. The total supply of goods offered on the market is restricted, which ultimately results in higher prices for consumers.

But the advantage reaped by the groups enjoying special government protection lasts only for a limited time. Domestic newcomers are immediately attracted by special government protection and the gain derived from it. New and additional competition then tends to eliminate the protection gain until the previous state of affairs is resumed. And so new and additional measures of protection will be necessary if the protected industry is to enjoy its original advantage.

The restrictive measures and the privileges of certain groups of producers bring about a structure of production that, because of each protective measure, grows apart from that of the free market economy. Additional factors of production remain employed in an industry that had shown symptoms of maladjustment and over-investment. Thus the structure of production as brought about by government measures will differ from that of an unhampered economy as long as the restrictive measures are not removed. A duty that was imposed one hundred years ago and never repealed shows its lasting effects in the structure of production. However brief the special gain from government protection may have been, the effects on the structure of production are permanent.

If restrictive measures are repealed, a new disarrangement of market data results. Although the effects are immediately beneficial to all consumers, they are detrimental in the short run to the special groups previously enjoying protection and privileges.

Many European industries have been protected and privileged by their governments for many decades. There is probably no European industry which has not enjoyed some protection in its past. And the pressure groups interested in the preservation of protection and privileges are numerous and powerful. They are well organized and possess many means of pressure which they can exert on their governments. And these groups would suffer most from the repeal of government protection under the unification plan. The crucial question which now arises is: *Are these protected groups of producers and their respective labor organizations prepared and willing to suffer temporarily from the abolition of inter-European trade barriers for which they have vigorously fought?* This is seriously doubted.

Special Groups Reject a Tariff Union. It appears inconceivable, for instance, that the German farm group, which constitutes the mightiest pressure group next to labor in German political life, would yield to an abolition of import restrictions on agricultural goods. Long before World War I, when the great Western nations in general conducted free trade policies, German agriculture and some industries enjoyed high protection from growing North and South American competition. German nationalism was determined to make Germany economically self-sufficient as far as possible, in order to free her from the necessity of importing agricultural and other vital goods in times of war and emergency. The great scarcity of foodstuffs during World War I proved to the German nationalists the insufficiency of their preparedness with regard to agricultural autarky. Therefore, in the years between the two world wars, the German government took recourse to even stricter anti-importation laws. In 1938, one year before the outbreak of World War II, more than ninety per cent of all agricultural goods consumed by this great industrial nation was produced by its own farmers. Germany was almost autark, and the war could begin.

An abolition of agricultural import restrictions would inevitably bring about heavy losses and severe unemployment for German farmers. Thousands of farms, often with ten or fewer acres of land, with high costs of production and medieval methods of cultivation, would become unprofitable. Thousands of farmers would have to sell their land which has often been in the possession of one family for hundreds of years. Their anger and indignation, together with their support by German nationalists, would force any government endeavoring to abolish agricultural protection out of office.

Other European nations encounter the same economic stumbling blocks to European union. Belgium, another highly industrialized nation, has maintained an important agricultural production by way of import restrictions. The effects of a policy of European free trade would be similar to those outlined for Germany. Holland, mainly an agricultural country, on the other hand, has become more and more industrialized as a result of her protective policies. It is unreasonable to assume that Holland is prepared to sacrifice her artificially protected heavy industry which, because of its lack of raw materials and high costs of production, could not endure Belgian and German competition. Large segments of the Dutch heavy industry would undoubtedly be abandoned and thousands of workers would be unemployed. Similar problems would arise in all other European countries. Industries that enjoyed protection and favors in the past would suffer temporarily from a return to an unhampered market economy.

Labor Unions Oppose Unification. A very serious opposition to European union and inter-European free trade would also come from the most powerful of all present-day pressure groups—labor. The workers in the countries with more favorable conditions of production and more capital invested per capita of population would denounce as "dumping" the free importation of goods from European countries with less favorable conditions and correspondingly lower wage rates. They would feel injured by their competition and oppose such an "unfair" policy. Labor, like all other pressure groups, enjoys special government favors because it possesses and exerts the power to influence policies in its favor. Now, could a national labor group or any other pressure group be assured that the supranational European state would continue to favor and protect them from other European states? Would they not run the risk of losing their power to influence government policies in their favor? Would it not be likely that the German farm group, farmers as well as agricultural labor unions, for instance, which have striven so successfully for high protection and high prices for agricultural goods, may be a minority in the Pan-European Parliament and be outvoted by an immense majority wanting low prices for foodstuffs? The whole structure of present-day national protection would collapse in the event of a supranational unification of Europe. But under contemporary conditions of ideology and policy it is the first and main function of national government to protect its pressure groups and do favors for its constituents. There is no room for a supranational European authority that cannot assume this function of national government. And it is the very feature of unification that the supranational European state could not do so.

Complete Abolition of National Sovereignty Required. The unification of Europe as designed by Coudenhove-Kalergi can only be unitary. All sovereignty can only be vested in the supranational authority. Yet this statement is contrary to the assertion of Coudenhove that "the member states would enjoy a maximum of freedom within the federation." [21] It is irrelevant in this respect whether a Pan-Europe as envisaged by Coudenhove may be classified as "federation" from the viewpoint of constitutional law. The real matter of concern is where the political center of gravity, the authority to government intervention, lies. The existence of inter-European free trade and of extra-European trade barriers necessarily shifts the political authority to the central government which would induce the formation of pressure groups on a supranational level. The struggle for privileges and government intervention would even grow worse since *national* coalitions of groups would be added to the present-day coalitions of national parties and "classes."

As has been indicated, *where there is struggle for privileges and government intervention, where there is interventionism or socialism, there can be only one central government—one planning authority.* Complete abolition of the sovereignty of national governments is a prerequisite for European unification as envisaged by Coudenhove. But are the European nations willing and prepared to take such a significant step?

The Destruction of Agriculture. Coudenhove-Kalergi outlines a means which is to lessen the harmful intermediary consequences which the abolition of inter-European trade barriers would bring

21 *Ibid.*, p. 175.

about. "In Europe," says Coudenhove, "a sufficient amount of land is still available for allotment; agrarian reforms could in most countries provide sufficient land to absorb the workers thrown out of employment by the abolition of customs frontiers and of the national industries." [22] As was demonstrated in the foregoing, agriculture in countries like Germany and Belgium would suffer severely if tariff protection were abolished. Thousands of farms with high costs of production would become unprofitable. Consequently they would be bought up and incorporated into larger land holdings with lower costs of production or would ultimately be more intensively cultivated as gardens, land for greenhouses, etc. If Coudenhove were to nationalize the large land holdings in order to distribute them among idle workers, he would counteract the effects of his own policy. At first he would bring about a tendency towards larger units of farming by making thousands of farms unremunerative. Then he would embark upon the destruction of larger units and partition them into smaller units with high costs of production. At the end, there would be few producing farm units left. Does Coudenhove really believe that all these consequences would be willingly borne by the nations of Europe for the sake of unification?

Property Rights Disregarded. It evidently does not occur to Coudenhove that the land which he would like to distribute to the unemployed is now the property of someone. Coudenhove fails to explain what will happen if the owner should refuse to sell his estate. Should he be forcibly removed from his property or be imprisoned for failing to sell as ordered by some authority? Nor does Coudenhove enter into a discussion as to whether the unemployed are to purchase this land, or whether they are to receive it from the European government as compensation for the loss of employment. Furthermore, he does not discuss the important problem of farm equipment. But these are minor technical questions about which Coudenhove does not bother.

The Individual's Freedom of Choice of Job Disregarded. Let us assume, however, for the sake of further illustration, that sufficient land is still available for nationalization and redistribution. It is inconceivable that millions of jobless of all walks of life should be willing to begin the life of a farmer for the sake of European unification. Thousands of workers of the Dutch heavy industry, for instance, engineers, foremen, accountants, clerks, directors, and secretaries, are to take up farming according to the plan of Coudenhove. What, however, are their alternatives if they do not choose

[22] *Ibid.*, p. 189.

to be farmers? Coudenhove refuses to answer. There is no question that all these people would rather vote against the realization of the plans of Coudenhove than to be subject to such planning.

Agrarian Reform Unrealistic. It is no less unrealistic to assume that the workers thrown out of employment by European unification will migrate from one country to another to begin life on a farm. The jobless Dane, Dutch, or German does not voluntarily choose to settle on a farm in France or Spain, or the Frenchman in Denmark or Germany.[23] It is also unrealistic to believe that the French government, for example, would nationalize large landholdings and expropriate its French owners so that Dutch, Belgians, Italians, and Germans could settle and take over.

Coudenhove's Program a Socialist Program. His plan of unification is unrealistic and fantastic. It is simply the result of daydreaming and worthless with respect to understanding the problem of European unification. Coudenhove-Kalergi's plan of Pan-Europe and the support which it finds in present-day Europe demonstrate the superficiality of present-day political and economic thought. We do not find anywhere in his treatise the slightest trace of economic reasoning; yet, "the foundation of a United Europe is economic," says Coudenhove. But Coudenhove never endeavored to be an economist. Why then does he write a book on a subject which is based on economics? We see him in full agreement with his socialist contemporaries clamoring for reforms, redistributions, unity, and solidarity. Coudenhove's plan is simply a variation of a socialist program with particular emphasis on unity. Let us look into this further.

Coudenhove Concurs with Lenin: "Competition Leads to Imperialism." It is one of Coudenhove's main objectives of European unification to protect every European state from being at the mercy, politically and economically, of world powers. Europe must repel the economic competition of the other powers if it means to safeguard its independence. In order to become independent in a material way, Europe must produce all the raw materials and foodstuffs

[23] This migration of the unemployed to the countries with "large" landholdings assumes free movement of individuals from one country to another. Almost all European nations, however, have very strict anti-immigration laws that are by far more rigid than the American acts. An abolition of the immigration barriers for the sake of unification would undoubtedly meet opposition by the most powerful European pressure group—labor. Immigration laws protect the wage rates of a country against labor from other countries in which wage rates are lower and living conditions are worse. The laws prohibit the immigration of labor that would compete on the labor market and reduce wage rates.

it requires.[24] Only then can Europe "maintain its economic independence with respect to the 'United States of America.'"[25] Only a United Europe can avoid bankruptcy and economic servitude.[26]

This thought of economic servitude of nations and loss of economic and political independence to other nations competing on the trade markets of the world is purely communistic and is taken from the ideology of modern radical socialism and communism. During his exile from czarist Russia, W. I. Lenin, while in Zurich, Switzerland, wrote the following remarks on capitalism: "It must be added," said Lenin, while discussing the development of capitalist competition to monopolies and trusts, and the evolution of capitalism to imperialism, "that imperialism leads to an increase of national oppression and subsequently to the growing of resistance not only in new territories just opened up, but also to territorial annexions among the old countries."[27] Lenin enumerated the features of imperialism which induced him to call it "putrescent capitalism."[28] They are: "monopoly, oligarchy, the striving for power instead of freedom, the exploitation of an increasing number of small and weak nations by very few and wealthy nations." Where Lenin discussed the "finance capital" (page 99) he stated: "Finance capital is such a prodigious, it may even be said, deciding power in all economic and international relations, that it is able to subjugate even countries which possess full political independence. And indeed it does so. . . . It is self-evident that those subjugations which are connected with the loss of the political independence of the oppressed countries and nations offer most 'amenities' and greatest advantages to high finance."

It cannot be the task of this work to refute socialism.[29] At this point it is necessary to demonstrate only Coudenhove's full agreement with socialist thought. Although Coudenhove fully concurs with Lenin on the explanation of political and economic phenomena, he differs regarding the inference he draws from his Leninian concept. Coudenhove summons the European nations to unification and socialization. Lenin, on the other hand, rejoices and waits for the collapse of capitalism and the dawn of socialism.

[24] *Ibid.*, p. 34.
[25] *Ibid.*, p. 74.
[26] *Ibid.*, p. 179.
[27] W. I. Lenin, *Der Imperialismus als höchstes Stadium des Kapitalismus* (Imperialism, the Highest Stage of Capitalism), Moscow, 1946, p. 151.
[28] *Ibid.*, p. 154.
[29] The reader who is interested in a detailed discussion of socialism is referred to the excellent study by L. v. Mises, *Socialism,* Yale University Press, 1951.

"Economic Competition Leads to War." Coudenhove's explanation of the Peace Treaty of Paris, in 1919, seems to be based on the same notion as stated above. The economic presuppositions of the Peace Treaty and all their harmful effects are explained by him as being due to the existence of inter-European competition which is a capitalist phenomenon leading to exploitation, war, and suppression. "Once economic cooperation in Europe has taken the place of the present competitive struggle, all economic presuppositions of the Peace Treaty will be automatically changed and will press forward for amicable settlement." [30] The "economic cooperation" which Coudenhove opposed to the "competitive struggle," in accordance with all rules of interpretation, can only mean the *elimination of competition through central planning.* There is no other alternative. With this plan of Coudenhove, socialists of all brands undoubtedly will concur.

Also, his notion of the unfair treatment of certain European nations "at the time the extra-European world was divided up . . ." is taken from Marxian ideology. According to the socialist's explanation of the distribution of colonies among the European powers, those countries with the earliest capitalism and largest capital accumulations have acquired most of the colonial territories. Young capitalist countries like America, Germany, and Japan only began to acquire colonies when their capitalist evolution proceeded rapidly and outdistanced that of the older capitalist countries like England and France. By this time, however, the world was divided, and a struggle resulted because of the divergence of capital concentration, on the one hand, and the spheres of colonial influence and power on the other.[31]

Melioration of Deserts a Truly Socialist Project. In order to make Europe autark and economically independent, Coudenhove suggests that Africa should be converted "into the future granary and source of raw materials for Europe." For this purpose, the Sahara Desert should be partially transformed into agricultural land which should be accomplished by the combined efforts of Europe. [32] It is evident that such a combination of forces can only mean central planning and regulation by the European governments, for no other organization could combine the European forces. Also it is hardly conceivable that an individual investor or banker would invest his savings in the melioration of some acres of sand somewhere in the Sahara.

---

[30] Coudenhove, *Ibid.*, p. 128.
[31] W. I. Lenin, *Ibid.*, p. 98 *et seq.*
[32] Coudenhove, *Ibid.*, p. 179.

Only socialist governments can spend their funds on such projects. They can tax the people or inflate the money supply. The European socialist government, for example, could obtain the funds through levying a "Sahara Sand Tax" or printing a "Sahara Issue" of new money.[33] A socialist supporter of Coudenhove may disagree on the details of his suggestions; in the approach to the problem, however, he will wholeheartedly agree with Coudenhove.

The Denial of Economics. Coudenhove's demand for social and land reforms fully agrees with similar demands by present-day European socialists and union leaders. Land and social reforms are designed and enforced by a socialist government to favor the agricultural and industrial workers. The underlying notion of such policies of reform is the denial of the existence of natural market laws or the belief in the deficiency of such laws. The adherents of social reforms cling to the notion that only through the exertion of power by strong labor parties and unions and through the enforcement of social laws and reforms by social and "fair" governments can the lot of the working man be improved. All these notions are socialist, called by one name or another.

Monopolist Industries and Agriculture Consolidated and Regulated. Coudenhove also discusses in a very ambiguous and unintelligible way the dangers "which threaten the economic development and realization of his 'Pan-Europe' idea from the outgrowth of the trust system."[34] He recommends "socialist controls" to counteract such dangers and the "consolidation" of all those industries, such as the agrarian and the monopolist industries, that have no foreign competition to fear. We can only imagine what Coudenhove conceives as "socialist control" of the trust system and the "consolidation" of the agrarian and monopolist industries. Whereas his demand for "socialist controls" of the trust system and "consolidation" of the monopolist industries will earn him the support of most European socialists, his demand for the "consolidation of agriculture" will align some socialist opponents for him, since only Marxian communists and the most radical socialists will support this program.

The "Strong Arms" of the Working Man. Coudenhove's views concerning the support of his Pan-European idea by present-day

[33] It is significant to recall in this respect the attempts of the British Socialist government after World War II to develop huge groundnut plantations in East Africa, to free Great Britain from the necessity of oil imports from non-sterling areas. The funds for these projects were obtained by taxation and inflation.
[34] *Ibid.*, p. 190.

political parties and European "classes" are very definite and clear. Any other socialist leader clamoring for social reforms, progressive taxation, redistribution and controls, and the nationalization of industries might have spoken the same words as Coudenhove. "The leaders of European socialism," he says, "more clearly recognize the necessity of Pan-European unity than do the leaders of the middle class. . . . The attitude of the European bourgeois toward the question of federation is less obvious; nevertheless, it will be decisive as regards their own fate. History once more gives them an opportunity to perform a great creative act. If they fail to pass the test, allowing petty interests to triumph over historic world necessities, they will be proving the bankruptcy of their class and their inability to guide the destinies of Europe in the future. Strong arms will take up their heritage and complete the task which proved too great for them." [35] The "strong arms" of the working man are Coudenhove's menace toward the "bankrupt bourgeois." The argument presented by Coudenhove is socialist to its final statement.

Coudenhove versus "Anti-Europeans." Finally, his fundamental distinction between adherents of his scheme of unification and "Anti-Europeans" finds its counterpart in the socialists' distinction between adherents of socialism on one hand, and "labor baiters" on the other. That a man can be a friend of labor without believing in socialism, in socialist government measures, and union policies is beyond the comprehension of a socialist. Similarly, Coudenhove apparently does not conceive that a European may oppose his scheme of unification and yet may not be anti-European with whom "a decisive struggle will arise for the fate of Europe." [36]

Coudenhove Ill-informed About American History. The "Pan-Europe" of Coudenhove is autark and economically independent, provided with socialist controls and consolidations of the monopolies and of agriculture. Yet, "the economic model for 'Pan-Europe' is provided by the United States of America," says Coudenhove.[37] This assertion is most dubious. Either Coudenhove is ill-informed on the history of the United States—on the nation of Washington, Jefferson, and Lincoln—or he endeavors to gain the support of unsuspecting readers with such a superficial remark.

Summary. It has been demonstrated that Coudenhove's plan is unrealizable for the following reasons:

1. The people of those countries who enjoyed the advantages of

---

[35] *Ibid.*, pp. 183 and 185.
[36] *Ibid.*, p. 193.
[37] *Ibid.*, p. 74.

trading with other continents and who attained a relatively high standard of living will not voluntarily submit to a lowering of their living conditions because and for the sake of unification of Europe.

2. Those groups of producers who, in the past, have vigorously fought for and received special government protection are neither willing nor prepared to suffer temporarily from an abolition of inter-state trade barriers.

3. Present-day pressure groups, enjoying special government protection, will not endorse a unification because they would lose their power to influence government policies in their favor.

4. The most powerful present-day pressure groups—labor—in countries with more favorable conditions of production, would oppose as harmful and "dumping" the free importation of goods from other European countries with less favorable conditions of production and correspondingly lower wage rates. Labor would also object to free immigration which would depress domestic wage rates.

5. Unification of Europe, under contemporary conditions of socialist and interventionist policies, can only be unitary. All sovereignty must be vested in one supranational authority. The nations of Europe, however, are not prepared to submit to such a complete abolition of national sovereignty and government.

Coudenhove's Pan-Europe plan, furthermore, is a scheme for the attainment of tacit socialism in Europe. Socialist thoughts are interwoven with all his explanations and with his pleading for unity. His book is addressed to millions of socialist readers all over Europe. Their reception of it made it popular and successful. Pertaining to the explanation and elucidation of the problem of European unification, however, it is of dubious value.

III

The Socialist Movement
for a United States of Europe

The Setting. At the beginning of 1947, several eminent European specialists met in London to discuss the problem of European unification. The growing importance and popularity of the unification problem had brought them together. After several days of discussion they decided to set up an "International Committee for Study and Action on behalf of a Socialist United States of Europe." The task which they assigned to the Committee consisted of the study of the unification problem and the publication of socialist literature on European unification. The result of its studies naturally had to be in agreement with the doctrines of socialism and ultimate socialist goal: creation of "a socialist Europe which is economically and politically independent." Moreover, the Committee was to fight against the creation of a Europe which is "capitalistic, reactionary, militarist and too submissive to American influence." Finally, a provisory commission was set up with the task of contacting the socialist parties throughout Europe and preparing the first constitutional congress for the "Socialist Movement for European Unification."

This Congress convened at Montrouge, near Paris, in June 1947, where the socialist parties of several European countries were represented. The strong participation of French socialist parties led to the election of one of their members, M. Marceau Pivert, as president of the movement. At this congress the representatives fully agreed that a "United States of Europe" was desirable, provided it was socialistic. All other schemes of unification were rejected as "capitalistic," "reactionary," or even "militaristic." Some representatives also emphasized that the social and economic successes won by the socialist parties for the labor class should not be sacrificed for European unification. If socialists had a choice between a united "capitalist" Europe and the contemporary disunited Europe with its socialist successes, they unhesitatingly would prefer the contemporary state of Europe.

The Conflict. Soon after the meeting at Montrouge the International Committee found itself in opposition to the official socialist parties which it felt called upon to criticize for their "inefficient bureaucratism." The party organizations, on the other hand, found reason to mistrust the Committee for being "too radical" and for "representing the viewpoint of the radical wing of European socialism." Furthermore, the socialist party leaders often occupied high positions in national governments. They naturally resented the Committee's criticism of their own policies. Sometimes the members of the Committee even had the audacity to label party policies as "liberal" and "capitalistic," which, indeed, is the greatest insult that can be dealt to a socialist party leader.

The International Committee uncompromisingly adhered to the idea of a *socialist* Europe and fought all other movements for European unification. When all other United Europe movements embracing different political ideologies met at The Hague in May 1948, the Executive Committee unhesitatingly rejected the invitation to attend. The statement that Mr. Churchill, "this reactionist and labor baiter" as he is called by European socialists, would attend and play a leading role in the meeting, was sufficient to cause this rejection. When the full Committee met at Puteaux about a month later, the position of the Executive Committee was upheld. The full Committee also discussed and accepted the annual report which set forth the danger of capitalism seeking to regain, under the cloak of European unification, the power it lost since the growth of the socialist parties. Committee members also repeatedly stated that a renunciation of national sovereignty in favor of a union would not necessarily constitute political and social progress; only the transfer of sovereignty to a *socialist* European government would signify such progress. A European federation would require abandonment of "national planning" in favor of "European planning." This would be all right and in full agreement with the socialist tradition and doctrine, provided European planning was also socialistic. However, under present conditions, there was the danger that abandonment of national sovereignty would be identical with giving up the socialist successes won over capitalism in recent years. Thus unification would only constitute social and economic decline and retreat in favor of European supercapitalism which in turn would be controlled by American big finance in Wall Street.

This attitude was and still is reflected in many socialist periodicals and newspapers in Europe.[1] Socialists want a United States of Europe, but they want their kind of union or none at all, for the important socialist successes, they feel, can be defended against capitalist attacks only by a socialist government of the union. Finally, the Committee also elected a new president of the movement, M. Rasquin, president of the Labor party of Luxembourg who was known for his radical-socialist outlook.

A Change of Policy. The attitude just described was prevailing among the majority of European socialists until the end of 1948. By that time a change of approach became apparent. The socialist party leaders realized that public opinion definitely wanted a United Europe and favored it even without the approval of the International Committee. The problem therefore had to be re-examined. It is true, it was said, Europe is in grave danger. At any moment, Europe might turn capitalistic and be subjugated to American imperialism and made subservient to Wall Street. But would it not be much easier for American big finance to attain its goal in a disunited Europe? Would it not be easier for Wall Street to deal with an isolated autark country, even a socialistic country? If Europe were united, would it not be able to defend itself more efficiently against the economic imperialism of the United States? Europe must unite, and its union is a matter of socialism or capitalism, indeed a question of life or death!

After two years of deliberation and hesitation, the official socialist parties in Europe began to revise their position with respect to unification. The foregoing arguments in favor of combined strength in defense against capitalism and American economic imperialism appeared too convincing. Also the British Labor Party, which was then at the height of its power, intervened discreetly by pointing at the necessity of union and the advantages of collaboration with capitalistic America. In November 1948, the new attitude was officially acknowledged. The "International Committee for a Socialist United States of Europe" was renamed "Socialist Movement for the United States of Europe." Individuals of all ideologies were invited to join. The new objectives were to create a United States of Europe and

[1] Oliver Philip, *Le Problème de L'Union Européenne*, Paris, 1950, pp. 189 *et seq.*; L. de Sainte-Lorette, *L'Intégration Economique de L'Europe*, Paris, 1953, p. 300; John Goormaghtigh, *European Integration*, Carnegie Endowment for International Peace, New York, 1953, p. 68.

then make it socialistic. A pamphlet on the goals of the Movement, which appeared in Paris mid-1949, clearly set forth the new outlook. "The actual equilibrium of political forces in Europe," it said, "probably does not allow us to attain immediately our goal, which is the creation of a Socialist United States of Europe, with a democratic organization of the European property of basic industries, and central management of the whole economy. However, the Socialist Movement does not declare itself less prepared to assist in the creation of a European Federation which does not realize these objectives . . . with the only reservation, that the political system be created in such a way that the objectives of socialism may be realized if, some day, the equilibrium of political forces should open a democratic way for their realization." [2]

There followed a considerable amount of publicity work by the Socialist Movement. The four large permanent commissions on "Colonial Questions," "Social Progress," "Economic and Financial Problems," and "Propaganda" busily prepared reports and publications. The following reports, for example, were published and presented to the public: "European Planning through Basic Industries," "The Coordination of European Agriculture," "European Security," "The Relationship between Europe and the People Dependent on It," "Germany and Europe," "The Political Authority of Europe," and "The Election of a Constitutional Assembly by Universal Suffrage." These reports were also discussed and approved at the Third Congress of the Movement in Luxembourg, November 1949. The fundamental dissension as to the objectives of the Movement also appeared at this congress. Some representatives advocated a socialist united Europe, or none at all. Others were willing to unite Europe first and make it socialist afterward. As to the reasons for unification, a deep divergence of opinion also became apparent. Some members advocated European unification as a means of defense against American economic imperialism; others hoped to make Europe the third power to rank with the United States and Soviet Russia, organized according to the system of socialism which would avoid the shortcomings of American capitalism as well as those of communism. There was also dispute as to whether the Socialist Movement should collaborate with other movements for a united Europe and join the over-all "European Movement" in which Winston Churchill played a leading role. A minority of the members feared that in joining the "European Movement" the Socialist Movement would tend to become "an instrument at the disposal of Mr.

2 O. Philip, *Ibid.*, p. 190.

Churchill in his fight against the workman."[3] Others believed that the Socialist Movement, under present conditions, should collaborate with other movements for a United States of Europe. The majority of representatives finally upheld this opinion and advised the Socialist Movement to collaborate henceforth with other movements in the unification of Europe.

SOME CRITICISM

Socialist Objectives Interpreted. The socialist attitude towards the problem of European unification is determined by the prevailing socialist doctrines in present-day Europe. Whoever undertakes to examine a socialist notion or policy must logically enter into detailed discussions of the underlying and fundamental doctrines of socialism. An exhaustive analysis must ultimately lead to a discussion of the Exploitation Theory, the Theory of Surplus Value, the Struggle of Classes, Lenin's doctrine of imperialism as the last phase of capitalism, and, finally, to the doctrine of the inevitable evolution of mankind towards its highest stage—socialism. In this survey of the doctrines and plans of unification, there is unfortunately no space for such a detailed discussion of socialist dogma. We must content ourselves with analyzing a few subjects which are closely connected with the problem of unification and the Socialist Movement for the United States of Europe.

In this chapter, the socialist unification movement will be analyzed by putting to test socialist principles in relation to basic principles of unification. The analysis leads to contentions that are diametrically opposed to socialist notions on the unification subject. These contentions are the following:

1. A society organized according to the system of socialism, because of its very nature, cannot, under any conceivable condition, voluntarily unite with another socialist society.

2. A socialist economy cannot conceivably be united with free market economies.

3. "American capitalism" pays for and upholds European socialism and finances its social and economic "successes."

Socialism Means Planning for National Disparity and World Disintegration. Under the system of socialism all the economic activities of the citizens of a country are consciously planned by a central planning authority. There is no private ownership in the means of production, only public ownership and control, which, of course, means state ownership and state control. It is insignificant in this

[3] O. Philip, *Ibid.,* p. 190.

respect whether the legal title in the means of production is directly transferred to the state, or whether legal title remains with the individual and the state assumes ownership control. That is to say, the state determines what shall be produced, how it shall be produced, at what cost and prices, etc. Both methods of socialization—legal acquistion of property and legislative and administrative control over property—are identical in their effects.

The alleged purpose of central planning and control is the direction of the means of production according to principles that benefit society. Plans and orders of central authorities are substituted for the functioning of the market economy because the latter is believed to be "wasteful," "unfair," and to benefit only the capitalists. Socialist planning is different. It logically follows that socialist planning would lose its justification if it concurred or endeavored to concur with the capitalist system of production and distribution. It necessarily means planning for disparity from market economies. Inasmuch as the world economy is a market economy, socialist planning irrefutably means planning for world market disintegration. These efforts are apparent in the system of bilateralism, formation of economic blocs, the political and erratic character of world trade, the disruption of international monetary and financial communication, the increased international immobility of production factors through nationalization and confiscation, and finally in all-round national protectionism.

Socialist Economies Must Be Secluded from Influences from Abroad. A basic condition for the realization of socialism is a tight seclusion of the socialist system from influences from abroad. Through numerous state controls over foreign economic relations, through government prohibitions, foreign trade quotas, and exchange controls, a socialist economy must be protected from "unplanned" imports and exports, from undesired monetary and capital intercommunication and other "undue" influences from abroad. How could a central planner realize his plan of forced disparity of prices if national borders were to remain open? How can he, for example, plan and enforce a butter price of $1, if businessmen are free to import butter at a price of 50¢? The first and inevitable step towards realization of a socialist or welfare plan is the closing of national borders.

A socialist economy within the framework of a supranational political union naturally can continue to exist, provided it is sufficiently sheltered from "unplanned" interferences. If the economic relations between the socialist system and other member states of the union continue exactly in the manner they were before the unification, no difficulties will arise. But if the outside protection of a socialist economy is abolished, it will instantly collapse because goods, capital, and even men will begin to cross the borders and tend to equalize the government-enforced disparities.

The assumption that Europe may be united by substituting one supranational economic plan for various national socialist plans is based on the failure to perceive the discrepancies of the various national economic structures. Although socialists enjoy talking about European unification and European central planning, they shun the mere thought of economic disparities as brought about by their own socialist or interventionist policies. The offered solution from this insoluble dilemma is the suggestion that the European central plan should be based on the national plans which are to be coordinated. Inasmuch as a coordination of national plans constitutes a compromise in national and social "successes," a mutual agreement is unattainable.

National Disparities Identical with National and Social "Successes." Coordination of national plans presupposes compromises as to economic plans and conditions. As has been pointed out, the essence of national planning is willful disparity according to national and social considerations. Strong pressure groups succeed in obtaining privileged positions which they consider as economic and social successes. Now assume, for a moment, that a supranational authority would attempt to eliminate these successes by abolishing the protection of certain national industries in order to eliminate the disparities. Then the question arises: "Will the privileged pressure groups, which are backed by national majorities, acquiesce in an elimination of their successes which were the sole objective of preceding socialist and interventionist policies?" It is obvious that neither a socialist nor a welfare nation is prepared for such a step.

The assumption that all the economies concerned must be socialist in order to assure unification is most fallacious. The more numerous the socialist economies to be united, the more numerous are the divergencies of national plans, structures of production, prices, wages, etc. It is self-evident that unification of ten heterogeneous "units" is more difficult than that of only two. To persuade ten nations to yield their plans and social "successes" in favor of one supranational plan, which can merely constitute a compromise of the ten plans, is unquestionably more difficult than to persuade two socialist or interventionist nations. But to induce any European nation to yield its protection and "social and economic successes" seems out of the question.

Unification of Socialist and Capitalist Economies Not Feasible. The same is true regarding unification of socialist and free-enterprise societies. Whether two heterogeneous socialist units are to be united or two heterogeneous economies of which one is a market economy and the other centrally planned, does not alter the problems involved. Although the national economic disparities may be smaller in degree because the socialist government only is planning and creating the disparities, the very nature of socialism requires divergency from a market economy. Through prohibitive tariffs, import and export licenses and quotas, exchange controls and government import and export monopolies, the socialist economy, for the sake of its own existence, must be efficiently sheltered from the market economy.

If a socialist economy and a free-market economy are to be united in one supranational organization of the socialist pattern, the market economy must necessarily be eliminated and conform to the socialist structure and plan. Such a unification presupposes an all-round adoption of the socialist structure of production, wages, prices, and an agreement on the central plan. It may be said that such an agreement is feasible if both parties would only compromise or submit their plans to arbitration. Indeed, this seems simple. But it must not be forgotten that such an agreement would entail the determination of who shall gain and who shall lose by the unification process. To find a compromise on the butter price of $1 and 50¢, for example, is extremely difficult. If the arithmetical mean of 75¢ should be accepted, the producers of the country with the $1 price would lose and the consumers in the country with the 50¢ price would lose by a like amount. On the other hand, the producers of the latter country and the consumers of the former would gain. Whatever aspect we may analyze, we would find inevitable gains and losses through the unification process. Of course, everybody would be eager to gain. But who would be willing to suffer losses for the sake of unification?

What Are Socialist Successes? Although an answer to this question is extremely difficult for the casual observer, we may find the answer by looking closely at the prevailing socialist doctrines and the way they are being carried out in present-day Europe.

The root idea of socialism is the idea that there are such things as a "social question," "labor problem," "class struggle," "surplus product," "exploitation through capitalism," etc. All these notions imply that the existence of capitalism harms the vital interests of the people—especially of the workers and the small farmers—and that radical reforms for the elimination of capitalism are indispensable.

Indeed, these radical reforms have been achieved in most European countries. An extensive price control system has, in general, eliminated the market economy. Basic industries have been nationalized and are now run by the state. Commercial and savings banks either are in the direct ownership of the state or are managed according to precise directives of the state. Furthermore, the state determines wage rates and other labor benefits. Private industries, i.e., industries that are not yet owned by the state, are heavily taxed and thus prepared for future nationalization. The central banks have successfully shattered the monetary systems through deficit financing, credit expansion, and outright inflation. These are a few of the socialist "successes."

The sphere of individual freedom and initiative is reduced with every increase in the authority of the state. As capital accumulation by individuals is deemed "unsocial" and rendered difficult, capital investment per head of population in several European countries has decreased steadily. Nevertheless, wages and other labor benefits are increased by order of the state and payment is enforced by its police. While wages are raised and paid with more paper money, real wage rates, or the purchasing power of the money wages, have declined in accordance with the lower labor productivity. As a rigid system of police-enforced price control prevents the necessary upward adjustment of prices, goods begin to flow into illegal channels of distribution. That is to say, the merchandise in the stores is getting scarcer while the waiting lines of consumers, the majority of whom are the workers, are growing longer. Government priorities, quotas, subsidies, price-fixing, rationing, trade inspections and penalties—all enforced by an army of bureaucrats and policemen—are the new socialist and welfare order of Europe which is supplemented by an illegal order: flourishing black markets and unlawful transactions termed "economic crimes" and "sabotages against society." And the number of "greedy" and "unsocial" people in prison increases correspondingly.[4]

Industries that government has taken over are bound to run at a loss. In spite of their tax exemptions, they are run at a substantial deficit and the quality of their services and products deteriorates. The national mining industries, steel and iron industries, transporta-

---

[4] For an excellent presentation of conditions under socialism in Great Britain, see John T. Flynn's The Road Ahead, Devin-Adair Co., New York, 1952, p. 26 et seq.

tion systems, telephone and telegraph industries, the postal service, and many other government-owned industries depend on the taxpayers for support.[5] But who are the taxpayers who pay the way for the nationalized industries? They are the millions of workers paying income taxes and thousands of corporations who, without the enormous tax burden, would expand and create jobs for workers. But, despite these abuses, this policy of nationalization is not termed a policy against and to the detriment of the worker; it signifies their economic and social "successes."

Although it is one of the main objectives of a socialist or interventionist government to provide homes for workers, despite free-handed government spending, the number of units built annually is decreasing. In the face of improved mechanization, financed by American government grants and loans, the productivity of labor, i.e., the per man-hour output, has declined in the government-controlled and -financed building industries as well as in all other nationalized industries. In the German mining industry which is government-owned or government-controlled, for example, the daily per man output during the first half of 1953 amounted to only 64.8% of the output in the first half of 1936.[6] And yet, Germany's recovery is considered most remarkable as compared with other European economies.

European governments often boast that production has increased in every year since the war. This is certainly correct, but for reasons other than they would like us to infer. At the end of World War II, production was greatly reduced or had entirely come to a halt. Production had to be resumed as long as there was will to survival. And production increased in spite of the controls and regardless of government checks and interferences. Governments are also boasting that some industries have increased their production over the pre-war level. This is also correct; but closer examination reveals that governments have neglected to acquire ownership of those industries or to enforce controls because they deemed them "unessential." Where private industries have suffered from the devastations of the tax collector and the regulations of price stabilizers, the socialist parties—in order to gain more economic and social "successes" —are demanding their nationalization.

[5] The relatively fortunate fiscal position of the government of the United States is due to the fact that it has to support only one nationalized industry: the Post Office, whose deficit in the last audited year (1952) amounted to only $4.50 for every man, woman, and child in the country.

[6] *Deutsche Zeitung und Wirtschaftszeitung*, Stuttgart, September 12, 1953, Series 8, No. 73, p. 9.

Under these conditions of "social and economic progress," the situation of the workers is deteriorating constantly. While producers often deflect part of the shrinking production from legal channels of distribution into illegal markets in order to avoid continuous losses, the worker must render his services on the labor market—the market most easily and efficiently controlled. Consequently, the worker bears more and more of the enormous tax burden. Of course, government control over wages and labor conditions are also rated as "socialist successes." Socialist policies by the worker and for the worker, in final analysis, thus mean his opportunity to wait in growing lines in front of crowded ration offices and empty retail stores. These are the socialist successes as seen and experienced by this writer in Europe.

American Aid Postpones the Alternative. The American aid which European governments received after World War II helped them to drag along and avoided the otherwise inevitable breakdown. Without the generous support by the United States government, the socialist policies of nationalization, government controls, and ample spending could not have been embarked upon without causing poverty and hardship. American aid meant the opportunity in many countries to push the realization of socialist programs further ahead than could have been done without it. There follows a partial list of countries receiving American aid via grants and credit. It covers the postwar period from July 1, 1945 through September 30, 1953.[7]

Austria	$ 990,000,000	Italy	$2,559,000,000
Belgium-Luxembourg	738,000,000	Netherlands	1,063,000,000
United Kingdom	6,800,000,000	Norway	295,000,000
Denmark	281,000,000	Sweden	108,000,000
France	4,929,000,000	Yugoslavia	616,000,000
Germany	3,745,000,000	Other western Europe	963,000,000
Greece	1,188,000,000		

It would be interesting to correlate the amount of foreign spending of the United States government per head of population in the receiving country with the number of its socialists "successes." Undoubtedly we would find a straight correlation between American aid and the growth of socialism.

Without the generous support of the United States government,

[7] Report in Appendix of *Congressional Record* for January 27, 1954, p. A604— "Foreign Handouts" by Hon. Daniel A. Reed of New York.

the nations of Europe would have faced an alternative between slow suicide through socialist and welfare policies or new life through return to the system of an unhampered market economy. It is characteristic in this respect that Western Germany, the socialist economy of which was almost at a standstill in 1947 and 1948, faced this alternative when American grants and credits per head of population were still small as compared with those to other European nations. And Germany chose, in spite of a long tradition of socialism and government omnipotence, a road of relative freedom and free enterprise. The other nations were temporarily spared this decision by vast grants and loans from the United States. Billions of American dollars were handed out for "economic reconstruction" and were spent to conceal the economic destruction which socialist and welfare policies brought about. The granting of additional billions of dollars in the form of military aid released domestic funds in like amount for purposes of nationalization, government controls, and social spending. And, yet, it is not enough. It is a matter of fact that the American aid, which is unprecedented in history, is not even sufficient to cover the deficits of the nationalized industries in Europe.

"American Economic Imperialism" the Motive for Socialist Unification. Although the American government has spent more than 43 billion dollars [8] for economic reconstruction in foreign countries, the greater part of which went to Europe, European socialists see in American capitalism and "imperialism" their most serious threat and enemy. It is America—"American imperialism"—against which they endeavor to unite. In the socialist literature on European unification, Soviet Russia is scarcely ever mentioned as an eventual aggressor or as a motive for unification. If Soviet Russia finds mention it is only in connection with a description of the objective of European socialism—the "middle road" between capitalism and communism. That is to say, Soviet Russia's economic system of central planning is approved and accepted by socialists—only the Russian methods are condemned. European planning is said to be less rigorous and more considerate of the rights and freedoms of the individual. Capitalism, on the other hand, is diametrically opposed to socialism. It is the system of exploitation and enslavement of the worker; it is the profit system of the millionaires in Wall Street.

These and similar socialist notions can only be understood as deductions from or as interpretations of the teachings of Marx, Lenin, and Stalin. They are unreal and contradict even the crudest rules

[8] From July 1, 1945 through September 30, 1953.

of common sense. Indeed, a person must be blind to the freedom of the American individual, his protection from encroachments by the state, and his standard of living and height of wage rates, if he embraces the socialist notions. It is a matter of fact that the American wage earner, in spite of more than twenty years of New and Fair Dealism, has an income equal to that of a French, German, or Italian state president and even the American tax exemption exceeds the income of the best paid workers in Russia. While the average income per man, woman, and child in the United States exceeds $1500 per year, the Russian income per head of population, according to Russian statistical sources, is less than $300 per year. As the reported money income in a socialist economy by no means constitutes real income for which additional ration cards and delivery rights must be acquired, we must discount even the reported Russian figures for the sake of a fair comparison. Furthermore, if we account for the ten to fifteen million slave-workers somewhere in Siberia, toiling for their bare existence, we arrive at a more realistic figure of perhaps $100 to $150 per year which the Russian worker may consume as his production and distribution planners deem fit. This is socialism as seen and experienced by this writer in Russia.

Wall Street and American Capitalism. The socialist contention that Wall Street and American capitalism are identical is as fallacious and superficial as all other socialist doctrines. If you look at contemporary American laws, the emptiness of this assertion becomes immediately apparent. It is a matter of fact that the highest taxes are paid in Wall Street. The American corporations owned by several million stockholders, for example, pay up to 82% of corporate income and Wall Street millionaires up to 88% of their remaining income to the federal government. In addition, state and city governments freely help themselves to revenues by taxing Wall Street income and transactions. Furthermore, numerous government controls have been imposed upon the credit and money market. How could this kind of taxation and the numerous Wall Street controls exist, if it were Wall Street that makes and executes the American laws? Is it not ridiculous to assume that Wall Street imposes these taxes and controls upon itself? Who pays the confiscatory taxes, Wall Street or the worker? If the socialist assertions regarding American capitalism, exploitation, and class struggle were correct, it would be the worker who would have to pay the 88% income tax and Wall Street would be tax exempt. This deduction is only common sense; and, yet, it is alien to socialist reasoning.

The Socialist Doctrine of Imperialism. According to Lenin,[9] capitalist imperialism is characterized by its final and desperate struggle for world markets. It is the last stage of capitalism after which socialism must inevitably follow. Nineteenth-century capitalism, with its full and perfect competition, exported goods and services into all parts of the world. Modern capitalism, i.e., mainly American capitalism, however, depends on the exportation of capital because the increasing poverty of consumers at home and abroad leaves an increasing part of total production unconsumed. As the growing wealth of a few capitalists lacks profitable employment at home, it seeks new outlets and markets in countries where capitalist parasitism may thrive. That is to say, foreign countries are subjugated by American imperialism and exploited by Wall Street. This is the official socialist dogma with respect to the United States.

Again we must refer to the fallacies of the underlying socialist doctrines of labor value, surplus product and exploitation, class struggle, etc., in order to understand Lenin's theory of imperialism.[10] Let us, therefore, look at a short presentation of capital movements in the past.

For more than one hundred years of American independence, the United States belonged to the underdeveloped areas of the world. Capital investment per head of population was small as compared with that in the countries of Western Europe. The opening of the vast North American continent was a constant drain on the formation of capital in the New England and Eastern states. But throughout this period of American past, European funds flowed into America and were invested in the construction of railroads, roads, canals, and factories. The European investors, especially in England, France, and Holland, preferred American investments to those in their home countries because America was poorer, the American interest rates were higher, American wage rates were lower, and opportunities for profits were large. If and when European investors reaped high profits, they could plow them back into business or freely transfer them to Europe. Throughout this period the American nation was the largest borrowing nation and *the* debtor nation of the world.

Under these conditions the vast North American continent was opened and America was built. Wage rates climbed steadily and the American standard of living increased rapidly. Towards the close

[9] W. I. Lenin, *Der Imperialismus als höchstes Stadium des Kapitalismus,* (Imperialism, the Highest Stage of Capitalism), Moscow, 1946.
[10] For an excellent analysis of socialism, see L. v. Mises, *Socialism,* Yale, 1952.

of the nineteenth century, American living conditions had almost crept up to the height of those in Western Europe. The American citizen was as free or freer than the citizen in Western Europe throughout this period of American growth. Who dares to maintain that he was unfree and enslaved by European capitalists? On the contrary, he was freer than he is today under his welfare government.

With World War I, conditions on the capital market of the world began to change. While the European nations began to consume their capital for war and "social experiments," American conditions continued to allow capital formation and consequently labor productivity and wage rates to rise. American capital began to flow to Europe and other parts of the world. Of course, capital left the United States in the expectation that it would yield a higher return abroad than at home.

For a few years it really did. As long as foreign debtors received more in capital than they had to pay in interest and repayments on the principal, no difficulties arose. American capital was used in the development of foreign industries, agriculture, commerce, public utilities, etc., and its employment raised the productivity of labor, created jobs, raised wage rates and the standard of living. But naturally, all these American investments were made with the tacit understanding that the principal would be repaid.

Unfortunately, this assumption on the part of American capitalists proved erroneous. In the following decades, scarcely a nation in the world did not nationalize American capital invested abroad. Compensation was often fictitious, its transfer prohibited, its value depreciated or annihilated through confiscatory taxation. And there is scarcely an American capitalist who did not lose all or part of his foreign investments. Whatever was left began to flow back through all legal as well as illegal channels. But this was not all. Not only were American capitalists eager to recall their funds, but foreign investors, and especially those of the underdeveloped areas, because of fear of nationalization and expropriation, began to transfer their funds to the safer harbor—America.

The economic effects of this capital migration are obvious. Living conditions in America improved more rapidly and conditions in foreign countries deteriorated at an accelerated rate. But was this due to capitalist and "imperialist" policies in Wall Street? Were the foreign debtors working with American funds or the foreign workers being employed in factories built by American funds being exploited? Or was it the American capital lender who was expropri-

ated by socialist or interventionist policies? Who caused the flight
of capital from Europe and other underdeveloped areas? The flee-
ing capitalist or expropriating governments? It seems unnecessary
to answer these questions.

Intergovernmental Aid and Private Lending. Socialists despise
private lending because they believe it to be the tool of capitalist
exploitation and imperialist subjugation. But let us compare for a
moment capitalist private lending with intergovernmental aid as it
is practiced among socialist and welfare governments.

Under modern political conditions, private capital, i.e., capital
accumulated by individuals, dare not leave the country without
running great risk of being nationalized, depreciated, blocked, etc.
But the underdeveloped countries need capital as urgently as did
America in the days of its growth. Since no private investor can
be persuaded to invest new funds in a country which has just
nationalized his old investments, other sources of capital must be
sought and found. This source was, and still is, the government of
the United States.

But what the private American lender could not expect, i.e., the
assurance of safety for his investment from expropriation by foreign
governments, the American government may demand for its intergovernmental loans. By international treaty and agreement the receiving countries promised to repay the loans. No matter what we
may think of governmental promises and international agreements,
the promise to repay constitutes the very basis of intergovernmental
loans.

The governmental indebtedness of underdeveloped countries to
the United States, however, constitutes a serious international problem. These loans are government loans, government obligations,
carrying government guarantees. If they are repaid at maturity, no
international problem will result. But what will happen if a foreign
government prefers to go in default rather than to meet its obligation? How is the American government to collect its funds from a
foreign government that is unwilling to meet its obligation? It apparently has the following alternatives: It may do what private
investors have done: forget about its foreign loans and write them
off. It also may grant moratoria of payments and write its investments off at a later date. Or, finally, it may attempt to collect by
use of sanctions, retaliation, and outright force. While this last
alternative is not open to a private lender, a government undoubtedly has the means for the use of violence. The question which now
arises is: "Will the creditor government, i.e., that of the United

States, employ its force to secure the repayment of its foreign investments?" Of course, it will not, since the various costs of collection by far surpass the amount to be collected. But, at any rate, an international conflict may be created through the existence of intergovernmental loans.

These deliberations must be taken into consideration if we evaluate intergovernmental aid as we know it today. Under the system of capitalism, individuals trade and deal with each other. A loan is an exchange of a present good for a promise of payment of a future good. If the debtor fails to deliver the future good, the only resort open to a capitalist lender is a forced collection via court. If the court should fail to bring about the collection, the claim is written off as a bad investment. The money lender suffers the loss and the problem is settled. As has been illustrated previously, conditions are different where governments deal with each other. Under socialism and Fair Dealism, intergovernmental debts lead to international conflicts.

Is Socialism a Barrier to Communism? European socialists want us to believe that a socialist Europe would provide an effective barrier to communism. They often cite the socialist governments of Australia and New Zealand and of the Scandinavian countries as examples of democratic socialism which, they assert, halt the march of communism and absorb the masses who would otherwise turn communistic.

A major fallacy in this contention is its tacit implication that there is an essential difference between a socialist state and a communist state. What, in all fairness, are these differences? There are none. In a socialist state as well as in a communist state the means of production are in the exclusive ownership of the state. Central planners control and regulate the economic activities of all members of society according to their own standards of fairness and expedience. A centrally planned economy has been substituted for the individually planned market economy. The market system of distribution with its sovereignty of the consumer has been replaced by a system of distribution in which the central planner and distributor is sovereign and his judgment the supreme order. The communist contention that in a future communist society each individual will contribute to production according to his abilities and receive according to his needs is no less fantastic than the contention that the communist state will "wither away."

From 1918 to 1921, Lenin tried to establish this kind of communism in Russia to the full extent, and millions perished in this attempt. In 1921 he had to retreat to the "New Economic Policy" which adopted more and more features reminiscent of the despised capitalist system. Great disparities in money and real incomes have since been introduced and the state, instead of withering away, has tightened its grip on the individual. The contention that, some day in the future, communism finally will be realized is uncontested here; but if this should ever come to pass, communism again will be a catastrophic failure and additional millions will perish in the new attempt. And as long as there is communism, there will be perishing and self-destruction.

The fact that socialism in Australia, New Zealand, Great Britain, and the Scandinavian countries differs from socialism behind the Iron Curtain does not disprove these statements. In all these countries strong oppositions which are backed by nearly half, and in some cases more than half, the nation keeps socialism within bounds. Also, the memory of the rights and freedoms of the individual to which he was accustomed in the capitalist past still lives and their remnants are tenaciously defended by the friends of liberty. Of course, it is readily conceded that a few more decades of socialism even in these countries will be sufficient to destroy the remaining rights and freedoms and prepare the way for communism, and its iron rule.

The experience of many countries has shown that socialism is no effective barrier to communism, but that it prepares the way instead. Socialists first destroy the barriers to communism; and when a determined group of communists begin to wrest the power from them, they can offer no effective resistance. On the contrary, they often join the forces of communism.

Russia is the classic example of the way in which socialism collapses before the determined onslaught of communists. Before the outbreak of revolution in March 1917, two moderate socialist parties had made their appearance in Russian political life and enjoyed many millions of adherents among the workers in Moscow, Petrograd, and other cities. The *Mensheviks* were a relatively moderate element of Russian socialism. They advocated realization of socialism in a democratic way. They despised revolution and differed from communism in many ways of party tactics. The second socialist party was the *Social Revolutionary party* which had its origin in an agrarian movement at the close of the nineteenth century. It had its strongholds among the poorer population in the country and was, in spite of its name, a relatively moderate socialist party. In addition to these two parties there was the *Bolshevik party*. The

Bolsheviks constituted the revolutionary Marxian element of Russian socialism. Its leaders, and especially Lenin, were prepared at any moment to seize and take control of the entire political and economic power of the country. They did not hesitate to employ the means of revolution to attain this end.

At the outbreak of revolution in March 1917, the Social Revolutionaries and Mensheviks were in the majority and gained control of the situation. In July 1917, a Menshevik leader, M. A. Kerensky, even became Prime Minister of Russia. That is to say, moderate socialism gained full control of the state. But now the small though determined group of Bolsheviks began to undermine the position of the party in power. Kerensky and his government, on the other hand, behaved with a helpless ineptitude in this time of crisis. How could they show firmness against the Bolshevik demands which were so similar to their own while they were in opposition? Being in power, how could they outbid the Bolsheviks remaining in opposition? On grounds of their own socialist ideology, what could they answer to the radical demand that the power should now be placed in the hands of the proletariat and the poorest strata of the peasantry? They could but plead for delay on grounds of untimeliness and inexpedience. On November 7, the Bolsheviks struck. Within twenty-four hours the government fell, its representatives were arrested, and the dictatorship of the communist party was erected. Socialism had paved the way for communism.[11]

The powerful *Polish* socialist party provides another example of the impossibility for socialism to meet the onslaught of communism. Although it is readily conceded that nothing could have been done in the years after World War II that would have prevented the domination of Poland from Moscow, we must point to the lame resistance of the socialist parties in their resistance against the communist party. Ideologically completely helpless, they first cooperated and finally merged with communism.

The same holds true of *Hungarian* socialism. We saw the same fatal cooperation of the socialists with the communists, the same final fusion of the socialist parties with the Soviet communist party, and the same acquiescence of the socialists in a totalitarian state.

Czechoslovakia is another case where socialism was particularly strong. After the liberation from German occupation in 1945, a coalition government with a strong socialist tendency under the premiership of Zdenek Fierlinger, a radical socialist, was in complete

[11] Ivor Thomas, *The Socialist Tragedy*, The Macmillan Co., New York, 1951, pp. 39-49.

power of the state. It nationalized the mines, national resources and big iron and steel enterprises, large enterprises in the food and drink industries, the banks and insurance companies and did everything in its power to appease the communists. Soon the socialists began to share the power with the communists who then seized it from their benefactors. If today Czechoslovakia lies in the grip of a communist dictatorship, it is because of the groundwork done by socialists.

Although the communists in *Italy* were unable to rise to power, we may observe the same readiness on the part of socialists to cooperate with communists and pave their way as did the socialist parties in the countries behind the Iron Curtain. The Italian socialist party was one of the oldest, strongest, and most cohesive socialist parties in Europe. Not only did it breed fascism and the dictatorship of Mussolini after World War I, but it fully supported the communist party in its struggle for power after World War II. Together with the communists they founded a single trade union movement and established the closest political collaboration in a "popular front." In a decisive election in April 1948, the socialist party, on a common list with the communist party, fought the Christian Democratic party for the power of the state. It was only through the brilliant leadership of the Pope and the Catholic Church that the "popular front" was decisively beaten.[12]

The history of the *French* socialist parties also shows convincingly that socialism cannot be a barrier to communism. The communists try to outbid the socialists, and the socialists try not to be outbid. Ugly waves of strikes, disorderly scenes, riots, and frequent changes of government are evoked alternately by the communist party or one or several of the socialist parties in opposition. Wherever the French socialists have been outbid by communists for the favor of the masses, they have not hesitated to support the communist actions which they themselves hated to employ. We may observe the same cooperation of both parties, the same agreements as to "popular fronts," in which the communists are the main beneficiaries, that have taken place in all other countries where socialist parties have enjoyed a popularity. In June 1946, an assembly election saw the communists in the second place of French political life, and as the chief aspirants for power with more than 5 million votes, thanks to the lengthy socialist groundwork laid for the communist party.

Great Britain offers another convincing example of how socialism cannot be a bulwark against communism. The British Labor party

[12] Ivor Thomas, *Ibid.*, p. 66 *et seq.*

is strongly entrenched. When it took office in 1945, it nationalized the "means of exchange," the coal mines, the gas and electricity industries, the iron and steel industries; it vested in a Central Land Board all development rights in land; it nationalized or acquired full control of the "means of distribution"; it made the Ministry of Food a huge state trading concern; it did its utmost to eliminate rent, profit, and interest, and made the whole nation subject to its conscious central planning. The British Labor party, indeed, carried Great Britain far towards the collectivist goal. And, yet, it could not stop, for the growth of its power brought in its train the radical opposition which tries to outbid the moderate elements of socialism. From anonymity Aneurin Bevan and his adherents have risen to strength and reputation and are now a growing wing of British socialism. There cannot be any doubt, if Clement Attlee should ever come to power again, Bevan will be waiting to seize the scepter from him. And then a more ruthless figure will be ready to replace Bevan, in a slow motion of communist revolution.[13]

Inasmuch as the fundamental tenets of the German nazi ideology did not differ from the social and economic ideologies of communism as applied behind the Iron Curtain, we must also refer to the growth of *German socialism* and the simultaneous rise of Hitler and his National-Socialist party to absolute power in Germany. For many years the great majority of the German nation had been both socialist and nationalist. Many millions were organized in the socialist parties and especially in the Social Democratic party; and there were millions of members of the trade unions affiliated with these parties. For many years during the interwar period, Prussia, the Reich's center of gravity, was ruled by the Social Democrats.[14]

With the sway of socialism in Germany two important socialist offsprings came to life. The communist party and Hitler's National-Socialist party were both determined to establish their totalitarian system. Hitler could finally triumph because socialists had first destroyed the cornerstones of democracy. Socialism gave birth to National-Socialism and helped to usher in the tyranny of Hitler, to the infinite misery of the German people and the calamity of the world.

Socialism and Democracy. Socialists universally condemn the institution of private ownership in the means of production. Under socialism the state acquires ownership and control and becomes the universal employer. The state controls the citizen's foreign exchange

[13] Ivor Thomas, *Ibid.*, p. 78 *et seq.*
[14] L. v. Mises, *Omnipotent Government*, Yale Press, 1948, p. 193 *et seq.*

transactions and his investments; it controls raw materials, prices, and the labor market. It determines the individual's rights to income, fixes wage rates, regulates rent, profit, and interest and determines spending and consumption. It is obvious that the socialist state is not compatible with individual liberty. And where liberty is lacking, there cannot be democracy, but submission of the individual to the party and state authority.

The undemocratic dependence of socialist representatives in the British Parliament on the leaders of the Labor party can best be illustrated by the pledge which candidates are required to give. They must promise to act in harmony with a party order which reads as follows: "For the purpose of securing concerted action in the house, members shall consult the officers of the parliamentary party before tabling any motion, amendment or prayer, or other proposal which may involve party policies or decisions and shall not vote for any motion, amendment or prayer contrary to the decision of the party meeting . . ." [15] Labor party representatives in Great Britain, the modern homeland of democracy, indeed are required to be what is commonly called "rubber stamps" in the hands of their party leaders.

Democracy is government for the people and by the people. Under socialism this relationship is reversed. Socialism means people for the government and by the government. It is the antipode of democracy.

[15] Ivor Thomas, *Ibid.*, p. 142.

IV

The European Federalist Union

Background. Immediately after World War II, throughout Europe movements were organized that proclaimed the noble goal to work towards future European peace by way of federation. Delegates of numerous national groups frequently met in international conventions to discuss the pacification of Europe through unification and federation. The first of these conventions was held in Geneva, Switzerland, a few weeks after the war. Others followed in Luxembourg, Basel, and Paris where it was first suggested that closer ties should be formed to facilitate collaboration among the various national groups. In April 1947, a convention was held in Amsterdam for the express purpose of deliberating on the question of collaboration and the eventual formation of a European Federalist Association. After it agreed on the principles of supranational organization, another convention of all federalist movements in Europe was called at Montreux, Switzerland, in August 1947. At this convention the "European Federalist Union" was founded—an organization comprising more than fifty movements, some dating from the inter-war period, with seventeen national committees and more than 100,000 members from sixteen countries. In France alone there are more than twenty federalist organizations collaborating through a central committee.[1]

Objectives. The objectives of the European Federalist Union are based on two basic principles of unification. For many of the members, federalism is the only conceivable way of collaboration among the European nations and national states; to others, federalism is not only a political doctrine of unification, but a way of life for all citi-

[1] O. Philip, *Le Problème de L'Union Européenne,* Paris, 1950, p. 196; John Goormaghtigh, *Ibid.,* p. 68; L. de Sainte-Lorette, *L'Intégration Economique de l'Europe,* Paris, 1953, pp. 301-2.

107

zens of a nation. To them the goal is not only the realization of European unity, but also the development of a movement for "federalism" in the national states themselves. The latter conception of federalism is especially held by the French section of the Union, which is the driving force in the European Federalist Movement because of its numerical strength and great activity. "For the sake of coherence and consistency," it demands a complete reform of national structures. The principles of federation are said to demand a federation from top to bottom—in the community, the workshop, industries, and, finally, in the central government. Federalism is to be substituted for our present system of parliamentarism. Max Richard, a leading advocate of the Federalist Union Movement, summed up the federalist criticism in the following words: "We may say that in the democratic countries the parliaments do not represent the true state of society, but they reflect its forces only incidentally and superficially, provided they do not ignore them entirely . . . Neither the diplomats, nor the most learned jurist, the statesman, the most zealous dictator, nor the parliamentarians, these adherents of coldest constitutional mechanism, can interpret that living reality which constitutes the European people." [2]

Organization of Society According to Fields of Solidarity. According to the federalists, a true representation is a federalist representation of the individual in his fields of solidarity as, for example, in his community, church, profession, school, family, etc. In each field of solidarity the citizens should form organizations of self-government; every branch of business should form its own self-governing body. Such a representation based on "social functions" is said to be the only authentic representation of the European nations. All other movements towards a European union are artificial and, sooner or later, are bound to fail. Such is the political and economic ideology held by most of the members of the European Federalist Union.

As the first and significant step toward realization of this system of internal and external unification, the European Coal and Steel Community, as introduced by the five leading coal- and steel-producing countries, is approved and celebrated. The Federalist movement indeed used its great influence to have the Schuman Plan accepted by the parliaments of the five nations.

The Ideological Foundations of the Movement. It is significant to note that a large number of its Italian adherents who have recently joined the Union were fascists prior to World War II. They

[2] Quoted by O. Philip, *Ibid.*, p. 196.

are busily advocating supranational and domestic federalism which, in fact, is merely another name for what was formerly called corporativism. The French wing of the movement seems to have its roots in the social philosophy of "solidarism" as it was developed in France during the decades before World War I. Solidarism is the social and political creed of all those who joined neither state nor Christian socialism, but who accept the socialist criticism of the capitalist social order. The statements of this wing of the movement are far from clear. In this respect the solidarist wing of the Union shows a striking similarity to another group of the Federalist movement that advocates a "new and better system of human organization" based on the teachings of the early socialists. The ideas of Saint-Simon and Comte are still reflected in the goals of many members and in their endeavors to reorganize society in such a way that "all social activity is given the proper form it needs," that is to say, an organization based on the individual's social function within society.

CRITICISM

A Federation of States. Federalism, according to many adherents of the Federalist Union, is the only conceivable relationship among national states. Because this argument enjoys enormous popularity in contemporary political literature, it has been analyzed at several other places in this work.[3] As has been illustrated, a federation of states is not feasible under present-day ideological conditions because of the prevalence of interventionist and socialist policies. Where public opinion approves or demands government control of domestic prices, foreign trade, and foreign exchange, people are not prepared to suffer from the temporary effects which an abolition of these measures would bring about.

Federalism as a Way of Life. The argument that is particular to the Federalist movement and that deserves our special attention is that federalism is not only a political doctrine of unification, but is also a way of life and organization of the relations among individuals. Federalism, according to this notion, is conceived as a political and economic system that is opposed to modern parliamentarism and to the free enterprise economy with its "waste and competition." It is federation from top to bottom—in the community, in the workshop, in industry, and on all levels of European collaboration. That this scheme of human organization is not realizable, on either the lowest or highest level of cooperation, shall command our imme-

[3] See especially Part I, Chapter I, p. 53 *et seq*, and Chapter II, p. 77.

diate attention. Furthermore, we shall elaborate and show that "federation" principles are pseudosocialist principles suffering from the twofold shortcoming of being socialist in basis and criticism, and of lacking completeness because of their hesitancy to take the last consistent step towards socialism.

The corporativist wing of the Federalist Union Movement advocates self-government in all spheres of social function—in the various branches of trade and industry, in churches and schools, in community and family. A social scheme is constructed that is said to lack totalitarian state supremacy and omnipotence, but "to reflect the true forces of society." The organizations of self-government are to enjoy full autonomy; they are free to settle their own affairs without interference by the state or anybody who is not a member of the functional organization. The relationship between the various organizations consists of bargaining on problems of mutual interest or acting on decisions reached by a European Assembly made up of delegates of the functional organizations. They are to represent the true forces of living European society in which the apparatus of state can either be completely abandoned or used as a tool of execution for the national assemblies and the supranational European Assembly as well.

Organization of Industries Leads to Restriction. The outstanding feature of this system is that the industrial organizations will no longer be subject to economic adjustments and pressures. There will be no competition and no supremacy of the consumers. At any rate, the interests of members will receive precedence over the interests of consumers. The collaboration of members will indeed be smooth and amicable. It is certainly very likely that they will agree to short hours of business and work, on high wage rates, on the employment of certain existing methods of production that exclude inconvenient and costly readjustment, on numerous business holidays, and on other problems of business and production. In all probability, all functional organizations will resort to the same policies. By mutual agreement production would be restricted and the prices for commodities and services would be raised. An all-round restriction of production would finally lead to a universal rise of prices and a concomitant lowering of living standards. And there would be no limit to the extent of this lowering process.

Industrial Federalism Means Conflict. Under these conditions there would be neither competitive nor monopoly prices. Those functional organizations that supply the vital necessities of life would attain a dictatorial position. Powerful organizations which already enjoy a favorable bargaining position would inevitably squeeze all the rest. The producers of vital foodstuffs, for example, could enjoy their position to the fullest extent. The suppliers of fuel, electric current, and transportation could easily restrict their production and yet enjoy high income and wage rates. Within a very short time, such a system of human organization would lead to violent conflicts between the suppliers of vital necessities and all the rest. Either chaos would result or the state would resume its role of arbitration and full control of all production activities.[4]

Such a development towards poverty and chaos would even be accelerated in a supranational union of all European states. Let us assume that the total supply of a vital necessity for the whole of Europe is produced only in a certain part of the Union. As soon as the organization of producers, in the name of social justice and progress, would begin to squeeze all other Europeans, a violent conflict would arise which would tend to become a national conflict between the country producing the vital necessity and all the others. Even the slightest attempt to realize this system of organization would soon result in destruction of the Union and in inter-European conflict.

Solidarism Leads to Socialism and Conflict. The schemes and plans of the solidarist and utopian-socialist members of the European Federalist Union are equally unrealistic and inconsistent. Solidarism proposes a solidarity of action in favor of the poorer members of society. While its *étatist* wing strives to achieve solidarism of human action by state coercion, a more ecclesiastically inclined wing appeals to conscience. The kinship between solidarism and "federalism," which characterizes the post-war solidarist literature, can only be explained by their common objective: the abolition of the contemporary system of society. The solidarist advocation of "federalism" is largely unclear and superficial in nature—a quality shared by all solidarist ideas, which do not distinguish themselves by depth of conception or clarity of expression. But this much can be said: wherever solidarism endeavors to substitute a "higher" norm of human collaboration for private property in the means of production, for competition and the profit motive, it is a variety of socialism. As such it must meet our criticism on socialism and on the unrealizability of a socialist union. Wherever solidarism advocates "federalism" as a new way of life and human organization, i.e., a "functional organization of society," it either leads to domes-

[4] See L. v. Mises, *Human Action*, Yale University Press, 1949, p. 812 *et seq.*

tic and interstate conflict or, in the case of state interference, to socialism. The failure of both these courses is inevitable.

Where There Is Socialism There Can Be No Union. A considerable part of the French section of the European Federalist Union seems to draw its arguments from the writings of the early French socialists, Saint-Simon and Comte. These writers, in their intention to "reorganize" society, made their starting point the English parliamentary system and endeavored to transform it into a more "scientific" and functional organization. Direction of economic activity was to be placed in the hands of the "industrialists"—that is, of all those who worked productively. The industrialists then were to be organized into three separate bodies: the "Chamber of Invention," to design the plans for economic activity; the "Chamber of Examination," to scrutinize and approve these plans; and the "Chamber of Execution," to execute or watch over their execution. Once such a scientifically directed social system would be universally established, society would no longer need a "government" but merely an "administration." The standard of living of the people so organized, these Federalists allege, would rise to new and unprecedented levels.[5]

The essence of socialism is that all means of production are in the exclusive control of organized society. It does not matter in what form socialism is realized. Control over the means of production may consist in ownership acquisition by the community, or control may be exerted by way of government laws and decrees. It is also immaterial whether the state with its division into legislature, administration, and jurisdiction holds the control, or whether "Chambers of Invention, Examination, and Execution" have exclusive control over the means of production. In both instances planning by authorities would be substituted for the planning by the individual. Saint-Simon and Comte designed plans of reorganization of society that undoubtedly are as socialist as are those of their successor, Karl Marx.

Our criticism, therefore, of their plans of reorganization must be essentially identical. A supranational unification of socialist systems of human organization, as has been stated in the preceding section on the "Socialist Movement," is not feasible because of the very nature of central planning. A socialist society is a closed unit society which is heterogeneous not only to free enterprise societies, but to other socialist systems as well. And the same holds true of inter-

[5] F. A. Hayek, *The Counter-Revolution of Science*, The Free Press, Glencoe, Ill., 1952, p. 132 *et seq.*

ventionist state organizations, that is to say, of every present-day state that is not outright socialist.

The presence of this group of socialist planners in the "European Federalist Union" instead of the Socialist Movement can be explained as follows: First, the desire for some vague and hazy reorganization of society makes this group welcome any scheme of organization that endeavors to abolish the free enterprise economy and substitute a new design, which, they hope, will be their own. Furthermore, these socialist planners hesitate to join the "Socialist Movement for the United States of Europe" because it advocates the realization of *Marxian* socialism. The Marxian socialists, however, are as radical, determined and uncompromising as to methods and ends as is this group of federalist socialists. Both groups claim having the true knowledge of the proper ends of society, and each group means to "defend" society's end and purpose. It is therefore entirely logical and natural that socialist groups not embracing the Marxian doctrines shun Marxian organizations and join another movement which also aims to abolish the present system but is less radical and can more easily be swayed and lead. But we must also be prepared for a secession of these socialist groups from the "Federalist Union Movement," if they should attain independent and sufficient strength to assure their being heard among the socialist parties in Europe.

V

The United Europe Movement

An Appeal to Winston Churchill. The numerous movements for European unification which, immediately after the war, arose all over Europe enjoyed lively public interest and support. But no real progress toward a European Union could be made as long as politicians and statesmen failed to support the movements and promote the plans of unification. In order, therefore, to force an actual realization of European unification, or at least of its initial steps, several leaders of the private movements appealed to Winston Churchill— the uncontested political leader in post-war Europe—to take part in the European movement. Having Churchill's support, they thought, would give the unification movement a real chance of success.

Churchill Urges Europe to Unite. As long as Churchill was in power, he refrained from giving support to the unification movements. But at Fulton, Missouri, in March 1946, when he was no longer Prime Minister of Great Britain, for the first time he called the world's attention to the continuing expansion of Soviet Russia in Europe and to the spreading of communism all over the world. He attacked Soviet Russia for enslaving the Eastern European countries and for making them satellites of communist Russia. A few months later, in September 1946, he made a famous speech at the University of Zurich, Switzerland, in which he appealed to the nations of Europe to unite against the rising threat from communist dictatorship. Churchill then declared that he himself would take part henceforth in the work for European unification. In May 1947, he repeated his call for unity before 40,000 listeners in London with the appeal to France and Germany to assume the initiative and leadership.

"United Europe Movement" Organized. Following this, Churchill founded in Great Britain an organization, "the United Europe

114

Movement," whose goal is to fight for a realization of European unification through mass education and create a popular unity movement. In this organization, members of all different political groups and walks of life—conservatives, liberals, socialists, Protestants, Catholics, etc.—are represented. Churchill himself assumed the presidency of the executive committee of the movement.

The Unification Desired. Although Churchill has never expressly stated which countries should unite, we may infer from remarks of eminent followers of the movement that France, Italy, Austria, Germany, Spain, Portugal, Belgium, Denmark, Holland, Switzerland, and the Scandinavian countries should unite. As compared with most other European movements which advocate "federalism" of some form or another, the Churchill movement advocates a "unitary" government with respect to essential government functions. Through a progressive creation of central organs, like those superficially designed and quickly established by the Allies during the war, a "United States of Europe" which is able to defend itself against communist Russia should be constructed. A uniform command with regard to national resources and energy and other essential functions of national life should be established and constitute the framework of an empiric union. It is in this sense that the United Europe Movement is unitary.

In all other respects unessential for European defense, the movement recommends the creation of a "Confederation" or a "European Commonwealth." The motives which may induce the European nations to join this confederation need not be identical. Some nations are urged to join for commercial reasons, such as the benefit of a tariff union or a system of commercial preferences; others may join for reasons of defense or for a combination of other reasons. The large area of economic collaboration would allow the greatest possible freedom of trade and enhance the economic prosperity of the nations. Cultural ties and an exchange of scientific information should also be developed. But above all, a consultation and discussion of all problems of mutual interest should reflect and constitute the fundamental solidarity and unity of the nations of Europe.[1]

The Organization. The work of the United Europe organization consists of propaganda through public rallies, publication of articles and reports, and, finally, study of the problems which the eventual

[1] L. de Sainte-Lorette, *L'Intégration Economique de l'Europe*, Paris, 1953, p. 302; E. Bonnefous, *L'Europe face à son destin*, Paris, 1952; O. Philip, *Le Problème de l'Union Européenne*, Paris, 1950; John Goormaghtigh, *European Integration*, Carnegie Endowment for International Peace, New York, 1953.

realization of the Union would create. It invites all eminent personalities who agree on the necessity of unification of Western Europe to organize and communicate with each other through the organization of the movement. The objective of the Churchill movement is clearly expressed in the first declaration of the executive committee. It reads: "This problem (of unification) is so urgent that if the governments find it impossible to undertake its realization at present, the people of good will in all countries should unite before it is too late. Europe must unite if she wants to preserve her civilization." Sir Samuel Hoare, an eminent adherent of the Movement, expressed a similar idea while pointing at the present state of European disunity. "The present position on the Continent," he says, "is indefensible—separate zones, impassable frontiers, exchange control, no freedom of movement, pernicious ideas of autarky and many more obstacles stifling European civilization. . . ." [2]

The United Europe Movement constitutes the nucleus of the movement for European unification in Great Britain. It collaborates closely with other movements on the Continent, especially the "French Council for a United Europe," which was organized on the initiative of General de Gaulle who also appealed for European unity against the rising threat of communist Russia shortly after Churchill had taken his stand.

CRITIQUE

British Commonwealth the Model of Unification. The United Europe Movement, in the opinion of this author, advocates a timely copy of the system of consultation and cooperation in the British Commonwealth. This pattern of cooperation, in the eyes of the fathers of the United Europe Movement and its British adherents, represents the most effective effort for the regulation of relations among numerous nations scattered over all parts of the world, comprising different ethnic groups, and having diverse interests. The machinery of Commonwealth consultation and cooperation is an empiric organization which has developed over a long time and which evidenced a striking absence of any planning. Because of its complex nature and its long process of development, statements about it are scattered and comprehensive evaluations are rare. In spite of the apparently haphazard and complex appearance which the Commonwealth pattern offers to the outside observer, there reappear continuously, however, three threads that bind the member

---

[2] Quoted by Alexander Galin, "Europe: Split or United?" in *Foreign Affairs*, An American Quarterly Review, Vol. 25, No. 3, April 1947, p. 417.

nations of the Commonwealth together. They are: (1) The Crown and the Common Law; (2) Sovereign Equality; (3) The Principle of Consent.[3] The last two threads are obviously also those which the fathers of the "United Europe Movement" envisage for a unification of Europe. The belief in the realizability of European unification on grounds of these principles reflects the idea that these threads are sufficient for the creation of a "United States of Europe."

Absence of Genuine Liberalism. However, another fundamental principle, as well as prerequisite, for interstate unification is consistently overlooked by the advocates of the United Europe Movement. The absence of this principle not only renders a realization of the ambitious plans of European unification unfeasible, but also assures the ultimate dissolution and destruction of the British Commonwealth. This prerequisite is *the economic freedom of the individual to plan and act according to his own motive and purpose.* Negatively expressed, it is the absence of nationalist, socialist, or interventionist principles of central planning by the member states.

The System of "Trade Preferences" Breaches International Unity and Cooperation. Modern policies, however, are policies of central planning for purposes of protection, national welfare, full employment, social and economic justice, and other collectivist principles. As has been shown repeatedly in other sections of this work,[4] a unification—and especially a tariff union—under the conditions of the foregoing principles is unrealizable. We may, therefore, content ourselves with proving that the specific feature of Commonwealth economic cooperation, the "system of trade preferences," which the United Europe Movement is also recommending to the free nations of Europe, is a *means of economic nationalism* and as such is breaching international unity and cooperation. It is a system designed for the detriment of outside countries and the temporary advantage of privileged groups of producers which it protects from foreign competition. Furthermore, the very ideas which gave birth to the system of Commonwealth preference must ultimately bring about the *destruction* of the Commonwealth rather than the strength desired and intended.

On the History of Commonwealth Cooperation. We may illustrate our contentions by briefly outlining the development of the pattern of Commonwealth cooperation. The old mercantile system of preferential duties upon British goods imported by the *Colonies,* which had been in effect for more than two centuries, was aban-

[3] Heather Joan Harvey, *The British Commonwealth,* New York, 1953, p. 4 *et seq.*
[4] See especially p. 69 *et seq.*

doned in 1855 when Great Britain and her Colonies adopted an "open-door policy." That is to say, British and foreign traders henceforth were treated alike. This liberal policy was expressly stated in treaties with Germany and Belgium and was later extended to other countries by the operation of the "most-favored-nation clause." The first minor infringements of the open-door principle were committed by the Colonies in favor of Great Britain in the years before the First World War. Towards the end of the war some substantial *export duties* on certain raw materials were levied by the Colonies. These levies, from which Great Britain was exempt, were mainly directed at Germany which used to import those raw materials. In 1922, when most Colonies had full sovereignty as to foreign trade policies, a *preferential tariff system* was adopted by various Colonies. This tariff system followed the old objectives of "protecting infant industries" in the process of growth to avoid "excessive" and "unfair" competition by foreign producers.

In the *Dominions* the first practical step towards Empire preference was made by Canada in 1897. Products from Great Britain were admitted at reduced tariff rates. Later, goods from other Empire countries were also included in this preference. Several other Dominions soon followed the Canadian example and introduced preferential rates in their tariffs. New Zealand followed suit in 1903, South Africa in 1904, and Australia in 1907. The preference margin amounted to from 5 to 15 per cent. In a few cases no preference was given to Empire producers because of their bothersome competition.[5]

In the *United Kingdom* tariff preferences for Empire producers followed very tardily. In the Tariff Act of 1919 the Conservative government introduced preference provisions which provided for a preferential reduction of one-sixth from the full tariff rates. But this preference was still designed mainly for fiscal reasons, so that the most important imports remained duty-free, and the protective character of the preference provisions was relatively insignificant. In 1921, the Safeguarding of Industries Act imposed new tariff duties from which Empire imports enjoyed a preferential reduction of one-third of the full rate. For a short period in the Mid-Twenties, the policy of preferential tariff duties was partially reversed by the Labour government in power, but was resumed by the Conservative government in 1926. Preferential reductions were then extended to all dutiable imports.[6]

[5] E. B. McGuire, *The British Tariff System*, London, 1939, pp. 257, 258.
[6] *Ibid.*, pp. 258-261.

The last remnants of the British liberal trade policy, finally, were systematically abandoned at the *Ottawa Imperial Economic Conference,* in August 1932. At this Conference preferential agreements were concluded among all members of the British Commonwealth. Such agreements were made possible by the preceding introduction of a general tariff by the United Kingdom. Its "Import Duties Act" of February 1932 imposed a duty of 10 per cent of value on all imported goods formerly duty-free but temporarily exempted Empire goods. Now, at Ottawa, the United Kingdom could bargain freely with Dominions and Colonies. The Conference resulted in a large extension of preferences in the Colonies for items produced in Great Britain and in the Dominions granting concessions to British and Colonial products. On the other hand, Great Britain promised to maintain her duty exemptions for Empire products.

The supreme preferential principle as manifested in the Ottawa Agreements was *"home producers first protection, Empire producers second protection, foreign producers none at all."* The agreements confirmed the abolition of Empire free trade and the substitution of bilateral trade relations. Eleven bilateral trade agreements were concluded at Ottawa after bitter struggles and endless bickering among the various groups of producers seeking protection. The Dominions desired to maintain and develop their manufacturing industries and feared almost equally the competition of British and foreign producers. They were not prepared to yield and submit to a substantial reduction in their tariffs. On the other hand, English producers fought for a continuance of the preference policy with respect to the exportation of manufactured goods to the Commonwealth. In the final preference agreements Britain submitted to almost all wishes of the other members of the Commonwealth. She agreed to maintain or impose substantial duties on most *foreign* foodstuffs and raw materials in order to grant trade preferences and privileges to Empire producers. She bound herself to continue the exemption of Empire products from duties imposed under the Import Duties Act of 1932. The Dominions, on the other hand, agreed to protect by tariff only those domestic industries "which are reasonably assured of sound opportunities for success." Furthermore, they promised to "avoid excessive protection" against British producers and allow a "reasonable degree of competition on the basis of relative costs." All concluding parties agreed to a method of fixing minimum margins of preference for Commonwealth producers.[7]

[7] See also J. Henry Richardson, *British Economic Foreign Policy,* London, 1936, p. 130 *et seq.*

The Destruction of the World Economy. Immediately after the Ottawa Conference, difficulties arose among the concluding parties regarding the interpretation of the preference agreements. British producers complained about the "excessive protection" of Dominion industries against British goods. On the other hand, the Dominions —especially Australia and Canada—increased the duties to the rate of 100 and more per cent of the product value, and they maintained that these rates were only moderately protective and allowed reasonable competition. While the markets for Dominion goods in Great Britain increased in subsequent years, those of foreign producers declined. Their complaints about unemployment and severe depression, of course, remained outside the sphere of Commonwealth interest. Since foreign producers were unable to sell to importers in Great Britain and thus earn British media of foreign exchange, they no longer bought goods produced in Great Britain. A decline in British exports to foreign countries and a corresponding depression in the British export industries inevitably resulted. Inasmuch as the policy of Commonwealth preference discriminated against foreign goods and foreign citizens, their states naturally took similar or even further retaliatory steps to discriminate against goods and citizens from the Commonwealth. All over the world the principle "home producer first and last protection" became paramount, and the obstacles to international trade and relations increased manyfold.

This system of Commonwealth cooperation would indeed be incomplete if it were limited to the use of tariff obstacles only. In the years following the Ottawa Agreements, modern and more efficient means of trade protection and preferences were developed such as the quota system with long-term guarantees of quantities and prices, the exchange control system with its priorities as to "essential" foreign trade, the system of monetary management, and sterling devaluations and manipulations supplementing or even replacing the tariff pattern of Commonwealth preference. It is this model of economic cooperation and unification which the fathers of the United Europe Movement are recommending to the free nations of Europe—a model of modern economic nationalism, a hindrance to international trade and reconciliation. It puts new duties on foreign products and imposes new taxes on goods consumed by the people; it closes the door towards freer world trade by binding the member nations to refrain from reducing tariffs without the consent of all other member nations; it limits the power to negotiate freer conditions of trade with other countries and perpetuates the sway of protectionism and interventionism. This is the pattern of cooperation of the British Commonwealth.

Europe Enjoys Greater Freedom than the Commonwealth. The difference between the present-day state of affairs in Europe and the British Commonwealth is only a matter of degree. Although it is true that the member nations of the Commonwealth have imposed lighter restrictions on each other's trade allowing for minimum margins of preference, a European nation at least enjoys the right and freedom to abolish its total restrictions at a moment's notice. It can return to free trade and enjoy its advantages without its neighbors' consent. Whoever values the aspect of return to free world trade and world cooperation must prefer the European system of "autonomous" trade restrictions.

Protectionism Must Destroy the Commonwealth. The very ideas that gave birth to the system of Commonwealth preference must ultimately bring about the destruction of the Commonwealth. The modern principle of government intervention in favor of domestic producers organized in political and economic pressure groups necessarily cannot differentiate as to the source of competition from which the domestic industry is to be protected. The objective of protective policies of intervention is *protection,* no matter with whom the industry is competing. The fact that government protection is granted gradually and discriminately does not refute this statement. The Commonwealth industry clamoring for protection from German, Japanese, or American competition is demanding *protection.* That the competition is German, Japanese, or American is irrelevant, although it is welcome since national, political and other considerations and feelings can be fully utilized in the advocation of protection. Once protection from foreign nations is secured, future desires for protection must necessarily be directed at other competition—Commonwealth competition.

There is no reason whatever stated for the elimination of *foreign* competition that cannot be cited in favor of elimination of Commonwealth competition. Once the Dominions have greatly eliminated foreign competition, they may begin to argue for protection from Commonwealth producers. They may raise their import restrictions to levels that are prohibitive not only for foreign importers, but for Commonwealth importers as well, even though they enjoy the minimum tariff preference. A prohibitive tariff may stay prohibitive even when the minimum preference is deducted. It is even conceivable that, under these conditions, the whole pattern of Commonwealth cooperation may become meaningless and the principle of national autarky paramount.

The Economic Link of the Commonwealth. The significance of the British Commonwealth as a pattern of cooperation lies in the existence of greater freedom of trade than in other parts of the world. That is to say, the Commonwealth enjoys real meaning and significance as long as its member nations enjoy a margin of liberty over other nations. A "minimum preference" in tariff duties obviously constitutes an insignificant margin, or even no margin at all, in this era of multiplicity of trade obstacles.

This knowledge leads us to another important conclusion. We may infer that the continuation of the Commonwealth's pattern of cooperation depends either on the trade policies of the Commonwealth nations themselves or on those of other nations. If the Commonwealth nations should resort to trade policies that are as restrictive as the policies of other nations, the British Empire will cease to be an area of relatively free trade and economic integration, no matter how many other historical, ethnological and cultural threads continue to bind the British nations. The Commonwealth as a pattern of cooperation then simply ceases to exist even though the member nations may continue to call themselves "British" and "member of the Commonwealth." On the other hand, the same disintegration may result from the trade policies of other nations. If other nations should return to an unhampered market policy, the Commonwealth nations' margin of economic freedom would be eliminated. And the British Commonwealth would then constitute an area of national trade restrictions and economic nationalism. That is to say, the British Commonwealth would cease to exist.

Consider the following example. If the United States were to conduct a free market policy without tariffs, quotas, and the numerous other restrictions now existing towards Canada, a large part of the production of the Canadian export industries, including agriculture, would be sold on the American market. Many goods that are now exported to Great Britain and other Commonwealth countries would be exported to the United States. The Canadian producers would earn large balances of American exchange which ultimately would lead to a corresponding expansion of American exports to Canada. On the other hand, assume that the Commonwealth nations would continue to apply the multiplicity of government restrictions on imports, although they may grant an insignificant "minimum preference" as to tariff duties on imports from Canada. Now the question may be raised: "With what economy will the Canadian economy be more closely integrated—the British, South African, or Australian national economies, or with the United States whose vast market is completely open to Canadians without any discrimination whatever?" It is obvious that, under these circumstances, the British Commonwealth, as far as Canada is concerned, would merely be a union in name, while the American-Canadian economic union would be a reality.

However, the latter road to destruction of the British Empire due to liberal policies by outside nations is unlikely under present-day ideological conditions. The United States, for example, is not likely to abolish its protection of grain, butter and egg producers and return to a system of free trade in the near future. But it is certain that the British Commonwealth must cease to exist, if and when the Commonwealth nations, animated by the ideas of protectionism and interventionism, resort to increasingly restrictive trade practices.

Summary. The invitation by Sir Winston Churchill and his followers to the European nations to unite as the Commonwealth nations are united must be rejected on the following grounds:

1. The Commonwealth economic system merely constitutes one of the many aspects and stages of the destruction of world economy.

2. The Commonwealth economic system is based on the relinquishment of the right to return to freedom of trade and world integration.

3. The Commonwealth economic system with its minimum tariff concessions has become meaningless through the application of a multiplicity of more efficient trade restrictions.

4. The Commonwealth economic system is in the process of dissolution and liquidation due to government restrictions of foreign trade.

5. The Commonwealth economic system is a system of cooperation of interventionist governments in their endeavor to control and direct the individual, be he Britisher or foreigner.

VI

A Coordination of the Movements for a United Europe

The International Committee of the Movements for European Unity. In December 1947 the several movements working actively for European unity decided to coordinate their efforts in order to avoid the danger of duplication and confusion and to conduct a joint campaign for unity throughout the European Continent. With the exception of the Socialist Movement the several movements decided to form the "International Committee of the Movements for European Unity." The Committee was "to inform and lead public opinion; to study the political, economic and technical problems of European Union and to suggest how they could be solved; to promote a sense of European consciousness and common loyalty to Europe; by every available means, to mobilize public opinion behind the policy of European unity and to provide a medium through which supporters of this cause could make their influence felt." [1]

The "Congress of Europe." One of the first actions of the Committee was to convene a Congress of Europe at The Hague from May 8 to 10, 1948. The aims of this Congress were: "(1) to demonstrate the widespread support for the cause of unity existing throughout the free countries of Europe; (2) to deliberate upon the issues involved, and make practical recommendations to governments; and (3) to provide a fresh impetus and inspiration to the European campaign." [2]

The Congress was attended by more than 800 delegates from almost all parts of Europe. Several former prime ministers and for-

[1] The European Movement, *European Movement and the Council of Europe,* Hutchinson & Co., London, 1949, pp. 35, 36.
[2] *Ibid.,* p. 36.

eign ministers, politicians of various parties, bishops and prominent churchmen of all denominations, business and labor union delegates, and other representatives of every important sector of European life were invited. The President of Honor of the Congress was Sir Winston Churchill who addressed the opening session with a speech on the urgency and desirability of European unification.

The Hague Congress resulted in the inauguration of a new organization under the name of the *European Movement* whose Presidents of Honor became Blum, Churchill, Gasperi, and Spaak. In each country a National Council composed of delegates of the various unification movements was formed. Where the countries had a totalitarian regime, National Committees of democratic leaders in exile were formed.

The discussions of unification problems by the Congress were conducted in three committees—political, economic and social, and cultural.

Resolutions on Political Union. The political discussions mainly dealt with the creation of a "Council of Europe" and a number of resolutions the most important of which read as follows:

"1. No attempt to reconstruct Europe upon the basis of rigidly divided national sovereignty can prove successful.

2. The nations of Europe must create an economic and political union in order to assure security, economic independence and social progress; and for this purpose they must agree to merge certain of their sovereign rights.

3. A European Consultative Assembly, whose members should be nominated by the Parliaments of the participating nations, must be convened forthwith.

4. The European Union or Federation should be open to all democratic European nations which undertake to respect fundamental human rights.

5. A European Court of Human Rights backed with adequate sanctions should be established to adjudicate in cases of alleged violation of these rights.

6. The special ties which at present link the countries of Europe with other States and dependent territories overseas must be preserved.

7. The creation of a United Europe must be regarded as an essential step towards the creation of a United World." [3]

These political principles were reaffirmed and given full expression at subsequent meetings of the International Committee.

[3] *Ibid.*, pp. 47, 48.

An Economic and Social Resolution. The Hague Congress also discussed and adopted a resolution on the economic and social problems of unification. It dealt with the broad principles of a European economic policy and was meant to be a common basis for future action. These principles of economic policy indeed were so broad that they were accepted through unanimous vote by all political parties and groups represented. It proved impossible, however, to formulate detailed proposals of European unification. For this reason the European Movement decided to convene an **economic** conference at Westminster which should discuss the important economic problems of unification.

Westminster Economic Conference. In April 1949, two hundred delegates including businessmen, trade unionists, economists, and politicians from all over Europe met at Westminster and discussed the economic aspects of the European problem. After several days of debates the Conference resolved that "Europe needs economic union in order to build a stronger, more efficient and more productive economy on the ruins and rubble left by the last war. This strength, efficiency and productive capacity can only be attained if Europe makes a rational use of all its resources, if it creates a market large enough to give full scope to the economies of mass-production, and if it allows all to share equally in the advantages of scientific invention and technical progress. Thus, and thus only, can the standard of living of Europe's peoples be raised as rapidly as respect for the inalienable human rights require that it should be." [4]

"Europe needs economic union," the resolution reads, "in order to promote a fuller and better understanding among its peoples by removing all those international obstacles which today restrict their freedom to seek work, to undertake business, to travel and live where they will. Thus, and thus only, can Europe create a civilization composed of distinct but integrated elements. . . . The purpose of the union must be to constitute within Europe an area in which men, goods and capital may move with no more difficulty than is experienced today within the frontiers of a single country." [5]

A Customs Union Advocated. The delegates proposed the creation of an economic union that was to be protected from outer-European competition by tariffs and other restrictions. Whereas the customs barriers, quotas, and all currency obstructions were to be eliminated within the Union, restrictions were to be continued towards other continents. "The first measure to be adopted as a re-

[4] *Ibid.*, p. 98.
[5] *Ibid.*, pp. 98, 99.

sult of this agreement," the resolution on the Customs Union reads, "should be a declaration of a truce both as regards tariffs and as regards quantitative trade restrictions. No modification of this truce should be permitted. . . . The second task which should be initiated forthwith, and accomplished while the truce is in force, must be the elaboration of a common tariff, *vis-a-vis* the rest of the world, which, in accordance with the accepted principles of commercial policy, must not be higher than the average of the tariffs of the participating states." [6]

According to this resolution, the participating European states are to effect the removal of inter-European tariffs and quotas within a period of ten years. To this end, a minimum annual rate of reduction of restrictions should be determined.

Government Protection of Workers to Be Continued. Although all forms of indirect or direct commercial protection and especially all forms of unfair competition, such as discriminatory transport tariffs, should be prevented, "the measures taken by the governments with a view to improving the living standards of the workers or their professional status should not be considered as having a protectionist character, so long as they are not disguised subsidies aimed at artificially lowering the cost price." Also in the determination of the annual rates of reduction of restrictions "due account should be taken of the need to ensure *full and productive employment* [7] in each country, and to maintain a satisfactory standard of living: and for these purposes, transitional measures should be adopted to facilitate the adaptation of national economies to the new conditions of the Union. . . . During this same period, every effort should be made to bring fiscal and social policies into line in a manner as favourable as possible to the workers, taking into account relative productivity."

In addition, collective bargaining on a Continental basis should be initiated and "collective European agreements should be discussed between the representatives of employers and workers in order to afford the latter minimum guarantees based on principles. It should be remembered that the standard of living of the workers is an element of vital importance in any plans for the realization of European unity. . . . The full employment of labour must be regarded as a moral, social and economic necessity. As far as possible, and taking into account family needs, each country should aim at providing adequate employment for its nationals through the in-

[6] *Ibid.*, p. 100.
[7] Italics added.

tensive exploitation of its natural resources and the development of its industry: a development which will be encouraged by the free movement of capital within the European Union." [8]

Convertibility of Currencies and Financial Policies. In a section dealing with the convertibility of European currencies the resolution reads as follows:

"No scheme for a European Economic Union can be fully realized unless Europe is organised as a zone within which there is free convertibility of currency. This free convertibility may, during a transition period, be limited to exchange requirements originating from current transactions. During such a period capital movements may continue to be controlled.

"The participating countries should co-ordinate their financial policies with regard to: (a) The extent to which provision is made for budgetary surpluses or deficits affecting monetary equilibrium;

"(b) capital movements from one country to another, in order to prevent such movements from upsetting the balance of payments of the countries concerned;

"(c) credit policy." [9]

The financial policies as well as the rates of exchange are to remain subject to the regulations of the Bretton Woods Agreement.

Socialization of Basic Industries. As to the European basic industries, the economists gathered at Westminster resolved the following:

"Study of the industries concerned reveals a variety of common problems regarding such questions as to co-ordination of investment, production plans and research; the study of markets; standardization; vocational training and co-operation in the prevention of unfair trade practices by governments or by commercial undertakings."

To this end "three organisations should be created in each of the four basic industries—Coal, Iron and Steel, Electricity and Transport —namely:

"1. A European governmental body which would have as its function the definition of general policies in the industry concerned, in particular the policies concerned with investment, volume of production, and prices, in order that it shall always be in line with the general policy and with the economic and social aims of a European Union.

"2. A consultative body consisting of employers, employees and

[8] *Ibid.*, p. 102.
[9] *Ibid.*, p. 103.

representatives of the public interest whose task would be to advise the European governmental body on matters of general concern to the industry. . . .

"3. One or more organisations of employers drawn from both publicly-owned and privately-owned undertaking, on whom would fall, amongst other duties, the task of carrying out the general directives and recommendations of the European governmental body. . . .

"In the event of an employers' organisation failing to act in accordance with these principles, the European governmental body would have power to institute proceedings with the competent judicial authorities, leading to the possible applications of sanctions such as:

the cancellation of certain decisions,

the award of damages to injured third parties,

the suppression of the employers' organisation concerned." [10]

Agricultural Production and Distribution to Be Regulated. The group of economists also recommended that Commodity Councils should be instituted in order to:

"1. consider the steps to be taken to promote a European agricultural policy in respect of production and distribution of agricultural products;

2. frame the necessary measures for stabilising European markets for these products at a level which will ensure to European farmers and agricultural workers a secure livelihood and an adequate standard of living in well-managed enterprise, whose existence is justified from an economic and social point of view;

3. in due course propose the establishment, in conjunction with the professional agricultural organisations, of the agencies required for the establishment of markets which might, if necessary, be entrusted with the task of handling stocks, effecting any carry over and generally administering international distribution schemes on behalf of a European Authority." [11]

Existing Preferential Systems and Other Economic Ties Should Be Continued. "To avoid unnecessary dislocations," the economists recommended that "it should be permissible for those nations which consider such steps desirable, to maintain the existing preferential systems and economic ties between themselves and associated overseas countries. In order to further the interest of European economic union, it is desirable to extend to all other members of the

[10] *Ibid.*, pp. 104-5.
[11] *Ibid.*, p. 106.

Union, on a mutual basis and as far as practicable, the benefits which members of existing preference systems now enjoy." [12]

As must be expected, a coordination of the several movements for a United Europe cannot present ideas and arguments in favor of unification other than those the various movements themselves advance. A coordination of various movements embracing diverging ideologies necessarily must be based on compromises and other middle-of-the-road solutions. If resolutions on unification are to be acceptable to the several member movements, they must be compromises between the various ideologies or be formed sufficiently broad to include the several ideologies. If one or several ideologies held by the member movements are found to be incompatible with interstate unification, a compromise solution containing an "incompatible ideology," too, necessarily must be incongruous with unification. If the ideologies of all member movements are found to render true unifications impractical for one or several reasons, the compromise solution containing ideas from each of the several movements necessarily must contain a multiplicity of unification obstacles.

The European Movement constitutes an agglomeration of movements whose political and economic ideologies do not render unification feasible. This assertion on the ideologies held by the member movements has been presented and evaluated in detail in previous chapters. It is obvious that an evaluation of a compromise solution which is acceptable to all member movements cannot lead to conclusions that differ from those on the proposals by the member movements. We may therefore dispense with a detailed analysis of the resolutions of the European Movement and content ourselves with a brief evaluation of its most important provisions. In one important aspect, however, an analysis of the compromise solutions adds considerably to our knowledge. Such an analysis reveals to us the relative importance of each movement in contemporary Europe and the significance of some fundamental notions which are found to be acceptable to all member movements. As shall be proven in the following, these fundamental notions are *socialist* notions accepted by the various movement representatives in the Westminster resolution.

The Obstacles to a Customs Union. "The first measure to be adopted . . .," the resolution on the Custom Union reads, "should be

12 *Ibid.*, p. 109.

a declaration of a truce both as regards tariffs and as regards quantitative trade restrictions." That is to say, whereas the member states are urged to bring about a "truce" in their trade relations, the policies of economic nationalism and warfare towards non-members may be continued and coordinated through the "elaboration of a common tariff vis-a-vis the rest of the world." This resolution apparently contains two serious fallacies. First, under prevailing ideological conditions, a "truce" among the member states cannot be achieved because the industries and groups of producers who enjoy government protection from the competition of industries and producers in other member states do not acquiesce in an abolition of their protection. Government protection, according to prevailing ideologies, is identical with "progress" and "social welfare." Furthermore, elaboration of a common tariff vis-a-vis the rest of the world is impractical because a union tariff would protect and subsidize particular groups of producers while it imposes a sacrifice on all the other producers and consumers. In a national state the representatives of a particular industry often succeed in persuading the rest of the nation to consent to a sacrifice in favor of a particular industry. In a federation comprising different nationalities, however, enormous difficulties arise. The sacrifice which the Union Tariff would impose upon the vast majority of population for the protection of certain minorities of producers would benefit other nationals in the Union. That is to say, a protective tariff in favor of German farmers would be rejected unhesitatingly by the Dutch, Belgian, French and Italian majority in the Union. Furthermore, any protection and restriction in favor of a particular industry would inflict serious harm on European export industries. Foreigners who cannot sell their goods to Europeans cannot buy from Europeans as they lack the European media of exchange. But would a Belgian export industry, for example, endure unemployment of labor and capital in order to benefit a Dutch industry clamoring for protection?

These are the problems of unification. Unfortunately, they are consistently overlooked by the schemers of European unification.

Policies of Full Employment and Protection of Workers Render Unification Unfeasible. "Due account should be taken of the need to ensure full and productive employment." This means that the member governments are called upon to continue their policies of spending, credit expansion, inflation, and protection of those branches of industry suffering from readjustment and unemployment. Naturally, all these measures bring about divergencies in the structures of economies. Divergencies are unification obstacles and the starting point for economic nationalism. Credit expansion, for example, depreciates the domestic currency and makes the price for foreign currencies rise. As this is considered undesirable, foreign exchange controls are imposed which then bring about a shortage of foreign exchange. This shortage then is met with import restrictions and allocations. Both these measures, however, are measures of economic nationalism and disintegration of the international division of labor.

The numerous provisions calling for special protection and benefits for the workers call for similar disparities of economies. Government measures in favor of the workers universally raise the costs of production. If one member government imposes higher costs on its industries than another member government, the industries of the former country are necessarily put at a competitive disadvantage to those of the latter. They will be undersold and will suffer from unemployment. As this is undesirable, imports will be restricted and the economic relations partially or wholly severed. But can these policies be considered to be "declarations of a truce"?

Furthermore, the most important government measures of protection of workers is the immigration legislation which protects the wage rates of the workers in wealthier countries from being lowered by workers immigrating from poorer countries. Now, what does the European Movement advocate? Protection of the workers in wealthier countries or European unification? It cannot have both.

Monetary and Financial Provisions Call for Economic Nationalism. The European Movement pretends to advocate free convertibility of European currencies. The exceptions which it concedes to its rule of convertibility, however, clearly indicate the hypocrisy of its provisions. "This free convertibility," the resolution reads, "may, during a transition period, be limited to exchange requirements originating from current transactions. During such a period capital movements may continue to be controlled." In the first place, what is a transition period? The International Fund Agreements of 1944 have a similar provision on a transition period in which capital movements may continue to be controlled. Up to this very day all members of the Fund but five have invoked this provision and continue to control capital movements. Furthermore, what are capital movements and what are current transactions? The impossibility of distinguishing them leaves all transactions open to arbitrary controls by member governments. There is no need for control on capital movements as capital invested in land, factories, buildings, machines, etc., cannot move anyhow. But why does the resolution make these provisions?

The participating countries are urged to coordinate their financial policies with regard to monetary equilibrium, balance of payments, and credit policy. That is to say, the member governments are urged to coordinate their planning and regulating of the economic activities of their citizens. The operation of the market economy in these important fields of human economy is to be eliminated and central planners are to establish their economic systems of production and distribution. But what yardstick are they to use for their economic order? The French yardstick as to "national interest," "social justice," "essentiality," etc., undoubtedly will differ from that of the Dutch, Belgian, German and Italian planners. As no true agreement can be reached, conflicts will arise and policies of economic nationalism will be continued.

Socialization of Basic Industries Leads to Socialism. Although it is common knowledge that the socialist parties in Europe strongly advocate a nationalization or socialization of basic industries to facilitate "more efficient economic planning," it is surprising to see the economists of the European Movement who represent *non-socialist* parties openly advocate fundamental objectives of socialism. This fact permits us to draw an important conclusion: *The prevailing ideology of Europe is socialist.* According to the Westminster resolutions, European governmental bodies are to define general policies in basic industries—in particular the policies concerned with investment, volume of production, and prices. Employers' organizations, under threat of penalties, are merely to carry out the general directives and recommendations of governments. But when government interferes with investment, volume of production, prices, etc., the results must be unsatisfactory, even from the government point of view, and other measures of central planning and regulation become necessary. And so the governmental body continues to plan and interfere until all-round socialism is established.

European Regulation of Agricultural Production and Distribution Not Feasible. The special steps recommended for the promotion of European agriculture and stabilization of its markets reveal an arbitrary preferential treatment of farmers to the detriment of the vast majority of European population. Is there any reason that can be advanced in favor of benefits to farmers that cannot be advanced for special benefits to barbers, writers, textile manufacturers, artists, etc.? Why should governments not stabilize the markets of books that do not sell, or buy and store up men's undershirts in order to insure fair prices and parity income to shirt producers and their workers? But let us disregard this inconsistency and inquire into the possibility of regulating agricultural production and distribution.

Various European governments have protected their farmers for many decades. But the national policies of protection have differed more or less as to the multiplicity of products, extent and nature of benefits, and groups of producers benefited. A European regulatory authority would have to cope with a vast variety of protective privileges which the farmers would defend vigorously. But there can be no common market if these privileges are continued. Let us assume that the German farmers now receive a price of 10 for a bushel of grain, Belgian farmers a price of 8, Dutch farmers 6, and French farmers 4. Now, would the German farmers acquiesce in a price of 8 for the sake of European unification? Or the French and Dutch population acquiesce in paying a price higher than they pay now? There cannot be any doubt that all parties concerned will reject a scheme of unification containing those provisions.

Preferential System or Economic Union: an Alternative. The Westminster resolutions urging European nations to unite find it permissible for nations "to maintain the existing preferential systems" and "desirable to extend to all other members of the Union . . . the benefits which members of existing preferential systems now enjoy." In other words, the European nations are to unite and to extend the British system of trade preference. One wonders what the European nations are really urged to do, to unite or to organize a system of trade preference. Certainly one precludes the other, and the European nations must choose—they cannot have both. Unification means non-discrimination among member states and absence of national policies of protection and economic nationalism. The Preference System of trade, however, means protection and economic nationalism in degrees. How can both systems be simultaneously realized?

If European governments should choose to join the British system of trade preference, they are faced with insoluble problems. The purpose of the British Preference System was to protect certain industries in the British Empire from competition afforded by all other nations. Admittance of outsiders to the preferential system is identical with abolition of preference. Now, is it likely that the protected Commonwealth industries will approve admitting European products in competition with their own? On the other hand, a great number of European industries enjoy government protection from the competition of efficient export industries of the British Commonwealth. As a matter of fact there would undoubtedly be some opposition on the part of protected European industries to exposure to the competition of efficient Commonwealth industries.

As we see contemporary political and economic conditions, there can be neither a European Union nor an extension of the Commonwealth preferential system to the countries of Europe. The modern predilection for government welfare and government regulation of the activities of individuals according to welfare principles has led, and still is leading, towards a disintegration of the international cooperation and division of labor. Predilection for government welfare is predilection for international conflict.

As has been shown, a coordination of various movements which themselves embrace a multiplicity of irreconcilable contradictions and fallacies cannot miraculously render unification feasible. A true unification of the nations of Europe is conceivable only if and when they decide to abolish the unification obstacles and abandon the ideologies of government welfare and world market disintegration.

Steps Toward Union

I_N THE spheres of politics and
economy, the endeavors to achieve European unification seem to
have made some headway. As can be readily seen in the chart on
page 141, all Western European governments have negotiated
treaties and have created several institutions for the promotion of
unity. Their insignificant achievements or total failures have caused
widespread disappointment. The success of each institution apparently depends on the unification achieved by all others. Without
political unity, economic unity—i.e., true freedom of migration for
men, capital, and goods—seems to be unattainable. But political
unity appears to be unattainable because economic unity is wanting. Problems of defense seem to be entwined with both economic
and political problems whose solution, in turn, seems to depend on
the solution of defense problems. The actual unification process
thus moves in circles.

Through *Aristide Briand,* a French politician and statesman, a
European government for the first time posed the problem of European Union and attempted to achieve the basic steps toward its
realization. Briand's plan of a "European Union," presented to the
world in 1930, provided for a regional union within the League of
Nations. It failed because of the ideological unpreparedness which
characterizes all nations of today. They prefer government interventionism and economic nationalism over international cooperation
and peace. Attempts at integration in 1930 failed just as all suc-
cessive attempts based on principles of government welfare and
economic nationalism must fail.

In October 1943 the governments-in-exile of Belgium, the Netherlands, and Luxembourg, whose countries were still under German
occupation, signed an agreement on monetary cooperation. This

137

agreement was the first step towards the *Benelux Customs Convention* which was signed September 5, 1944 in London. It provided for the abolition of interstate tariffs and established a uniform tariff on goods imported from other countries. The member states, however, remained free to resort to a system of import licenses and quotas. The member states' power to tax also remained unimpaired. It was hoped that ultimately a full economic union would develop from this Customs Convention.

The *Economic Commission for Europe* (ECE), which was set up in March 1947, is a permanent organization of the UN Economic and Social Council with its seat in Geneva, Switzerland. It is the only European organization which the communist states of Eastern Europe have joined, although they play no active role. The Commission works and cooperates with nearly all organizations that are occupied with unifying Europe. It has established a series of permanent committees dealing with Electric Power, Industry and Materials, Inland Transportation, Timber, Coal, Steel, Agriculture, Trade, and Manpower. The United States too, is a member of ECE.

In April 1948 in Paris, representatives of 16 nations signed a convention that created the *Organization for European Economic Cooperation* (OEEC). This institution, which has its permanent seat in Paris, was the outcome of Secretary of State Marshall's invitation to European nations to join in detailing their common needs, which were then to be considered by the Congress of the United States. When Congress approved the Foreign Assistance Act in April 1948, the Organization for European Economic Cooperation served as the receiving and distributing agent for American aid. The supplying side of Marshall's vast "European Recovery Program" was handled by the American "Economic Cooperation Administration" which approved and financed the supply of goods. The objective of the Organization for European Economic Cooperation is to make the best collective use of the member states' individual capacities and potentialities and to execute a joint recovery program.

The *Council of Europe,* which was established in May 1949, is an assembly composed of parliamentary representatives from all European countries that wished to join. The aim of the Council is "to achieve greater unity between its Members for the purpose of safeguarding and realizing the ideals and principles which are their common heritage and facilitating their economic and social progress. ... This aim shall be pursued through the organs of the Council by discussion of questions of common concern and by agreements and common action in economic, social, cultural, scientific, legal and administrative matters."

The *European Payments Union,* which was set up in September 1950, constitutes the second step toward European monetary cooperation and integration. It is an institution whose provisions on the full and automatic settlement of bilaterial balances are based on the "International Monetary Fund Agreement" of July 1944. Trade balances are reported monthly to an agent—the Bank for International Settlements—which determines the balance position of each country toward the Union. Settlements take place between each country and the Union only. Furthermore, net monthly surpluses and deficits of each member state are offset against one another to establish a cumulative position of each member state. Debtor states receive credit by the Union; creditor states grant credit to the Union. Thus a clearing of interstate accounts is facilitated with the smallest possible transfer of media of foreign exchange. With Great Britain as a member of the Payments Union the whole sterling area participates in the Union.

The *European Coal and Steel Community,* which was established in April 1951 for a period of fifty years, is the only supranational authority with independent power to act. The Community combines the coal and steel industries of the member states and purports to establish a common market for coal and steel. This common market is also supposed to promote economic expansion and full employment, and to improve the standard of living in the participating countries. The Coal and Steel Community has become a model for other plans projecting similar pools in other economic sectors, such as the Green Pool to coordinate European agriculture and the Transport Pool to coordinate the European transport system under a High Authority. The Coal and Steel Community, as well as the plans for similar communities, constitutes the "functional approach" toward European integration.

The *Brussels Treaty* of March 1948 was concluded by the governments of Belgium, France, Luxembourg, the Netherlands, and the United Kingdom for a duration of fifty years. In October 1954, Italy and West Germany were invited to join. It established a military alliance as well as collaboration in economic, social and cultural matters and provided for permanent organs and commissions designed to facilitate consultation and cooperation. While the military purpose of the Brussels Treaty Organization, commonly called Western Union, was later assumed by the North Atlantic Treaty Organization, its other objectives were assumed on a much broader basis

by the Organization for European Economic Cooperation (OEEC)
and by the Council of Europe.

The *North Atlantic Pact* of April 1949 is designed to preserve the
"peace, security and freedom" of the member nations through collective defense. It is based on a common pledge to consider an
armed attack against one or more of the signatories as "an attack
against them all." The North Atlantic agreement is an alliance for
defense and its articles deal with armed attack on and with threat
to one or more member states.

In all these institutions for unification the cabinets of the member
states play the deciding role. Parliaments only take active part in
one organization—the Council of Europe. With the exception of the
Coal and Steel Community, decisions in all these organizations are
made through unanimous agreement by all member governments
involved. They are not supranational but international institutions.

In the following chapters these important steps toward union are
analyzed as to the purposes and achievements. Their shortcomings
are traced back to their ideological foundations which are examined
in the light of their compatibility with the objectives of the institutions. Where the ideological foundation is found to be incompatible with the objectives proclaimed, failure is believed to be
inevitable.

(as of January 1, 1955)

MEMBER STATES	Benelux Customs Union 9-5-1944	ECE, Eco. Commission for Europe March, 1947[1]	OEEC, Org. for European Eco. Coop. 4-16-1948	Council of Europe 5-5-1949	European Payments Union 9-19-1950	European Coal & Steel Community 4-18-1951	Brussels Treaty Organization 3-17-1948	North Atlantic Treaty Organization 4-4-1949
Austria		x	x		x			
Belgium	x	x	x	x	x	x	x	x
Denmark		x	x	x	x			x
France		x	x	x	x	x	x	x
W. Germany			x	x	x	x	x[3]	x[4]
Greece		x	x	x	x			x[4]
Iceland		x	x	x	x			x
Ireland			x	x	x			
Italy			x	x	x	x	x[3]	x
Luxembourg	x	x	x	x	x	x	x	x
Netherlands	x	x	x	x	x	x	x	x
Norway		x	x	x	x			x
Portugal			x		x			x
Sweden		x	x	x	x			
Switzerland			x		x			
Turkey		x	x	x	x			x[4]
United Kingdom		x	x	x	x[2]		x	x
Yugoslavia		x	x					
Canada								x
U.S.A.			x					x

[1] Also the USSR, Ukraine, Poland, Czechoslovakia, and Byelorussia are members.
[2] The entire sterling area is a member.
[3] Italy and W. Germany were invited to join in October 1954.
[4] Greece and Turkey joined NATO in 1951, W. Germany was invited to join in October 1954.

I

Aristide Briand and the Initiative of the French Government for a European Union, Prior to World War II

ARISTIDE BRIAND was a French politician and statesman who, between 1909 and 1930, was Premier of France eleven times and Minister of Foreign Affairs twelve times. At other times he was Minister of Justice or held other cabinet posts. He was humanitarian, i.e., broadly philanthropic and humane, anti-chauvinist, and anti-militarist; throughout his life he hated and opposed war. This fundamental characteristic was chiefly responsible for Briand's joining the political group that condemned militant nationalism and finally led him to champion the idea of European unification. Because the socialist parties advocated peace and unity among the working classes of all nations, he became a socialist, and he remained one all his life. Another factor that induced him to join socialism was that he happened to be the son of poor parents, and socialism was commonly believed to be the true political and economic ideology of the worker. Briand, who for longer than a quarter of a century was one of the most eminent socialist leaders in Europe, never studied the doctrinal side of his ideology. During his whole life Briand wrote as little as he read, but he was a brilliant speaker with an unexcelled ability for compromise and conciliation. His lack of dogmatic knowledge and his natural inclinations were probably responsible for his never maintaining a dogmatic position.[1]

[1] See Emil Ludwig, *Leaders of Europe*, London, 1934, p. 116.

The two highlights of his diplomacy were the Treaty of Locarno and the Kellogg Pact by which Briand changed the nature of international relations in postwar Europe. When he became Premier in 1925, he adopted a German plan of guaranteeing mutual security against attack, not only for France but also for Germany, and put it through at Locarno. It was a treaty of non-aggression, of conciliation, arbitration, and mutual guarantees.[2] The Kellogg Pact, which had been an American proposal of a bilateral pact between America and France, was broadened by Briand to contain elements of elastic expansion, so that it might include other nations and secure an abiding peace.

E. Herriot Advanced First Plan of Unification. Aristide Briand was not the first French statesman to propose the unification of European nations. Premier Edouard Herriot had recommended the creation of a United States of Europe in a speech in the Chamber of Deputies on January 25, 1925. But his suggestion had found no response in other European governments—except indifference and sometimes downright hostility. Weeks after Herriot's proposal his government fell before further steps could be taken to assemble an international conference for the study of the unification problem.

Briand Appeals for Cooperation. It was four years later that Aristide Briand, who was then Minister of Foreign Affairs, decided to take up the suggestion of Herriot and present to the League of Nations a plan of a United States of Europe. In a ministerial declaration Briand appealed to the nations of Europe to unite in a common effort for conciliation, peace, and security. "Europe can never live in peace," the declaration read, "until certain questions are settled and the nations have found the road of cooperation."[3]

Briand's appeal immediately created a world-wide sensation. The public opinion of the world was in almost unanimous approval. The few dissenting voices of the extreme nationalists and communists were not taken seriously. Even Mussolini, the Italian dictator, declared himself in favor of the plan, provided a United Europe would also assume the common administration of the European colonies in Africa. Only in Great Britain were skeptical and dissenting views heard. Prime Minister MacDonald, for example, expressed

[2] It seems noteworthy to mention that in signing this treaty of conciliation Germany tacitly acknowledged the loss of Alsace-Lorraine to France. However, Germany refused to accept the loss of eastern German territory to Poland. The Treaty of Locarno implied this refusal and enabled Germany to direct her attention to the East. Fourteen years later German troops crossed the Polish borders. World War II had begun.

[3] Quoted by Edouard Bonnefous, *L'Europe face à son destin,* Paris, 1951, p. 62.

his doubt regarding the immediate realizability of the plan, which he considered premature.

Briand Addresses League of Nations. In June 1929, Briand personally contacted several ministers of foreign affairs who expressed themselves in favor of his plan. Weeks later, on September 7, 1929, at the opening of the Tenth Assembly of the League of Nations, Briand posed the problem of European Union. In his famous plea for Union and collaboration he declared: "I think that among nations geographically located like the European nations there should exist a kind of Federal Union. Nations, at all times, need the possibility to get in touch with one another, to discuss their interests, to make resolutions, and to establish among them a tie of solidarity which would allow them to face serious situations as soon as they appear. It is this tie which I endeavor to establish." [4] The German Minister of Foreign Affairs, Stresemann, immediately agreed to Briand's suggestion and emphasized the necessity of unification because of its economic aspect. Other ministers of foreign affairs also expressed their approval. The only objecting voice at the assembly was that of the British delegate, Henderson, who maintained that a mere restoration of the freedom of foreign trade and the mutual agreement not to increase existing national tariffs would signify a great achievement. After long and enthusiastic discussions the League of Nations delegates assigned to Briand the task to draw up a memorandum outlining a European union. The memorandum was to be approved by the Assembly and then submitted to the national governments for ratification. It was to constitute the basic step towards European Union.

Briand Advances Plan of Unification. On May 1, 1930, Aristide Briand published his memorandum. It provided for the creation of a "European Union" which was to constitute a regional union within the League of Nations. The memorandum was explicit and precise on the organization of the Union government. The legislature, which Briand called the "European Assembly," was to consist of delegates from member governments; the executive branch, which he called the "Permanent Political Committee," was to be elected by the European Assembly. The Committee was to organize a "Secretariat" as the administrative organ of the Union with its seat in Geneva. Finally, a "European Court of Arbitration," the judges of which were to be appointed by the European Assembly, was to constitute the judicial branch of the Union government.

All European governments were invited to participate. The mem-

[4] E. Bonnefous, *Ibid.*, p. 63.

orandum provided that the sovereignty of the member states should not be touched, although the federal government should have certain functions. The economic and social provisions of the memorandum were very vague and fragmentary. They merely foresaw an economic union with "economic collaboration" and a "common market." The important problems with which Europe was occupied during this period were not even mentioned as, for example, the problem of colonies, national minorities, revision of the peace treaties, etc. His proposal was mainly concerned with the development of a system of arbitration, security, and extension of the guarantees given at Locarno.

Governments Take Exception. A long and deep silence in the capitals of Europe followed the publication of Briand's memorandum. Then, voices of disappointment were heard. To some governments the document was much too long; to some it was too vague. Although every government approved the principle of unification, every country had reservations with respect to the consequences of such union. Only three governments, those of Bulgaria, the Netherlands, and Yugoslavia, were willing to accept the memorandum without major objections. A mere diplomatic alliance and an economic collaboration now seemed to be most suitable to most governments concerned. The government of Germany declared its fullhearted agreement, provided the Treaty of Versailles was revised and Germany be granted full equality of rights. Belgium objected against the abandonment of sovereignty as outlined in the memorandum. Sweden, Norway, and Switzerland declared the League of Nations to be entirely sufficient under the present situation. Great Britain expressed her reluctance to abandon the British Commonwealth and its preferential trade. Soviet Russia bitterly opposed the plan because a United Europe would constitute a menace to her own security. Italy, finally, preferred to stay silent altogether.

Aristide Briand had drawn up this memorandum and published it in order to be able to present it officially to the national delegates at the following General Assembly of the League of Nations. But when the Eleventh Assembly met on September 1, 1930, Briand, because of all the opposition and criticism which his plan had encountered, merely suggested creating a "Commission for the Study of European Unity." He dared no longer mention a serious discussion of his memorandum or an early realization of its objectives. The delegates finally agreed to a commission that was to examine the fundamental problems and possibilities of unification. It was set up with Sir Eric Drummond of Great Britain (then Secretary Gen-

eral of the League) presiding, and altogether convened six times.
When its discussions proved entirely fruitless, the whole idea of European Union was dropped.

Last Appeal for European Unity. A few months later Aristide Bri-
and, the Great French Conciliator, died of a heart ailment. His
dream of a United States of Europe and his spirit of conciliation and
cooperation appeared once again when in 1931, with the great depression on its way, the French government suggested a European
Union for the express purpose of European economic cooperation.
But this last appeal for European Union suffered the same fate as
did the earlier one by Aristide Briand.

Explanations of Failure in Contemporary Literature. To seek the
reasons for Briand's failure of attempts at European conciliation and
cooperation in a few historical facts would indeed be easy and superficial. We could lay blame, as is done almost without exception
by contemporary writers, on the refusal of present-day governments
to abandon even the slightest part of their sovereignty—an abandonment which is said to be a prerequisite for a Union; or on the existing division of Europe in victorious countries which endeavored to
consolidate Europe as it existed, and defeated Germany which was
clamoring for revision of the peace treaty and equality of rights; or
on the hostility of Great Britain towards a European Union because
she would not abandon the ties with the Commonwealth and inte-
grate with a tariff union of Europe. Or we may become even more
superficial by stating that Briand was bound to fail because Stresemann, the German minister of foreign affairs who for several years
worked with Briand for European conciliation, had died in October
1929, and that Briand's suggestions came too late. We may even say
that, in 1930, the great depression was on its way, or that the Nazis
were on their rise in Germany, and Briand's plans were too late for
these reasons. But such explanations hardly touch the core of the
problem. Briand's project of European conciliation and unification,
in reality, was bound to fail because it was built on a basis that suffered from its heterogeneous double nature upon which neither a
union nor conciliation can be solidly rested.

The Fundamental Conflict. Briand's greatness lay in his *humanitarian or humane* approach to the problem of unification. His motivating power was his humanitarian nature and his anti-chauvinist
and anti-militarist outlook. But these noble characteristics con-
flicted with his *collectivist ideology,* for humanity and collectivism

are two heterogeneous worlds of ideas and human action. The humanitarian idea proclaims that man and his happiness are paramount; that he not be neglected in favor of the different aspects of his life, like nation, race, sex, faith, profession, and social groups. The collectivist proclaims and enforces moral imperatives upon the individual in favor of the collectivist whole. In a collectivist society man ceases to be an end, but becomes a means for the ends of state and society. These two worlds of ideas and human action are diametrically opposed. If collectivism attains supremacy, it must overthrow whatever has been built and achieved by humanity; if humanity is to be paramount, whatever collectivism brings about must be removed.

The heterogeneity of these two philosophical principles is reflected in the life work of Aristide Briand. Every step in the direction of his ultimate goal of European peace and collaboration was taken on the humanitarian road for the peace and happiness of the individual; and every step on this road was undone by the collectivist ideologies which animated Briand as well as the politicians and statesmen of his time.

The following criticism is solely based on this aforementioned duality. We may content ourselves with a presentation of the fundamental fallacy of Briand's intentions and refer to a detailed analysis of the specific prerequisites and effects of a realization of a Union in our treatment of other writers' plans elsewhere in the book.[5]

Humanity versus Collectivism. Humanity, i.e., the principle of humane or philanthropic disposition, maintains that the noble side of mankind is the dominant feature of his nature, that goodness, kindness, and love are man's motivations. Man is more important than any of his part-aspects of life—nation, race, sex, faith, profession, and social group. The world law of human collaboration is gentle and peaceful; war is bad and detestable. Peace and man's happiness are the highest objectives. To deliver man from war and strife is a principal goal of humanity.

This concept is rejected by collectivism which maintains that the "immoral" concepts of individual rights and individual supremacy must disappear. Collective society must recognize no private persons—only collective wholes which the individual must serve. The dignity of the individual results from his homogeneity with society as a whole. The individual, in final analysis, is a "pure abstraction" and society a single "collective being."

It is obvious that this conception of individual and society, which

[5] See Part II, Chapters I-V.

is clearly stated by August Comte, the founder of Positivism,[6] necessarily must lead to a totalitarian view and an eventual realization
of a totalitarian society.

It is characteristic for the various schools of collectivism to attack
the idea of "humanity" under misleading and presumptuous names.
August Comte rejected "humanity" by designing plans for a "new
religion of humanity" which is a thoroughly anti-liberal scheme for
human regimentation and submission. The followers of Comte then
fully developed this "new religion of humanity." But since nomen-
clature is immaterial for the purposes of scientific analysis, which is
concerned with the essence of the matter, we may disregard this
misleading terminology and call the prevalence of the collective
over the individual by the more suitable name—collectivism or anti-
humanity.

The doctrine of collectivism makes the happiness of others the
directing force of the individual's conduct in life as well as the principle of his happiness. It is obvious that this fundamental principle
must rest on the knowledge of what makes up the happiness of
others and of the kind of happiness which all others enjoy. But it
is easily recognized that such a knowledge is unattainable to the
human mind. Collectivism, in this respect, does not reveal at what
the individual is supposed to be aiming. What sort of happiness
shall the individual secure for others? Collectivists thus are asking
the individual to aim at collective happiness before they can tell us
in what it consists. They are arguing in a circle by declaring that
the happiness of others is the directing force of the happiness of the
individual. The individual is supposed to be happy because others
are happy who, in turn, are to be happy that others are happy. But
this is absurd. Collectivists do not know what collective ends consist of, but they proclaim moral imperatives for which they claim
authority to make and execute laws.

Economic Collectivism Means Oppression and Tyranny. Collectivist policies in the economic world find their expression in government measures in favor of the collective entity—the nation or the
"class." The institution of private ownership in the means of production is universally condemned by collectivists, and entity ownership, which means state ownership and control, is substituted. Thus
all power of ownership is concentrated in the hands of the state.

---

[6] August Comte, *Système de Politique Positive*, Paris, 1824; *Cours de philosophie
positive*, 1830-1842; *Système de politique positive* (4 vols., 1851-1854).
    For an excellent discussion of "collectivism" and social sciences, see F. A. Hayek,
The Counter-Revolution of Science, The Free Press, Glencoe, Ill., 1952.

When ownership is widely diffused, it is impossible for any one man or a few to employ it all at once to evil use. But when all ownership is concentrated in the hands of the state, it is relatively easy for one man or the few in control of the state to turn all that concentrated power to evil use. A diffusion of property in private hands thus is a check on the evil propensities in man, whereas state ownership is the tool for evil to reign. Private ownership of the means of production also has the beneficial effect of giving security to the owner whose liberty of thought and action it promotes. It enables man to pursue courses that he would not be able to pursue if he were the servant of a universal employer. The great thinkers in human history—the leaders, the pioneers, and the discoverers—have been men who enjoyed a sufficient security to free them from dependence upon anyone else and to enable them to pursue their tenor of life without fear or favor.

Collectivists universally condemn private incomes from rent, profit, and interest. If these incomes are abolished, then all individual incomes must be derived from the state or state institutions in the form of wages, salaries, pensions, and allowances. In addition to this contrast in earning income is the opportunity for spending it. The keystone of the profit system is the consumer's freedom to choose and spend his income as he sees fit. Through the operation of the profit motive on the part of producers the consumers' wishes are met. Only through the satisfaction of consumers can profits be made. Thus the whole system is built around the wishes of consumers. The abolition of the profit system means abolition of man's freedom to decide for himself what to consume; the central planners take that prerogative.

Collectivists universally condemn the "wasteful competition" of "planless" individuals. They substitute central planning for the freedom of the individual. They introduce controls of foreign exchange and investment, the control of raw materials, the control of prices, and the control of labor. The free choice of a job is abolished and the citizen is coerced to "more useful work" in the service of the state or of "more essential" industries. Central planning necessarily involves the direction of all factors of production including labor. The control of labor like all other controls, however, is a direct limitation of individual liberty. It concerns everybody as it subjects everybody.

Economic Collectivism Leads to International Conflict. Collectivist policies not only infringe upon fundamental liberties of the individual, but also bring about the destruction of international relations. They erect obstacles to international trade in order to realize their collectivist schemes. These obstacles may be classified and summarized as follows: (1) monetary controls which the collectivists introduce as an essential means for the realization of collective programs; (2) full-employment controls which are to restrict individual activities in accordance with the program of the full-employment planner; (3) price controls which are to fix prices at a different height from that of the world market; (4) controls connected with government programs for the development of national resources and the protection of infant industries; (5) controls for purposes of war preparedness.

All these obstacles to international trade and relations impede the international exchange of goods and services, thereby reducing the standards of living and rendering more difficult the most practical and essential means by which nations communicate with each other. Among all the fields of international cooperation, foreign trade is the most important. Whoever plans to wage an effective war of aggression must first eliminate ties of trade relations and attain a considerable degree of national self-sufficiency. Cultural, political and other aspects of international relations do not, by far, have the same importance as economic relations have in the daily lives of so many people. But in this important field of international relations it is the collectivist ideology, i.e., the preference of the nation and not of the individual, that directs contemporary policies. Is it humanity that makes us exclude goods from domestic markets simply because they are produced by foreigners? Or for a worker to be prohibited from working at a job simply because he is a foreigner? All national trade restrictions are government acts of discrimination in favor of certain groups against others. They are direct measures of compulsion and coercion granting privileges to certain citizens and excluding foreigners or restricting and prohibiting the economic activities of foreigners.

These were the policies of the European governments at the time Aristide Briand advocated peace and European cooperation. While Briand and a few government delegates at the League of Nations were discussing "eternal peace" and "European Union," economic collectivism triumphed all over Europe. Parliamentary democracy as a form of government was finally abolished in several European states, and systems of government omnipotence were established. All over Europe the ideology of collectivism seized power and became diastrous to humanity and mankind. The inevitable outcome of the supremacy of collectivism over humanity was the final catastrophe which came over Europe through the doctrines and deeds of German National Socialism.[7]

[7] See also Wilhelm Röpke, *Civitas Humana*, 1944, Part 2, p. 200 *et seq.;* Karl Jaspers, *Vom Ursprung und Ziel der Geschichte*, 1949, p. 280 *et seq.;* Henrich Hoffmann, *Die Humanitätsidee in der Geschichte des Abendlandes*, Bern, 1951.

II

The Benelux Economic Union

Origin and Purpose. The driving force towards an economic unification of Belgium, Luxembourg, and the Netherlands was the desire of their governments-in-exile during World War II to bring about full economic cooperation among the three countries. As early as October 1943, when their territory was still occupied by German armies, the governments-in-exile signed a monetary agreement on the relative values of the Belgian franc and the Dutch florin which indeed paved the way for the *Customs Convention* of September 1944. This convention reflected the governments' desire to create an economic unit that would be sufficiently large to compete successfully in the postwar world market. It called for the elimination of existing tariff barriers among the signatories and for the levying of common tariff duties on imports from other countries. Inasmuch as economic unity had existed between Belgium and Luxembourg since 1921, the agreement was to create a Customs Union between the Belgian-Luxembourg Economic Union and the Netherlands.[1]

Although this Customs Convention suppressed the existing duties on goods passing from one member state into another, it did not include provisions abolishing either the differences in excise taxes or the elaborate system of import licenses and quotas as well as exchange control. Nevertheless, it was hoped and expected that this "customs union" would develop into a complete union with a common market in which goods would flow freely among the territories of the member states with no restrictions whatever.

The Organization. The 1944 Customs Convention also provided

[1] "Texte de la Convention douanière belgo-luxembourgeoise-néerlandaise," in Jean Van Der Mensbrugghe, *Les Unions Economiques: Réalisations et Perspective,* Institut des Relations International, Brussels, 1950, pp. 349-351.

for certain organs which were to implement the provisions of the Agreement and to prepare the way for further agreements on unification. It provided for the following three councils which are composed of an equal number of government representatives from the Netherlands and the Belgo-Luxembourg economic union:

1. A *customs council* which is to assure uniform legislation as to import duties. After World War II a special commission was created to assist this council in the examination of disagreements and disputes arising from the interpretation of the Customs Convention;

2. A *union council* which is to coordinate the commercial policies of the three member states;

3. A *foreign trade council* which is to assure a coordination of commercial relations with third countries.

These were the first steps of the governments of Belgium, Luxembourg, and the Netherlands on the way towards an economic union.

Implementation of the Agreement Delayed. The Agreement was to go into effect as soon as the three countries were liberated. However, its implementation was delayed in 1944-1945, at the time of actual liberation, because the attention of governments was fixed on other problems as, for example, the immediate problems of reconstruction, credit and money reforms, economic production and fair distribution, etc. But finally, in April 1946, some ministers from the member states met to examine and discuss the possibility of realizing the 1944 agreement. It immediately became apparent that the tariff list which was drawn up as an annex to the Customs Convention was unsatisfactory to all signatories and that a new tariff list had to be drafted. But this was a very difficult task. Great disparities of duties "on account of different needs for protection" existed between the two areas, and even the methods of calculating the tariff duties were different. In order to iron out numerous conflicts which had arisen among the member states, a permanent institution, the "Meeting of the Prime Ministers," was set up in March 1947. The Prime Ministers were to attempt to coordinate the work of councils and thus hasten the process of unification. It was also decided that another institution was needed whose task would be essentially administrative, and thus a "Secretariat General" was established with its seat in Brussels.[2]

Customs Convention Ratified. After several meetings of the

[2] Department of State Publication 4944, *Regional Organizations*, April 1953, p. 6; L. de Sainte-Lorette, *L'Intégration Economique de l'Europe*, Paris, 1953, p. 92 *et seq.*; J. Van Der Mensbrugghe, *Ibid.*, p. 26 *et seq.*; William Diebold, *Trade and Payments in Western Europe*, Harper & Brothers, New York, 1952, p. 319 *et seq.*

Prime Ministers and after considerable work on the part of all councils, the Convention and annexed documents were submitted to the parliaments of the three member states and ratified in July and August 1947. The Customs Union went into effect on January 1, 1948.

As it was soon recognized that the economic policies of the member countries must necessarily be coordinated in order to give meaning to a customs union, the governments decided to broaden the aim of Benelux to an "Economic Union." The following objectives were agreed upon by the Prime Ministers attending a conference in June 1948: (1) to return to a system that allows freedom of consumption; (2) to reduce government subsidies to producers and consumers; (3) to coordinate their citizens' investments; (4) to unify fiscal and social policies; (5) to conduct policies that guarantee monetary equilibrium. It was hoped that this Economic Union, in operation, would bring about free movement of persons, goods, and capital within its area.

The Prime Ministers even went so far as to set a tentative date for formation of this union: January 1, 1950.

Progress Slower Than Anticipated. Once again the governments of the three member states were in agreement, and harmony reigned during the meeting of the Prime Ministers at The Hague in March 1949. Again plans and projects for future unification were agreed upon. Special attention was given to the necessity for free convertibility of the members' currencies, harmonization of agricultural policies, coordination of wages and social security, and coordination of systems of taxation. But as to the realization of this and previous plans of unification, the Prime Ministers decided to postpone the date six months. They also made arrangements for a "pre-union period" lasting from July 1, 1949 to July 1, 1950, during which the governments pledged to remove the barriers to interstate trade and to unify Benelux trade with other countries.

The Conference at The Hague in 1949 probably constituted the climax of the Benelux Union movement, "an example of unity in a divided world." All conceivable plans and projects were drawn up —only realization had to follow.

The first difficulties arose out of "trade deficits" of the Netherlands to Belgium. Financing of these deficits depended on the European Payments Union, then in the process of being revised. Other domestic problems, such as Holland's colonial problems in Indonesia and Belgium's problems connected with the abdication of the Belgian king, began to overshadow the problem of unification. Both governments grew reluctant to accept new obligations, and when the date for the "pre-union" arrived, postponement for the time being was agreed upon.

Towards the end of 1949 it seemed as if some progress could be made. In September 1949 the Dutch had devalued their currency to a larger degree than the Belgians and new credits were advanced to the Dutch central bank by the Belgians. But during the following spring the "balance-of-payment deficits" began to plague the Dutch government again, and so it was concluded by all parties concerned that realization of a full economic union could not be considered until the imbalance of trade was overcome. Also, the desired removal of certain Belgian levies on agricultural imports from Holland and the coordination of turnover taxes were very difficult. During the first half of 1951 the Dutch "balance-of-payment" problems became so great that some of the preliminary work towards union was even undone. The governments concerned therefore pledged to take the necessary steps internally to correct the causes that had led to the reimposition of trade restrictions.

After that, silence enveloped the Benelux Union, which had been the example of unity in a divided world. Only occasionally does one read of hopes and new plans for Benelux unification.

The "Economic Stumbling Blocks" in Contemporary Literature. The fact that the Benelux nations have made so little progress towards the unification desired during the decade since the Customs Convention was signed, is explained and interpreted in many ways by contemporary writers. The *difference in internal economic policies* is most frequently quoted as the main obstacle in the path of unification. The London *Economist,* for instance, stated, "For the moment the chief obstacle to the realization of the Benelux idea is the difference in the internal policies of the two countries: rigid State interventionism in Holland and qualified liberalism in Belgium. Holland cannot accept the free circulation of goods within the Union so long as price levels and conditions of supply and demand cannot find their conditions of equilibrium." [3] Another article in the same periodical expressed a similar concern regarding the *lack of equilibrium.* It reads as follows: "As the Belgians and Dutch are discovering, it is not schemes of union that create economic balance but the attainment of balance that alone makes schemes of union—either of currency or of customs union—feasible. There are no short-cuts." [4]

[3] *The Economist,* May 31, 1947, p. 853.
[4] *The Economist,* August 20, 1949, p. 389. For criticism see further below: "The Great Fallacy."

Shortages of foreign exchange are said to have led the Dutch government to use quotas and foreign exchange control in order to restrict imports from Belgium. In spite of numerous complaints by Belgian producers who were eager to sell in the Dutch market, the government of Holland refused to remove the quotas because it feared the loss of gold and foreign exchange reserves. As long as the Belgian government advanced substantial credits to Holland for imports from Belgium no difficulties arose. But the Belgians felt that they could not go on lending additional funds indefinitely. They insisted that Holland remove her rationing and quota regulations; the Dutch government insisted on continuing government controls as long as there was disequilibrium. When Belgium once again advanced new credits to the Dutch central bank and when the European Payments Union granted it considerable amounts of drawing rights, the government of Holland allowed Dutch imports from Belgium to rise. But when Dutch credits were almost exhausted and deficits were still growing during the first half of 1951, the Dutch government once again curtailed imports from Belgium, and old controls and restrictions were reimposed.[5]

Another offered explanation of the Benelux failure, an explanation with which we entirely agree, refers to the *divergencies of agricultural prices* between the two territories. Any divergency of national prices from free-market prices is government-created and desired by the respective producers who are backed by parliament. Abolition of price divergencies inescapably runs counter to the well-entrenched interests of the protected producers. In the Netherlands agriculture is the mainstay of the national economy, and agricultural products, especially dairy products and vegetables, are the country's main export items. They are better and cheaper than in Belgium or any other neighboring country. Furthermore, the Dutch government paid high subsidies to the Dutch farmers for social, economic, and other reasons. Naturally, Holland expected to sell large quantities of her cheap farm products to Belgian consumers. But here the Belgian government stepped in. How could it allow its higher-cost farmers and producers to be exposed to Dutch competition, especially since the Belgian farmers were protesting against Dutch "flooding" of the Belgian food market with cheap and "unfairly priced" goods? The problem was finally solved by negotiating a protocol that assured minimum prices and "fair profits" to producers. It also emphasized the right of a member government to "protect its home market against third countries and partner

[5] William Diebold, *Ibid.*, p. 336 *et seq.*

countries." [6] This provision naturally meant that Dutch farm products being imported into Belgium were levied with a tax that raised their price to the Belgian level. Of course, these taxes on imports were not custom levies—at least, their names said they were not.

Another issue that contributed to the defeat of the Benelux idea was the existence of different *excise taxes* on similar products. Excise taxes are revenues for government treasuries. The multiplicity of social and economic functions of modern government requires vast revenues which are either collected through taxation, outright inflation, or both. At any rate, modern governments largely depend on all kinds of taxes and, among others, on excise taxes. As Jacob Viner pointed out, standardization of these taxes was a major problem whose complexity "may, in fact, have been a significant factor in preventing customs union agreements from being reached." [7] He also quoted G. de Molinari who stated that "the most serious difficulty, and we can even say the sole genuinely serious difficulty which the formation of an international *Zollverein* will face, rests in the standardization of excise regimes." [8] We agree, with the sole reservation that modern tools of government control—foreign exchange control, quotas, government monopolies, etc.—are even more formidable obstacles to unification than excise taxes. The latter in general owe their existence merely to fiscal need for revenue, while control and planning are the basic functions of modern government. It is obvious that abrogation of a fundamental function of government is more difficult to obtain than a mere renunciation of revenue.

Unification of excise taxes can be effected by raising the lower rates of one country to the higher rates of the other. Such a solution is acceptable to both governments since one loses no revenue while the other even gains. Of course, the Dutch and Belgian governments wanted to try this, but their parliaments would not agree. The Belgian parliament, for example, refused to raise the tax on beer because considerable Belgian opposition among producers and consumers was encountered. The Belgian producers even organized a real campaign of opposition under the slogan: "Benelux perhaps—but pay more a pint for our beer, never!" [9]

Another popular explanation for the failure of Benelux refers to

[6] William Diebold, *Ibid.*, p. 334.

[7] Jacob Viner, *The Customs Union Issue*, Carnegie Endowment for International Peace, New York, 1950, p. 61.

[8] G. de Molinari, "Union douanière de l'Europe," in *Journal des économistes*, 4th Series, 2nd year, V (1879), pp. 314-315.

[9] John Goormaghtigh, *European Integration*, International Conciliation, Carnegie Endowment for International Peace, New York, 1953, p. 77.

World War II. Eight months passed between the liberation of Belgium and the freeing of the greater part of Holland from German occupation. And this difference in time of liberation with all its effects on reconstruction and development is cited as a difficulty in unification. In addition, the war destruction of capital and wealth was much more severe in Holland than in Belgium. Van Der Mensbrugghe estimated the extent of war damages per head of population to have amounted to $274 in Belgium and $418 in the Netherlands. War destroyed about one-third of Holland's national wealth, while Belgium's losses amounted to less than 4 per cent. These figures are offered to us as explanation for the contradictory political situation in both countries and as reason for the Benelux failure.[10]

Considerable opposition to Benelux was also offered on the part of *Belgian workers and trade unions.* Wages are much higher in Belgium than in the Netherlands. Unification of these countries would also mean free migration, thus allowing thousands of Dutch workers to pour into Belgium and compete with Belgian workers in the labor market. Belgian wage rates would naturally drop—and Belgian workers would strike and complain. Importation of cheap Dutch goods was also opposed by labor in Belgium on grounds of "unfairly low labor costs" in Holland. But similar arguments were also advanced by Dutch workers and trade unions. The Dutch heavy industries greatly rebuilt and renovated by American means out of Marshall aid funds, worked with much higher costs than Belgian competitors. Unification would therefore mean unemployment of capital and labor in the heavy industries in Holland. But such a price was far too high; unification yes—but never readjustment and unemployment!

Customs Union and Governmental Intervention. As we have repeatedly pointed out, the removal of interstate barriers between countries with important economic relations is a very difficult matter because of the growth of governmental intervention in economy. It is especially difficult if the two countries have centrally planned economies. Nowadays, tariffs, quotas, exchange controls, import licenses, state import monopolies, rationing and allocating, etc., protect the desired national price and wage structures, the volume of employments, social security programs, artificial foreign exchange rates, monetary and fiscal policies, and so forth. There is no longer a well-functioning international division of labor or an equilibrium of price structures. Whatever balance there is left within a national

10 J. Van Der Mensbrugghe, *Ibid.*, p. 40. For criticism see further below, p. 165.

economic unit depends on the maintenance of appropriate barriers to imports or subsidies to exports. An economic union, therefore, presupposes an equalization of economic controls, central plans, and objectives. It even presupposes an harmonization of social structures, of powers of pressure groups, and their future intent. It is obvious that such a union is not only difficult to attain, but also involves a more complete degree of political unification than a union under free-market conditions.

During the nineteenth century, when the world was an interrelated market economy, prices were flexible and unhampered by government decrees. Exchange control was an unknown phenomenon, exchange rates were relatively stable, and costs were flexible because of absence of government wage regulation, cartelization, or extensive collective bargaining. Under these circumstances lowering or removing tariff barriers could be taken in stride, although it might still cause a temporary shock. Tariffs merely constituted an element in cost and their removal brought about limited repercussions in the structure of cost and production. Otherwise world economy was an unhampered market economy.

Union and Readjustment. Under contemporary economic conditions any removal or reduction of trade barriers must be extremely disturbing. Prices and costs have been made rigid by innumerable government regulations which have to be changed or revoked in case of unification. Government regulations, however, are based on the express desire of a nation's majority for just such a price and cost structure. Consider the example of the heavy industry in Holland, formerly an agricultural country. Because the Dutch government decided that Holland should have a heavy industry, such an industry was built. Many millions of dollars were spent by the government for construction of blast furnaces and other installations, and more millions were invested in housing for workers. Whole towns and cities were built. However, these installations and cities are far removed from the sources of raw materials—iron ore, coal, etc.—and so the industry is faced with enormous transportation costs. With these greater costs the new industry has to be permanently protected from foreign competition, especially Belgian and German competition. It is obvious that a Customs Union between Holland and Belgium would require an adjustment in the form of a liquidation of the Dutch heavy industry. Government investments in the amount of many millions of dollars, and even many millions of Marshall Aid Funds granted for modernization and expansion of this industry, would be lost, and thousands of Dutch workers of the heavy industry would be unemployed. In this case, like many others in both Holland and Belgium, unification would mean an adjustment that would render futile all preceding government attempts at national and social planning. Are the nations prepared to pay this price for the Customs Union?

Customs and Other Trade Barriers. Under existing conditions, the term "customs union" as used in economic history, and especially in that of the last century, is not only ambiguous, but downright misleading. As long as customs duties were the sole barrier to international trade, absence of interstate customs really constituted an economic *union*. If the territory of the union was exposed to the unhampered influence of the world market, we spoke of open-door policies which made the world a vast economic union. If the territory of the union was free from interstate tariffs, but remained separated from the world by certain outside customs, we could speak of "customs union." Today, however, the absence of tariffs between states is unimportant because of the multiplicity of modern trade obstacles at the command of governments. By freely resorting to import and export quotas, exchange controls, import licenses, state trade monopolies, and rationing and allocating, governments may prohibit a single good from crossing its country's borders, even though no tariff is in effect. But can this be called a "customs union"? We believe a more logical and appropriate term for what was formerly called a "customs union" would be "controls union." It is a "controls union" that the Benelux nations are striving to attain.

Use of this term would immediately indicate that it extends to all trade barriers and not merely to ordinary import duties. It would also reveal at first glance that it is much more difficult to achieve, unless brought about through a process of essentially political unification. Thus, in final analysis, the problem of "customs union" becomes a problem of political unity. That such plans are empty and utopian, under socialist or interventionist conditions, has been proven repeatedly.

The Great Fallacy. The great fallacy in almost all attempts at explanation of the Benelux failure is the doctrine of the "national balance of payments." The lack of payments equilibrium, the chronically unfavorable balance of payments on the part of the Netherlands, the gold and foreign exchange shortages of the Dutch central bank, the Dutch payments deficits towards Belgium—all are aspects of the same fallacy: the balance-of-payments doctrine. It is one of the oldest mercantile doctrines which, though exploded again and

again, has lived throughout the ages. It survives and lives in spite
of devastating criticism by the economists.

The balance of payment of an individual, group of individuals,
or a nation is always in equilibrium. The money equivalent of all
incomes of an individual, group, or nation during any particular
period equals the money equivalent of the amounts employed—
whether used for consumers' goods, producers' goods, investments,
charity, savings, or cash holdings. The balance of payment of an
individual living on loans or other people's contribution, or even on
thievery or robbery, is always in equilibrium; his income equals his
funds employed.

What the advocates of the balance-of-payments doctrine have in
mind is the following: they assert, although in a rather hazy and
nebulous way, that the individual who reduces his cash holdings
and employs his funds for the acquisition of goods and services has
an unfavorable balance of payment! An increase in cash holdings,
they say, is identical with a "favorable balance of payment." Similarly, they maintain that a nation intent upon reducing the amount
of money by importing foreign goods or services suffers from an
unfavorable balance of payments. The fundamental error in this
assertion is the notion that the reduced cash holdings of an individual (or nation) are the unintentional outcome of his acquisitions
and that he may spend his total cash holdings unintentionally. A
nation, they say, may spend its whole stock and reserve of money
and media of foreign exchange on imports of commodities and foreign services. It is obvious that such a notion is fantastic and beyond all imagination.

"But how do you explain the Dutch payments deficits towards
Belgium and the gold and foreign exchange shortages of the central bank of Holland?" a balance-theorist will ask. The answer lies
in one of the most easily understood economic laws: Gresham's
Law. "Bad money drives better money out of the country." That
is to say, whenever a government depreciates its domestic money
through inflation and credit expansion, but continues to enforce the
former exchange rate, foreign money disappears from the market
and depreciated domestic money remains. Arbitrary exchange rates
bring about the effects described by Gresham's Law.

Union and Exchange Control. Government control of the foreign exchange transactions of citizens is not only instrumental in
creating foreign exchange shortages, but also constitutes the most
important of all international trade barriers. This control, which is
even required by certain provisions of the International Fund

Agreement, forces citizens to exchange foreign currency at a rate fixed by governments. If a government, let us say that of the Netherlands, now embarks upon a policy of inflation and credit expansion, the price of foreign exchange as determined in Dutch guilders tends to rise to a point corresponding to the diminished value of the inflated guilders. If the government nevertheless continues to enforce the old exchange rates, it enforces prices for foreign exchange below the true market price, and immediately the effects appear which Gresham's Law describes—foreign media of exchange become scarce.

We may illustrate this law briefly as follows: suppose you are a Dutch businessman from Rotterdam. You have cash holdings and bank deposits in Dutch guilders and Belgian francs, which you need for your transactions with Belgian businessmen. Let us also suppose that a unit of both currencies is equal to one purchasing power unit. You conduct transactions smoothly on this basis. Now your Dutch government begins to inflate and expand credit, and the purchasing power of your guilders decreases to half a unit. Naturally you will cease to exchange both currencies on a one-to-one basis. You will expect to receive or pay two guilders for a Belgian franc. But your government interferes and says: "In the name of our authority and the majority of your fellowmen, we order thee to exchange guilders against francs on a one-to-one basis!" Of course, you will protest and say: "This is ridiculous. Our guilders have lost half of their purchasing power!" But your protests are in vain. As a loyal and obedient citizen you exchange your Belgian francs having one purchasing power unit against guilders having half a purchasing power unit. Soon, however, you will find that your total units of purchasing power are rapidly decreasing in number. With every franc-guilder exchange you are losing half a purchasing power unit. You are on the way to bankruptcy. So you determine to bring a halt to this deterioration of your business and well-being. First, you stop exchanging your Belgian francs on a one-to-one basis. But since you cannot sell them legitimately, you either seek a buyer who is willing to give you two guilders (i.e., *one* purchasing power unit) for each Belgian franc, and thus become a "black market trader," or you attempt to transfer your Belgian franc holdings out of your country to a place where you will be able to get the full value for them. In all likelihood you will transfer them to Belgium, which means your media of foreign exchange will leave the country. Of course, if you should have earned Belgian francs for exports in the meantime, you make arrangements to leave them and all future franc earnings abroad.

But now you hear that there is still one bank which exchanges Belgian francs against Dutch guilders on a one-to-one basis: your own central bank. It still is ready to buy and sell Belgian francs on the one-to-one basis. Of course, you are not interested in selling francs on this basis; but to buy them on this very basis is quite another thing. It would be very lucrative to buy francs having one purchasing power unit with your guilders which have only half a unit. If you should be able to conclude such a transaction, you would reap an enormous profit. Indeed, a wonderful thing! You apply immediately for an exchange transaction with your central bank. You want to get as many francs as you can. You offer to buy a million francs (i.e., a million purchasing power units) for a million guilders (i.e., 500,000 purchasing power units). If your central bank should find your application worthy of consideration, you will get a million purchasing power units for the half a million you give in exchange. You are rich!

Not only you and other businessmen, but also thousands of others in all walks of life, will apply for such an exchange. And thousands of applications will pile up in your central bank which will pay until its supply of Belgian francs is practically exhausted. Your central bank now suffers from a foreign exchange shortage.

In the postwar period the Dutch government decided not to tolerate any rise in foreign exchange rates. In an effort to prevent a possible shortage, and do it efficiently, the government nationalized foreign exchange transactions. This meant that it decreed that every citizen holding or acquiring media of foreign exchange was under compulsion to sell it at the official rate to the government office of foreign exchange control. Importers, on the other hand, had to buy it at the official rate from the government office. Under these circumstances, officials could "eliminate" the "excess demand." Goods that were unessential in the eyes of the foreign exchange officials could no longer be imported. Payment of interest and principal on debts owed to foreigners were either prohibited or allowed within the limitations described by the officials. Traveling and spending abroad were declared "unessential" and made impossible without foreign exchange. Thus government determined the purpose of spending, where to buy, what to buy, from whom to buy, and, above all, who may do the buying. Foreign exchange control was the most efficient government tool to regulate the foreign transactions of its citizens.

After World War II, the Dutch government followed a course of rigid socialism while a policy of qualified liberalism was conducted in Belgium. The Dutch government inflated its currency and expanded credit, while the Belgian government refrained from inflating to the same degree. Consequently, the Dutch inflation in connection with Dutch exchange control led to scarcity of Belgian media of exchange and trade restrictions. The Union of the Benelux thus was an area of trade restrictions instead of one of unity.

Union and War. The difference in circumstances under which Belgium and Holland emerged from the war is often blamed for the difficulties of unification of these two economies. The difference in time of liberation and the extent of destruction in capital and wealth are said to have led the two governments to conduct different policies. The diverging economic policies, which defeated the attempts at unification, were caused by facts, say these spokesmen, they were not ideological. The state of both economies at the end of the war called for different measures: one for strict governmental control and socialist policies; the more prosperous economy, for a greater degree of individual freedom. Circumstances and human surroundings thus did not render unification feasible.[11]

The advocates of this explanation of Benelux failure obviously believe that man's surroundings determine his system of social organization, production, and distribution. The Dutchman's set of facts called for a socialist system of society, while the Belgian's called for a more liberal system of organization. Similarly, we may infer, American surroundings call for a Fair-Deal system, while Russian facts require communism. As facts and surroundings change, the system must change. Until several decades ago, we may say, American facts required a capitalist system of society and, when time and facts changed, the system of society changed and Fair Dealism was ushered in. The advocates of this explanation obviously mistake cause and effect. It is not man's material surroundings that determine his social organization, but his conception of ends and means which decide his political actions and his choice of social organization. An individual, group of individuals, or a nation that considers socialism as the system most suitable for the realization of its ends will turn socialistic and apply socialist measures. On the other hand, a nation imbued with the idea of individual liberty and initiative as the best means for the realization of its ends will rely on liberty and initiative of the individual.

The Dutch government conducted a policy of inflation and credit

[11] Van Der Mensbrugghe, *Ibid.*, p. 202.

expansion because easy money was believed to enhance the national welfare; it was not national welfare that forced upon the reluctant Dutch a policy of inflation. Actually, at that moment, stable monetary policies were called for. The Dutch government imposed strict foreign exchange controls because it considered them a means to overcome foreign exchange shortages; but shortages do not demand foreign exchange control, they demand abolition of such controls. The Dutch government imposed price and wage controls because it considered them advantageous for the well-being of the workers; it was not the well-being of the workers that required such controls. On the contrary, the workers' well-being depended on the very absence of such controls.

The assertion that eight months of earlier liberation for the Belgians and the additional damage of $144 per head of Dutch population made all the difference in the choice of policies and for the future of both nations for all times to come is as popular as it is fallacious. It is true a loss of $144 makes me poorer by this amount, but it does not require me to select and apply means that make me still poorer. The assertion that the additional $144 of war damages required the Dutch to resort to government controls tacitly implies that a poorer nation must resort to controls, while a richer nation can afford individual liberty and freedom of trade. Such an implication, however, is tantamount to a denial of all economic thought. What a poor nation needs above all is freedom of the individual to plan his life as he sees fit, freedom to build and to create. Liberty is not the offspring of wealth but its very genitor.

The Economic Commission for Europe

T_{HE} Economic Commission for Europe is a regional commission established by the *United Nations* to deal with the special economic problems of Europe and contribute to raising the standards of living. It collaborates with many other international bodies in bringing about important aims of the United Nations: economic and social progress and development; solutions to international economic, social, health and related problems; full employment. The Commission, popularly called ECE, was created in December 1946 with headquarters in Geneva through a decision of the United Nations General Assembly. The annual plenary sessions of ECE are attended by representatives of all the countries of Europe—United Nations members and non-members alike, except Spain. The United States of America is also a member of ECE.

ECE's Task. The particular task of this Commission is "to maintain and strengthen the economic relations of the European countries both among themselves and with other countries of the world." [1] It is to promote government cooperation in European economic reconstruction and recovery from the appalling destruction and disorganization of the war. The economic conditions in Europe, it is said, reveal the close relationship of each country's problems with the problems and policies of other countries. The Commission therefore received broad powers from its parent body and was authorized to negotiate formal as well as informal agreements on national policies to conform to international goals. But it must refrain from study and action with respect to any country without the agreement of that country. With permission of the gov-

[1] United Nations, *The Economic Commission for Europe,* June 1953, p. 2.

ernments concerned the representatives of ECE may study the over-all European economic situation, review progress made by member governments, assign work to committees and working parties of experts, discuss difficulties of cooperation, and, finally, bring about agreement on measures to remove the difficulties.

Postwar Emergency Activity. Numerous shortages in basic services and materials after World War II, due to price controls and other government regulations, hampered reconstruction everywhere. State-owned public utilities and transport industries had to be entirely reestablished; coal, steel and timber output, largely regulated by governments, had fallen significantly and had to be raised. All kinds of raw materials for reconstruction falling within the allocation and distribution programs of governments had become very scarce. At this time ECE committees and expert groups working singly or together went into operation. They often succeeded in obtaining government agreements on the distribution of scarce supplies and on special allocations of certain raw materials to certain countries and industries. ECE, for example, effected an allocation of household coke to Sweden in order that that country might burn less timber and make more of it available to other countries for building purposes. Special allocations of coal were made to Belgium and Italy for production of more fertilizer. ECE also allocated pit-props for certain coal mines, and briquetting pitch so that coal dust could be made into usable fuel. Some ECE specialists collaborated to increase timber production and distribution; other experts studied and estimated each country's needs for coal mining, electric power, timber and transportation equipment; together with producers' and consumers' representatives they studied the shortages in ball-bearings, conveyor belts, ceramic insulators, and other commodities.[2]

Committees at Work. The Economic Commission for Europe is an organ at the service of governments promoting the development of their national economies through government planning and regulation or through government enterprise. The several committees of ECE cooperate with governments on a technical level, studying problems, and endeavoring to find solutions. The *ECE Committee on Agricultural Problems,* for example, has conducted studies on the problems of relative prices, the bread-grain situation, livestock production and fodder, fertilizers, and assistance to small and medium farmers. It also recommended to governments general provisions and government regulations for the commercial stand-

[2] *Ibid.,* pp. 5, 6.

ardization of grading, marking, packaging of commodities, and quality control of fresh fruit and vegetables moving in international traffic. Definite standards have been recommended for citrus and certain other fruits, and draft standards have been prepared for eggs, tomatoes, and other vegetables and fruit.[3] The *ECE Coal Committee* seeks three goals: to secure the satisfaction of European needs in solid fuel, both as to quantity and quality; to promote the "rational" use of fuels; and to render the coal market as stable as possible. To this end the Committee has already made specific recommendations to governments to promote and enforce better utilization of fuel. Furthermore it has conducted an extensive study of a uniform system for classifying coal. After three years of work in Geneva and in the laboratories of nine European countries and the United States, ECE experts finally agreed upon a scientific and practicable system for describing all European and North-American hard coals by their characteristics. This agreement must still be approved and enforced by governments.[4] The *ECE Committee on Electric Power* deals with problems relating to the use and development for hydro purposes of rivers and lakes belonging to two or more countries, with economic and legal problems relating to European electric needs, especially in rural areas. The *ECE Housing Sub-Committee* aims to promote more and better building at a reduced cost. It also examines points where intergovernmental action in Europe might be useful in the field of town and country planning. Committee studies are in progress on special aspects of housebuilding, such as: strength, stability and safety factors; the influence of laws and regulations on the cost of building; methods of awarding building contracts and placing orders; and productivity. It thus hopes to cope with the need for housing at low rental rates. The *ECE Industry and Materials Committee* deals with questions pertaining to the supply of primary materials and the problem of government cooperation in supply and allocation matters. It has also decided to solve the need for an up-to-date machine-tool glossary which will contain definitions and drawings for 1000 concepts in English and French, describing each product or sub-product in terms of its characteristics and functions. The study group preparing this glossary is receiving the assistance of the International Standards Organization and the cooperation of UNESCO. When completed the glossary is to be accepted by governments and enforced in respective industries. The *ECE Inland Transport Com-*

[3] *Ibid.*, p. 6.
[4] *Ibid.*, pp. 10, 11.

mittee endeavors to formulate a general transport policy for Europe, work out international tariffs, and coordinate private as well as public investments in the various branches of transport. It initiated agreements on refrigeration transport equipment and proposed standard conditions of transport, such as temperature control and uniform packaging for perishable foods. The *ECE Steel Committee's* major attention is directed to insuring a balanced development of sectors in the industry and markets for European steel products. The balanced development is to be achieved through government restrictions of certain sectors and stimulation of others. "Balance," of course, is what the ECE representatives conceive as balance. The *ECE Timber Committee* studied and expressed concern over the extent to which the scarcity of timber in Europe has caused timber prices to go beyond price rises for other basic materials and thereby to encourage an "abnormal use" of substitutes for wood. It urged all European governments to take appropriate action in order to insure the development of European forests and adequate timber supplies.[5]

ECE, GOVERNMENT AND ECONOMIC PLANNING: AN APPRAISAL

The Economic Commission for Europe is to promote government cooperation in the field of economic reconstruction and development. This task obviously presupposes the existence of such a government function. It presupposes that government shall either fulfill its economic function through government-owned enterprise or through control and regulation of the economic activities of individuals—or through both. There is no other interpretation conceivable.

European governments indeed fulfill their economic function through government ownership in the means of production and through government regulation and control. We may assume with complete objectivity that about 25 per cent of the economic system of most European nations has been nationalized and transferred into the ownership of governments. The following 13 fields of basic economic activity are nationalized by either all or most European governments:

1. The Central Bank
2. Commercial banks and other large financial institutions
3. Postal service
4. Telephone and telegraph service

[5] *Ibid.*, p. 19.

5. The overseas communication system—cables and wireless
6. Radio and television
7. Civil aviation
8. Railways and other means of transportation
9. Coal mines
10. Steel industry
11. Electric industry
12. Gas industry
13. Medical services

In this large sector of *government economy* within the national economic system it is the task and function of government, as legal owner, to reconstruct and develop the enterprise. However, inasmuch as government enterprises are generally run at substantial deficits, the reconstruction and development of the government sector must necessarily be financed and facilitated through contributions by the remaining sector—the privately owned sector of the economy. These contributions are made through loans, heavy taxation, or outright inflation. Additional contributions are claimed through the system of quotas and priorities according to which raw materials are distributed. That is to say, the government sector enjoys absolute priority over the private sector in all allocations and distributions of materials. Numerous other government controls over the private sector, such as government fixing of prices, labor quotas and wages, government plans of investment and credit, etc., also favor the government sector to the detriment of the private sector.[6] *Government reconstruction and development thus means reconstruction of government-owned enterprise, through levies on and subsidies by private enterprise.*

This conception of government reconstruction and development clearly indicates not only the nature of contemporary government policies but also the only conceivable way to genuine recovery. A successful economic policy of reconstruction and progress must contain two objectives: (1) it must endeavor to reduce the size of the government-owned economic sector and thus decrease its annual deficits; (2) it must reduce the burden and abolish the shackles on the private sector which is supporting the former. Any economic policy falling short of these objectives cannot justly be called "reconstructive" and "developing."

The Economic Commission of Europe is a United Nations organ

[6] The main difference between the various national economies in Europe lies in the extent of government control over the private sector. As to the government sector, a general conformity exists.

at the disposal of governments conducting socialist or intervention-ist policies. It collaborates in the planning of government inter-ference with private enterprise; it designs systems of allocation and distribution; it endeavors to promote the government-owned sector of economy by restraints on the "unessential" private sector; it urges government to take appropriate steps of planning and coercion; it seeks to direct the economic development according to its own pat-tern of balance; it criticizes the "abnormal" use and consumption of materials according to its own conception of normality, etc. In all these actions and endeavors ECE deliberately and willfully runs counter to the laws of the market economy and to the choices and wishes of the millions of consuming Europeans. The structure of production and distribution in a market economy is determined by the choices and preferences of consumers. Any planning and co-ercion on the part of government or any other institution toward a diverging structure necessarily run counter to the will of consumers. Since planning of divergencies can be realized only through force and coercion of the individual, ECE, in the last analysis, advocates government coercion of the individual to actions which ECE deems fit. In other words, ECE advocates substitution of government co-ercion for the freedom of the individual.

The Economic Commission for Europe derives its task and author-ization from its parent body "the Economic and Social Council" of the United Nations. In discussing the Economic Commission for Europe we may not withhold our analysis and judgment regarding the nature of the parent organization which provides the framework within which ECE operates.

International Economic Cooperation and United Nations. Article 55 of the Charter of the United Nations provides for the promotion of the following objectives:

"*a.* higher standards of living, full employment, and conditions of economic and social progress and development;

"*b.* solutions of international economic, social, health and related problems; and international cultural and educational cooperation; and

"*c.* universal respect for, and observance of, human rights and fundamental freedoms for all without distinction as to race, sex, language, or religion."

In Article 62 the Economic and Social Council is authorized to "make recommendations for the purpose of promoting respect for, and observance of, human rights and fundamental freedoms for all."

These are the most significant and illustrative economic provisions

of the United Nations Charter. They are *two kinds of provisions*
whose fundamental natures are diametrically opposed to each other.
One kind provides for the attainment of international cooperation,
peace, and prosperity; the other kind promotes economic nationalism, which brings about economic war and international conflict.
One kind of provision is incompatible with the other.

Let us look at the provisions under Article 55 *a* and *b*. The member governments are to promote "higher standards of living." What
does that mean? It means that the signatory governments have
pledged to interfere actively with the economic actions of their
citizens for the "common good." And how does a government promote "higher standards of living?" To improve the living conditions
of farmers, for example, it endeavors to raise farm prices through
restriction of farm production and reduction of foreign imports and
competition. The latter step is identical with economic nationalism.
In order to promote the living conditions of the workers, governments burden employers with additional social and labor costs
which put them at a disadvantage towards foreign competition and
bring about unemployment. In order to avoid these undesirable but
inevitable effects, imports are restricted. This too is an act of economic nationalism which means international conflict.

Member governments are to promote "full employment." What
does this mean? It means one of two things: A government either
inflates and depreciates its domestic currency, which leads to foreign exchange control, import quotas, and other import restrictions—
all measures of economic nationalism and international conflict; or,
in order to promote full employment, a government merely restricts
imports. In order to promote full employment in the watch manufacturing industry, for example, a government merely restricts importation of watches from abroad. Such a restriction of imports
constitutes a means of economic nationalism and ultimate international conflict.

Member governments are to promote "conditions of economic
and social progress and development." What does this mean? It
means that governments through active interference are to bring
about conditions which governments conceive as "progress" and
"development." As these conditions differ from those of an unhampered market economy, imports must be restricted in order to
protect the domestic conditions of "progress" and "development."
This protection, too, is an act of economic nationalism and international conflict.

All these United Nations objectives require still another means of economic nationalism. In order to promote higher standards of living and bring about full employment as well as conditions of economic and social progress and development, governments restrict the free migration of people. This too means economic nationalism with its attendant international conflict.

Member governments are to promote "solutions of international economic and social problems." What does this mean? It means that governments are to conclude agreements on the stabilization of prices of certain raw materials and foodstuffs. In other words, production is to be restricted and world market monopoly prices are to be established. Since such agreements favor the producing countries and harm the importing countries, international conflicts are created.

This is the one kind of provision, which, if carried out, can lead only to economic war and international conflict. The other kind apparently endeavors to promote international cooperation, peace, and prosperity. Article 55 c, for example, speaks of "universal respect for, and observance of, human rights and fundamental freedoms for all without distinction as to race, sex, language, or religion." And Article 62 authorizes the Economic and Social Council to "make recommendations for the purpose of promoting respect for, and observance of, human rights and fundamental freedoms for all." Of course, we must take into consideration that this provision allows a manifold interpretation which even permitted the communist signatories to accept this provision. But if we disregard the ambiguity of the terms under the cloak of which suppression of individual rights and freedom frequently reigns, we may assume the objective to be international cooperation and peace.

The United Nations organization suffers in all its aspects of existence from this double nature of incompatible foundations and objectives. While few voices are heard in favor of human rights and fundamental freedoms, a chorus of voices defends and advocates economic nationalism and economic warfare. This is especially true in the Economic and Social Council where its numerous committees have become ready instruments in the service of economic nationalism. Their voluminous studies on recent economic history are pervaded with the spirit of economic nationalism and international conflict.[7]

[7] See ECE, *Economic Survey of Europe in 1948*, Washington 1949; *Economic Survey of Europe since the War*, February 1953; A *Survey of the Economic Situation and Prospects of Europe*, Geneva 1948; *Economic Bulletin for Europe*, published in April, July and October.

But can we expect it to be otherwise? We cannot, for the United Nations delegates are representatives of the very governments conducting policies of national "welfare" and economic nationalism. They receive precise instructions from their governments and represent and defend strictly national interest as public opinion conceives it. The United Nations consists of an assembly of brothers of economic nationalism before the eyes of the world. How can delegates imbued with the ideas of government welfare and economic nationalism bring about international cooperation, peace, and prosperity? How can the representatives of the United States, for example, successfully defend the cause of world cooperation when their own employer, the U. S. government, prohibits the import of foreign grain, sugar, potatoes, butter, or cheese? Or when it holds huge quantities of surplus goods from government storage over the world market? Of course, the representatives may continue to speak of cooperation and peace while their own governments indulge in acts of economic nationalism and warfare, but the cause of world cooperation and peace can hardly be furthered under these conditions.

The United Nations must fail, like the League of Nations has failed, because it lacks the spirit of genuine liberalism. It is a convention in which academic talks on world peace, humanity, and cooperation are held while economic warfare continues. Insofar as the United Nations organization is an organ at the disposal of an ideology that is hostile to a world economy and world cooperation, its every step and every move further its own liquidation.

IV

Organization for European Economic Cooperation

Background. In April 1948, nineteen countries of western Europe established an Organization for European Economic Cooperation in order to launch a coordinated attack upon their economic problems. Western Europe was on the verge of breakdown as a result of the socialist and interventionist practices of almost all European governments. Inflations and credit expansions were running wild. All-round price and wage controls strangled economic activity. Large and important sectors of industry were nationalized and turned over to government officials. The remaining private industries were levied with confiscatory taxation. All these and many more socialist shackles on the activity and initiative of the individual resulted in decreased productivity and lower real incomes and standards of living. The stock of capital equipment was no longer maintained, and productive techniques remained stagnant or even deteriorated. These conditions naturally impeded every attempt at reconstruction and reparation of the damages caused by war.

In these dark hours of the system of central planning and government control in Europe a light suddenly began to shine. On June 5, 1947, the Secretary of State of the United States, General Marshall, made a historic speech at Harvard University in which he invited European nations to join in detailing their common needs which then were to be considered by the Congress of the United States. Immediately European governments responded and set up a "Committee of European Economic Cooperation" which developed into the "Organization for European Economic Cooperation" when Congress approved the Foreign Assistance Act providing for billion dollar aid for Europe in April 1948. OEEC henceforth served as the

receiving and distributing instrument for American aid. On the supplying side of Marshall's vast "European Recovery Program" the
American "Economic Cooperation Administration" (ECA) was set
up to approve and finance the purchase of goods for Europe.

Convention for European Economic Cooperation. While the
American Foreign Assistance Act laid down the basic policy of assistance and aid as far as the United States was concerned, the
European governments laid down their principles of cooperation in
the "Convention for European Economic Cooperation." In it they
declared "that their economic systems are interrelated and that the
prosperity of each of them depends on the prosperity of all. . . . Only
by close and lasting cooperation between the Contracting Parties
can the prosperity of Europe be restored and maintained, and the
ravages of war made good." [1]

Article I of the Convention defines as an immediate task "the
elaboration and execution of joint recovery programs . . . to achieve
as soon as possible and maintain a satisfactory level of economic
activity without extraordinary outside assistance." Then follow specific objectives which the contracting governments pledged to pursue.

The governments will "both individually and collectively, promote with
vigour the development of production, through efficient use of the resources at their command, whether in their metropolitan or overseas territories, and by the progressive modernization of equipment and techniques."

The governments will "within the framework of the Organization . . .
draw up general programs for the production and exchange of commodities and services. In so doing they will take into consideration their several estimates or programs and general world economic conditions."

The governments will "develop, in mutual cooperation, the maximum
possible interchange of goods and services. To this end they will continue the efforts already initiated to achieve as soon as possible a multilateral system of payments among themselves, and will cooperate in relaxing restrictions on trade and payments between one another with the
object of abolishing as soon as possible those restrictions which at present
hamper such trade and payments."

The governments will "continue the study of Customs Unions or analogous arrangements such as free trade areas, the formation of which might
constitute one of the methods of achieving these objectives. Those Contracting Parties which have already agreed in principle to the creation of

---

[1] *Convention for European Economic Cooperation, with Related Documents*, Paris,
April 16, 1948, U. S. Department of State, Publication 3145, Preamble.

Customs Unions will further the establishment of such Unions as rapidly as conditions permit."

The governments will "cooperate with one another and with other like-minded countries in reducing tariff and other barriers to the expansion of trade, with a view to achieving a sound and balanced multilateral trade system such as will accord with the principles of the Havana Charter."

A government will, "having due regard to the need for a high and stable level of trade and employment and for avoiding or countering the dangers of inflation, take such steps as lie within its power to achieve or maintain the stability of its currency and of its internal financial position, sound rates of exchange and, generally, confidence in its monetary system."

The governments will "make the fullest and most effective use of their available manpower. They will endeavor to provide full employment for their own people and they may have recourse to manpower available in the territory of any other Contracting Party. In the latter case they will, in mutual agreement, take the necessary measures to facilitate the movement of workers and to ensure their establishment in conditions satisfactory from the economic and social point of view." [2]

Organization. The following national governments are members of OEEC: Austria, Belgium, Denmark, France, Western Germany, Greece, Iceland, Ireland, Italy, Luxembourg, the Netherlands, Norway, Portugal, Sweden, Switzerland, Turkey, the United Kingdom, and the Anglo-American Zone of the Free Territory of Trieste. Also the United States and Canada associated themselves informally with OEEC and, although they are not full members, they are usually represented at its meetings.

The Organization, which has its seat in Paris, is composed of a Council consisting of all the members, a seven-member Executive Committee, and a Secretary-General with several directorates. The *Council* is the policy-making body of the Organization and is responsible for all major decisions which are binding for all members having voted in the affirmative. The Council consists of cabinet ministers of the member governments or their deputies. It meets at least once a month at the executive level and every two months at the ministerial level. The Council also designates the Members of the Executive Committee and its officers and appoints the Secretary-General and the directors.

The *Executive Committee* is charged with carrying out the policies of the Council and directing the work of the numerous com-

[2] *Ibid.*, Part I, Articles 2-9.

mittees. It consists of seven member governments elected by the Council; it reviews and makes recommendations on matters before they are considered by the Council.

The *Secretary-General* prepares the meetings of the Council and of the Executive Committee. He insures the execution of their decisions, presents to the Council for approval the Organization's budget, and stays in contact with other international organizations. There are also a variety of *committees* which meet on a regular basis throughout the year. The "vertical" technical committees deal with questions relating to specific commodities as, for example, food and agriculture, coal, nonferrous metals, or certain sectors of the economy as inland transport and shipping. The "horizontal" committees are concerned with broad questions such as balance of payments, trade, government planning, and manpower.

In order to eliminate the payments difficulties among OEEC countries the *European Payments Union* was developed by OEEC and is operating under its authority. The Union was created by a special agreement signed by all OEEC countries in September 1950. The Managing Board of EPU is responsible to the OEEC Council, the policy-making body of the Organization. It is also responsible for the execution of the September 1950 agreement and has the power to make decisions concerning the operation of the Payments Union.

Aid and Counterpart Funds. In each country where assistance is provided by the government of the United States, a special local currency account is created in which the local currency equivalent to the dollar grant received is deposited. During the first four years of American recovery aid, 95 per cent of the counterpart funds were available for use by the *depositing* governments; since 1952, this part has been reduced to 90 per cent.

Under the Economic Cooperation Act of 1948, counterpart funds were employed for (a) promotion of reconstruction, expansion, and modernization of industrial capacity, (b) stabilization of internal financial and monetary conditions, and (c) development and expansion of the productive capacity of basic industries. The Mutual Security Act of 1951 extended the use of counterpart funds deposited for current dollar grant aid by the U. S. government to include "military production, construction, equipment, and matériel." The Mutual Security Act of 1952 provided that counterpart funds were to be used primarily for military assistance and defense support. This Act also provided that "the counterpart derived from

100 million of dollars aid be used to stimulate free enterprise and
the expansion of the economies of the participating countries with
equitable sharing of the benefits of increased production and productivity between consumers, workers and owners." The employment of funds is subject to supervision and control by the American
administration providing the dollar aid.[3]

The cumulative status of counterpart funds accounts from April
3, 1948 through September 30, 1953 was reported as follows: [4]

Country	Balance for Use By Recipient Governments (millions of dollars)
Total of all countries	10,579.7 [5]
Austria	698.2
Belgium-Luxembourg	28.0
Denmark	222.5
France	2,677.3
Western Germany	1,256.9
Greece	661.5
Iceland	25.1
Ireland	17.3
Italy	1,153.2
Netherlands	833.2
Norway	347.1
Portugal	19.4
Trieste	34.3
Turkey	192.0
United Kingdom	2,216.6
Yugoslavia	153.7

The cumulative amounts and the purposes for which withdrawal of
counterpart funds by the recipient governments were approved by
the American administration were reported as follows: [6]

[3] The Economic Cooperation Administration, *A Report on Recovery Progress and United States Aid*, February 1949, p. 157; Foreign Operations Administration, Statistics and Reports Division, *Local Currency Counterpart Funds*, data as of September 30, 1953, p. 1.

[4] Foreign Operations Administration, *Ibid.*, p. 3.

[5] The total of all foreign grants and credits by the United States Government in the postwar period from July 1, 1945, through September 30, 1953, amounted to $43,076,000,000. See Appendix of "Congressional Record" for January 27, 1954, p. A604.

[6] Foreign Operations Administration, *Ibid.*, p. 6.

Cumulative Withdrawals
April 3, 1948–September 30, 1953

Purpose		*(millions of dollars)*
Military		1,270.0
Retirement of debts of national governments		2,510.8
Promotion of national production through government grants and spending....		4,244.8
Subsidies to agriculture	906.4	
Subsidies to mining	494.8	
Subsidies to manufacturing	742.5	
Subsidies to transportation	1,787.5	
Subsidies to public housing and buildings	884.2	
Other subsidies	313.7	
Total of all approvals of government withdrawals and spending		9,304.0

An Annual OEEC Program. According to Article I of the Convention, the Organization is to elaborate and execute a joint recovery program. The first annual program which was handed to the American ECA representative in Europe in October 1948 was most illustrative as it laid down the principles of future European cooperation. Representatives of nineteen countries had cooperated in its preparation and had agreed unanimously upon its terms. The program covers the following points:

1. Allocation and use of $4,875 million of United States aid.
2. Introduction of a system of intra-European payments linked to United States aid.[7]
3. Rules of commercial policy to guide the future financial, economic and commercial relations of the member countries.[8]

As the basis for the division of American aid the program recommended the *dollar deficit* of each country's central bank with the central banks of the non-member countries, account being taken also of its creditor position *vis-a-vis* the central banks of the member countries. The primary objective of this approach towards division of American aid was to cover dollar deficits and encourage "the development of a free system of payments through the extended use of Western Europe's own currencies."[9]

---

[7] On this point, see detailed presentation, p. 196 *et seq.*

[8] Organization for European Economic Cooperation, *Report to the Economic Cooperation Administration on the First Annual Programme*, July 1, 1948-June 30, 1949, Foreword, p. 7.

[9] *Ibid.*, p. 9.

In order to reduce future dollar requirements, OEEC suggested that the chief imports from the United States should be those capital goods that would most likely result in future dollar earnings or savings. It also recommended government restriction of certain dollar imports and the shifting of other imports from the dollar area to European or other non-dollar sources. Recommendations were based on an attempt to forecast in detail for a year the supply and demand for each commodity. OEEC finally appealed to the member governments to develop domestic production, improve labor productivity, coordinate the investment plans of their citizens, and embark upon other measures of government aid.

A Quota Removal Program. Quotas which limit absolutely the amount of goods that may be imported accounted for most of the postwar increases in government restrictions of foreign trade. It is obvious that there cannot be effective economic cooperation and integration where the economic relations are rigidly limited by complete sets of government quotas. OEEC therefore decided to center its attack on the removal of import quotas in intra-European trade.

Early in 1949, OEEC embarked upon a quota removal program. In its *Interim Report* it invited the member governments to consider abolition of import quotas and their substitution by a system of "global quotas" or "open general licenses." [10] Global quotas which only limit the total amount of imports of a certain product do not specify from what country within the OEEC area imports are to come. Open general licenses allow free imports of certain products from certain countries. Both forms of trade liberation, of course, are subject to the limitations imposed by government exchange control. The *Interim Report* also emphasized the following conditions for these steps towards intra-European trade liberalization: the suppression of inflation, the correction of excessive disequilibrium, the balancing of the area's dollar accounts, the restriction of trade with the dollar area, and other preliminary steps.

Until 1951 the member states really abolished a considerable part of their quotas on intra-European trade. Most OEEC governments reached a 60 per cent liberalization by the end of 1950, and the 75 per cent mark was reached in the summer of 1951. When it became apparent that the liberation list of every OEEC government differed from that of all other governments, and not a single good appeared on the liberalization list of every OEEC country, it was proposed that all governments remove quotas on a "common list" of goods. About 70 commodities comprised this list which most

[10] OEEC, *Interim Report*, p. 92.

member governments agreed upon and for which trade was tentatively freed from quota restrictions.[11]

Bearing in mind that import quotas are merely one of many tools of government planning and restriction upon foreign trade, we may deliberate on the extent and meaning of the liberalization of trade quotas as brought about by OEEC. At first glance, the liberalization of intra-European trade at the rate of 75 per cent of all commodities is undoubtedly impressive. We gain the impression that European nations are really heading towards unification and integration of their economies. Upon second glance, however, the OEEC liberalization program appears in a different light. A distinction becomes apparent that is of greatest importance for the understanding of government quotas of foreign trade—the distinction between *restrictive* and *non-restrictive* quotas. A true liberalization of trade quotas naturally means the removal of those quotas which led to a restriction of trade. Abolition of non-restrictive quotas, of course, is meaningless. For example, a country whose system of government quotas consists of 99 per cent non-restrictive quotas, may abolish 99 per cent of its total system, and, yet, its quota restrictions would remain unimpaired. Switzerland, for example, may abolish her quotas on imports of watches, clocks, and similar products of precision instruments which, of course, does not lead to any expansion of trade, because she is *exporting* these goods and need not fear any foreign competition whatever. However, if she would remove import quotas on American automobiles, more automobiles could be imported and consequently more Swiss goods could be exported. Removal of such restrictive quotas would lead to expansion of foreign trade.

But let us assume for the sake of further illustration that the quotas removed within the OEEC area were really restrictive and that their removal lead to an expansion of trade. We yet must bear in mind that the *liberalization applies only to imports from OEEC countries.* Quota restrictions upon trade with non-member countries either have remained unimpaired or have even increased. If we see the effect of the OEEC liberalization program in the light of a nation's *total* foreign trade, we arrive at more illustrative results. According to a conservative estimation by William Diebold, compliance with the OEEC liberalization program by the spring of 1950

---

[11] See also William Diebold, *Trade and Payments in Western Europe,* Harper & Brothers, New York, 1952, p. 158 *et seq.*

meant "the removal of quotas of 40 per cent of the total imports of Belgium, Ireland and Switzerland. For Denmark, Sweden, the Netherlands and Portugal the figure was 27 or 28 per cent; Norway, 23 per cent; Germany, Italy and Greece, 14-16 per cent; and France and Britain, only 10 per cent." [12] Diebold then proceeds to compare the liberalization of trade within the OEEC area with the gross national product of each member country. According to him, "liberalized imports amounted to 12 per cent of Belgium's gross national product, and 11 per cent of Switzerland's, but in France and Germany they were only 1 per cent and in Britain, Ireland and Italy, 2 per cent. The other countries fell in between, ranging from 3 per cent in Greece to 9 per cent in the Netherlands." [13]

If we now bear in mind that the quotas removed were mainly non-restrictive and that quota restriction is merely one of many government restrictions, we perceive the full extent of the "liberalization" as achieved by the OEEC countries.

The Reforms Needed. Europe at the end of the war was economically very poor. The destruction of capital equipment and the depletion of resources expended in the war against the Axis had deprived the countries of the capacity to produce at the rate that would have allowed the pre-war standard of living. It was clear enough to all observers that the European nations had to curtail their consumption and, in order to improve living conditions, had to get things straightened out. The elements in the problem of reconstruction were the following:

1. Almost all European governments had unbalanced budgets. They were borrowing and spending far more than the tax revenues collected. All of them conducted policies of inflation and credit expansion which were wrecking the currencies. All of them had currencies that were increasing steadily in volume, fluctuating violently, and depreciating rapidly. The utmost need for Europe was that of balancing government budgets and stabilizing currencies.

2. When the government of the United States, the only strong creditor country, offered to make grants and extend credit to the European governments, the proceeds were to be taken partly in gold, to build up the reserves of the central banks. The measures of currency stabilization in connection with adequate gold reserves would have allowed free convertibility and redeemability of currencies—the only measures that could bring about reconstruction and recovery.

[12] William Diebold, *Ibid.*, p. 182.
[13] *Ibid.*

3. Finally, if the European nations wanted to benefit from the advantages of an international division of labor and desired access to international capital markets and, especially, to that of the United States, tariffs had to be lowered and quotas, exchange controls, and other trade barriers had to be removed. If men are free to transfer balances, capital, and goods from one country to another without encountering government-created difficulties, an integrated world economy can develop and bring in its train strength and prosperity.

The Opportunity of a Creditor. An industrial corporation that is compelled to undergo a reorganization does so because all other remedies or treatments for bankruptcy have failed. Like the simpler remedies of refinancing, reorganization is designed to prevent the disintegration of the business and, as a going concern, make it more valuable than it would be in liquidation. A common objective of reorganization, which is usually forced upon the corporation by its creditors or prospective creditors, is to raise new funds for working capital and other rehabilitation. In this process the creditors have the opportunity to impose adequate requirements for internal reform upon the corporation. Bankers as creditors have an obligation towards their own depositors to do just this.

In the case of intergovernmental loans the creditor government has a similar opportunity and obligation. The United States government, from the close of World War II through September 30, 1953, had more than 43 billion dollars' worth of opportunity to bring reason and order to the world. The United States government also had a 43-billion-dollar obligation towards its own citizens and taxpayers to do just this. When the question of aid and loans arose, the United States government was in a position to impose adequate requirements for internal reform upon the country which was receiving the grant or credit. To fail to do this would mean prolonging the misery of the debtor and the chaos of the world.

If we see the foreign aid spending of the United States government from this point of view, we must conclude that the United States government not only missed this rare opportunity but also failed entirely to discharge its 43-billion-dollar obligation towards its own citizens. Never in history has such an amount been spent and been poured into 43 countries with such a disregard for prudent principles of economy. But could we expect the American government to lead the other countries to sound financial and economic reforms while similar policies of ample spending and currency depreciation were conducted at home? Obviously, we could not, for the American leaders were inspired with the same kind of New-Deal ideas abroad as recent administrations have desired to enforce at home. Instances are even related where American officials interfered with foreign governments which endeavored to abolish controls and return to sounder principles of government. American Fair-Deal officials repeatedly exerted pressure on the Belgian and German governments to inflate their national currencies at a greater degree and create more credit through simple expansion. Fortunately for these nations, their governments usually resisted this Fair-Deal pressure.

A Windfall for Socialism. The true meaning of the foreign aid spending of the United States government can be recognized only if we analyze the purposes for which the billions of dollars of American aid were used by the recipient governments. Let us look, for example, at the uses of the Marshall aid by European governments which are required to deposit the local currency proceeds from such aid in counterpart accounts before they are authorized by American authorities for government spending. As of September 30, 1953 the *Austrian* government was allowed to spend the following amounts for the following purposes:[14]

Retirement of government debt	$12.5 millions
Agricultural programs of government spending for research for government-owned forestry, etc.	75.0
Subsidies to government-owned or government-controlled mines	28.9
Subsidies to government-regulated manufacturing industries considered essential	153.8
Subsidies to government-owned railroads run at a deficit	52.3
Subsidies to government-owned or government-regulated electric, gas, and power facilities	111.5

The uses of the *French* counterpart funds during the five years' period by the French government are similiarly revealing. The expenditure statement reads as follows:[15]

Military production	$493.6 millions
Retirement of government debt	171.4
Agricultural programs of government spending and subsidies to farmers	253.0
Subsidies to government-owned mines run at substantial deficits	308.6

[14] Foreign Operations Administration, *Local Currency Counterpart Funds,* p. 8.
[15] *Ibid.,* p. 11.

Subsidies to other government-regulated industries considered essential by central planners 230.8
Subsidies to government-owned railroads run at deficits   125.1
Subsidies to government-owned or government-regulated
electric, gas and power facilities 563.9
Public housing and other housing under government rent
control 350.3

The *German* government enjoyed a similar windfall for its spending
programs. Through September 30, 1953 American recovery aid
provided for under the Marshall plan was employed as follows:[16]

Agricultural programs of government spending and subsidies to German farmers .... $106.3 millions
Subsidies to government-owned or government-con-
trolled coal mines 107.1
Subsidies to industries considered basic and essential ...   268.2
Subsidies to government-owned railroads run at substantial deficits 17.1
Subsidies to the government-owned system of telephone,
telegraph, and other communication facilities run at
deficits 10.6
Subsidies to government-owned or government-regulated
electric, gas, and power facilities 200.1
Subsidies to public and social housing under government
rent control 130.8

In *Italy* spending of the counterpart funds by the Italian government was authorized by American officials for the following purposes: [17]

Military production .... $ 54.4 millions
Agricultural programs of government spending and sub-
sidies to farmers 233.6
Subsidies to the government-owned railroad system run
at substantial deficits 220.4
Loans to industries considered essential and regulated by
government 193.5
Subsidies to housing under government rent control ...   161.2

Similar statements on Marshall aid spending by other recipient
governments would reveal similar purposes of government spending
and hand-outs. We readily admit that the purposes of spending as
indicated in the expenditure statements were most urgent and bene-

16 *Ibid.*
17 *Ibid.*

ficial. A railroad system that is government-owned and run at substantial deficits year after year undoubtedly is in urgent need of modernization and reconstruction. Public utility facilities that are government-owned or government-run, which break down at sunset or supply only part of the public, are in need of reconstruction. A government-owned telephone system whose "across the street" telephone service requires more effort and patience on the part of the public than a "cross-continent" call with the American Telephone and Telegraph Company undoubtedly is in a bad condition and needs to be reconstructed. Housing conditions in a country whose government practises strict rent control for twenty or more years must be deplorable and call for improvements. But a lasting improvement of this unfortunate state of affairs cannot come from some reconstruction subsidies, similar to those drawn by the industries from their own governments for many decades. It only can come by eliminating the root of the evil: the nationalization or regulation of these industries by their own governments.[18]

It is obvious that the American government is not concerned with the cause of the evil but merely with its inevitable effects. It poured more than 43 billion dollars' worth of aid into old channels of government spending which, in the past, had swallowed vast amounts and which will gulp similar amounts in the future. The American government merely relieved temporarily the recipient governments from an activity to which they themselves were committed.

In this connection, one decidedly detrimental effect of American aid to European governments must be mentioned. The billions of American dollars at the disposal of the recipient governments have strengthened enormously the position and authority of government. The system of government interference and handouts gained new

[18] An excellent example of the operation and "expansion" of nationalized industries is the German postal, telephone and telegraph service, which for many decades was considered to be an efficiently run government enterprise. The following data must be considered in the light of the monopolistic position of these government industries and the enormous growth of many private industries.

Service	1911	1936	1951	1952	1953
Letters handled (in millions)	5994	6437	4443	4815	5511
Parcel Post (in millions)	271	296	178	191	203
Telephone calls (in millions)	2074	2562	2156	2323	2499
Telegrams (in millions)	50	21	26	26	27
Personnel emp. (in thousands)	310	382	294	303	334
Surplus or deficit as presented by government accountants (in millions of Marks)		+72	+102	—51	—146

Source: *Deutsche Zeitung und Wirtschaftszeitung*, April 21, 1954, p. 4.

support and enjoyed new popularity with each dollar distributed among the constituency. And while railroads, public utilities, and other government enterprises are rebuilt and modernized with American money, people find their belief in their system of government confirmed, in nationalization of industries, in central control, and in government hand-outs. With every new train passing by people infer: socialism works; our system of government regulation works. Government orators confirm their belief: it works! it works! But it is obvious that this inference, sooner or later, must lead to further economic breakdowns, to new poverty and chaos.

The Dollar Mystery. "The number one financial problem of the world is the shortage of the United States dollar." The United States government is therefore urged by foreign governments in concert with most contemporary writers on foreign affairs to make dollars available for countries that suffer from this malady. The explanations commonly offered for the dollar scarcity are "the emergence of the United States as an overwhelmingly dominant economic power and the hostility between the West and the Soviet Bloc." The United States, it is said, has 50 per cent of the world's purchasing power and 75 per cent of total investment capacity. These conditions cause maladjustment and call for planning on the international plane. They also explain, it is asserted, why other countries' currencies are often "overvalued" when compared with the United States dollar. American productivity rises faster than elsewhere, thus creating greater competitive power and industrial supremacy, which finally results in the elimination of foreign countries from the most productive lines of production. Thus the difference between rich and poor nations grows and the dollar shortage brings about "a continued deterioration of (at least the relative) standard of life of countries other than the United States." [19] To remedy such unfortunate world conditions international loans are said to be unsuitable because the poor nations can scarcely be expected to repay loans. "Stability in the world economy, therefore, could be expected to depend on the capacity of the United States to maintain activity by domestic measures or on arrangements of a non-commercial nature which would use United States productive power threatened with unemployment for the reconstruction or development of foreign coun-

[19] T. Balogh, *The Dollar Crisis,* Oxford, 1949, p. 9; see also OEEC, *Comments by the Economic Committee on the Report on International Financial Stability,* Paris, 1952; OEEC, *Financial Stability and the Fight Against Inflation,* Paris, 1951, pp. 13, 16, 32.

tries." [20] In other words, the United States government is urged to conduct policies of full employment and turn over a larger share of American production to the poor nations of the world. Through sharing American wealth the dollar shortage in the world is said to disappear.

In the first place, such an assertion contradicts reality. From July 1, 1945 through September 30, 1953, America indeed has shared its wealth by granting more than 43 billion dollars' worth of foreign aid. And yet the dollar shortage has not been overcome. If 43 billion dollars of foreign aid constitute no sharing of wealth for the reconstruction and development of foreign countries, what amount would earn this designation? Should the United States government double its aid? Or treble it? Great Britain alone has received $6.8 billion via grants and credits for reconstruction. And yet the pound sterling is still inconvertible and subject to British exchange control because of the alleged dollar shortage. If $6.8 billion were insufficient to stabilize the pound, what amount, if any, could achieve the stabilization?

Secondly, the foregoing explanation lays the blame for the dollar shortage solely upon the United States. In reality, there is only one convincing explanation for the dollar shortage: the monetary and fiscal policies of governments. A government that enforces an exchange rate between domestic money and foreign money at which the sellers of the latter are shortchanged, will experience foreign exchange shortages. This is the essence of one of the oldest economic laws known to economists: Gresham's Law. But we need not be economists in order to understand this economic phenomenon. It is just common sense.

The contention that it is American productive power that throws the world into a state of imbalance and forces foreign governments frequently to devalue their "overvalued" currencies is meant to be a popular excuse for policies of inflation and depreciation. It is true, increasing productivity tends to increase the purchasing power of the domestic currency. But this tendency has a limit because international transactions are based on gold parities. The movement of gold from one country to another tends to equalize the purchasing power of currencies. Inflow of gold in one country tends to raise its prices for commodities; outflow tends to lower prices. In the United States the inflow of gold has raised commodity prices considerably. Since the United States government has also inflated its

[20] T. Balogh, *Ibid.*, p. 7.

currency, the purchasing power of the dollar has even declined below its legal gold parity—that is to say, the United States dollar is traded at 37-40 dollars per ounce of gold on the free money markets of the world. This dollar-gold relationship on the money markets reveals that any government refraining from inflating its own currency would experience an immediate inflow of American gold and a *surplus* of United States dollars. Such a government could also embark upon a very lucrative undertaking. For one ounce of gold it could buy $37-$40 on the free currency market and then purchase one ounce of gold for only $35 from the United States Treasury. That means, as long as the United States dollar would sell at a gold discount, it could earn the spread on each transaction. The United States government indeed would suffer from a heavy drain on its gold and foreign exchange.

However, conditions are such that most governments are inflating and depreciating their currencies at a faster rate than the United States government. Consequently the phenomenon of "dollar shortage" is inevitable, unavoidable, and brought about by the very governments complaining about it.

The fact that American citizens export more goods than they import stems from one reason only: the granting of credits and outright gifts by American citizens and the United States government to foreign citizens and governments. How could foreigners import more from the United States than they export without a settlement of the balance? Who would sell to a foreigner without receiving payment or being willing to extend credit for the time being? If American citizens or the United States government were not willing to extend credit and make outright gifts, foreigners could not buy more than they sell. If the United States government would discontinue its vast foreign aid spending, foreigners would have to restrict their buying to equal their selling. It is obvious that it is not additional purchases which call for more American aid, but American aid allows and calls for additional purchases. If you do not have the means and are unable to obtain a consumer's loan for the purchase of a new car, you must abstain from buying. If you should obtain a loan, you can purchase the car. This principle of exchange naturally is valid not only in your transactions with fellow citizens but also with foreigners.

V

The Council of Europe

Background. The several movements advocating a United States of Europe not only supported cooperation on an intergovernmental basis, but also considered it most important and urgent to form an organization which would represent people and parliaments as well as administrations. In May 1948, the Hague European Congress, convened by the International Committee of the Movements for European Unity (later called the European Movement), passed a resolution supporting the creation of a European Assembly. It subsequently submitted detailed recommendations to the Brussels Treaty Powers for realizing such an Assembly. When the French and Belgian governments immediately endorsed the recommendations, they were submitted to the Brussels Treaty Council in September 1948 for official discussion.

The European Movement's recommendations were considered by the Foreign Ministers of the five Brussels powers at a meeting in Paris in October 1948 where divergent views arose between the British and other members of the committee. The British suggested the formation of a European Committee of Ministers, whereas the other members favored the idea of an Assembly. After negotiations among the member countries, a draft of a Statute was prepared that provided for both institutions—a Committee of Ministers and a Consultative Assembly. During the following spring, the Western Union powers invited Italy, Ireland, and the Scandinavian countries to participate in a preparatory conference for the creation of the Council of Europe. The ten powers concluded final negotiations and signed the Statute on May 5, 1949. It went into effect in August 1949 after ratification by seven signatory governments.[1]

[1] Department of State publication 4492, 1952, *Council of Europe,* Foreign Affairs Outline No. 26; *European Movement and the Council of Europe,* Publication on be-

191

Aims of the Council of Europe. The Statute instituted a Consultative Assembly to represent European public opinion and a Committee of Ministers to represent the governments. The aim of the Council of Europe is to achieve greater unity among its members by discussing questions of common concern and by agreeing on common action to be taken in economic, social, cultural, scientific, legal and administrative matters, and to maintain and further human rights and fundamental freedoms. The Council of Europe thus is intended to be an institution for the coordination of the political activities of its member states.[2]

Member States. The original signatory governments were Belgium, France, Ireland, Italy, Luxembourg, the Netherlands, Norway, Sweden, and the United Kingdom. Greece and Turkey also joined the Council in August 1949, and Iceland in March 1950. The German Federal Republic became an associate member in March 1950 and a full member in May 1951. The Saar became an associate member in March 1950, which entitles her to representation in the Consultative Assembly but not in the Committee of Ministers.

Organization. The Statute of the Council of Europe provides for the creation of three organs—the Committee of Ministers representing the governments of the member states; the Consultative Assembly composed of representatives from the national parliaments; and finally the Secretariat which is at the joint disposal of the organs of the Council of Europe (Articles 13-37).

The Committee of Ministers is the organ which takes executive action on behalf of the Council of Europe. It decides on the measures required to further the aims of the Council and may recommend to governments the enactment of agreements and conventions.

The Consultative Assembly submits recommendations to the Committee of Ministers. Its members are nominated by their respective parliaments in whatever manner the parliaments determine. The number of seats each member state may hold is determined by the size of its population. Each representative speaks and votes as an individual.

The Secretariat, which consists of a Secretary-General, a Deputy Secretary-General, and such other staff as may be required, is ap-

---

half of the European Movement. Hutchinson, London, 1949; John Goormaghtigh, *European Integration,* International Conciliation, Carnegie Endowment for International Peace, New York, 1953, p. 90 *et seq.;* Council of Europe, *The Union of Europe: Its Progress, Problems, Prospects and Place in the Western World,* Strasbourg, October, 1951.

[2] Council of Europe, *Ibid.,* pp. 16-17; see also *Statute of the Council of Europe,* Article 1, in *European Movement and the Council of Europe, Ibid.,* p. 170, also in Department of State publication 3748, 1950.

pointed by the Consultative Assembly on the recommendation of the Committee of Ministers. It is located at the seat of the Council in Strasbourg.

The Work of the Council. After the Council of Europe was established, the Assembly proclaimed the political aim to be the creation of a European political authority with limited functions but real powers. In the economic field, the Assembly adopted several resolutions regarding the European Payments Union and the formation of the Coal and Steel Community. Debates in the Assembly played an important role in the negotiations which led to the Community. Other debates and proposals of the Assembly have dealt with the establishment of a European code of social security. A European Convention for the protection of human rights has been signed by the members of the Committee of Ministers on the basis of a draft presented by the Assembly.[3]

These are the achievements of the Council of Europe during the first five years of its existence. Measurable and tangible results have been very few. Of course, innumerable speeches on European cooperation and integration were made in the Assembly which served as a useful sounding board for the several unification movements. But when the sterile character of the numerous discussions and debates became quite obvious, many of the Council's ardent supporters resigned or refused to serve as delegates in the meetings of the Assembly. Gradually public interest declined to the point of indifference.

SOME CRITICISM

Welfare and Socialist Ideologies Are the Reasons for Failure. When the several movements striving for unification of Europe realized the failure of the Council in bringing about any degree of unification, they decided to attempt another approach towards European unification. If only the true representatives of the people, the parliamentarians, or the people themselves could be brought together, they said, unification could be achieved. Where people can discuss their problems and settle them in mutual understanding through honest bargaining, cooperation and unification can be achieved.

But let us look more closely at this popular point of view. The institution of democratic government reflects the state of public opinion. Its mandate is received from the constituency whose opinion decides what policies shall be conducted and who shall put them into effect. The assumption that the constituency may favor the

---

[3] Council of Europe, *Ibid.,* p. 18.

project of European unification while the government it elects may oppose unification is erroneous. It contradicts the fundamental principle of democratic government.

The true obstacle to unification is ideology. Wherever the ideology of economic nationalism prevails, policies of economic nationalism are conducted. Wherever public opinion favors government protection of industries or other policies of government intervention, protectionist policies are conducted. Wherever public opinion rejects the inevitable effects of interstate unification, they are rejected on all levels of government. If, for example, the Dutch people approve of the project of unification except in the area of their own industries, which would suffer from readjustment and unemployment, their representatives in the Dutch parliament and in the Council of Europe, too, will basically agree to unification, Dutch industries excluded. The Dutch Prime Minister will also approve of unification, except in industry. If the German farmers say: "Unification yes, but not for us farmers," the German representative in the Council of Europe, too, will say: "Unification yes, but not for farmers." And the German chancellor will echo the same approval with the same limitation. If public opinion in France approves of unification but not its consequences, the French parliamentarians will say, "Unification yes, but also protection from the consequences of unification." And the French Premier will also "basically approve" of unification, but continue to conduct policies of protection from unification. Of course, no matter how convincingly the statesman or politician speaks for unification in one speech and for protection from the effects of unification in another, he will not promote both causes to simultaneous fruition because of their incompatible natures.

An Opportunity for Representatives. The failure of the Council of Europe to attain its admirable objectives is currently attributed to several causes. The actual provisions of the Statute itself are blamed: the lack of power of the Consultative Assembly and the veto right of the Committee of Ministers. The fact that governments are not prepared to accept more binding obligations and that the representatives are responsible to no one but themselves also comes in for a share of the blame.[4] At this point we need not enter into an analysis and detailed refutation of these spurious and superficial notions inasmuch as we have already found the ideologies of government welfare and socialism to be the true reason for failure. However, we wish especially to reject the statement that the cir-

[4] Max Sorensen, "The Council of Europe," in *The Year Book of World Affairs* 1952 (London Institute of World Affairs, London, Stevens and Sons), p. 88 *et seq.*

cumstance which made representatives solely responsible to themselves largely contributed to the failure of the Council of Europe. It is our belief that this very freedom of the representatives provided them with rare opportunity to further the ultimate aim of the Council of Europe.

Being responsible to no one but themselves the parliamentarians convening in Strasbourg have the excellent opportunity to discuss the sole and true obstacle to unification: the policies of government welfare and economic nationalism. The decision and common resolution by the parliamentarians gathered at Strasbourg henceforth to refrain from such policies would have an enormous impact which may usher in a new era of peace and international cooperation. If each single representative of the Council of Europe, who is also a representative in his national parliament, would pledge to his colleagues at Strasbourg henceforth to refrain from voting for policies of economic nationalism and discriminating measures against other nationals, a most essential and important step towards peace and cooperation would be achieved. Such a decision and common pledge on the part of the parliamentarians of Strasbourg, however, have never been discussed nor even considered. The representatives rather prefer to talk about cooperation and brotherhood while in Strasbourg, and advocate government welfare and protection from foreign competition while in their national capitals. Of course, we may assume that they merely fail to perceive the heterogeneity of their activities.

The weekly schedule of a Strasbourg parliamentarian may look as follows:

Monday—advocating farm parity prices and government restriction on imports of farm products
Tuesday—voting for easy money policies and foreign exchange control
Wednesday—voting for extensive import restrictions because of foreign exchange shortages
Thursday—speech on cooperation and unification before the Council of Europe
Friday—returning to his capital and advocating higher tariffs for the protection of a particular industry
Saturday—speech on government welfare and international cooperation before his constituency.

Meanwhile, our politician gains great reputation for his sincerity, assiduity, and ability. Of course, actual unification of Europe at the end of his busy week is further away from realization than it was at its beginning.

VI

European Monetary
Cooperation and Integration

Two Steps Toward Cooperation. The first major step on the road toward socialism is the extension of government control over the national monetary system. In order to finance policies of "fair prices," "fair distribution," and nationalization programs, planners cannot do without the most desirable instrument of government planning—power over the currency system. Through credit expansion and inflation the government purse is made inexhaustible for vast projects of spending for public and social works. Once government control over money and credit has been established, a policy of "abundance" and "fair distribution" can be conducted.

The gold standard, whose very eminence consists in limiting government spending and leaving the monetary purchasing power independent from government measures, is the first victim of the central planner. As soon as the gold standard has fallen, a slow but incessant destruction of the monetary order begins. That is to say, the monetary system is increasingly shattered through inflation and credit expansion. The inevitable rise in prices then is followed by price controls, rationing, exchange controls, and import restrictions because of "unfavorable" balances of foreign trade. All these measures finally result in a thorough dissolution of the international system of monetary settlements. Once this stage has been reached, the same planners who advocated abundance through credit expansion and inflation now begin to demand *international monetary cooperation*—so they may be allowed to continue with their old plans and policies of ample spending, unperturbed by the inevitable effects of their monetary policies.

During two world wars and the great economic crisis of the inter-

196

war period, nearly all national monetary systems were shattered by governments conducting interventionist policies. When the disorganization of international trade and payment was almost complete during the years preceding and especially during World War II, the clamor for monetary stabilization and reconstruction of an international settlement system through international action and cooperation became louder. It finally found expression in two major international efforts which were made to bring about monetary cooperation. The first of these efforts was made during the Second World War when, at Bretton Woods, New Hampshire, in July 1944, all free governments of the Allied nations agreed upon a policy of cooperation through the operation of a new organization, the *International Monetary Fund.* These international agreements on the establishment of the Fund are of a fundamental nature and reveal most clearly the underlying ideas on contemporary money and credit policies. Although the agreements are "international," an analysis of them is essential for the understanding of purely European cooperation and "monetary integration."

The second of these attempts was made through the establishment of a *European Payments Union* whose objective is to reconstruct the monetary organization of Europe. The root idea of this Union is the notion that continuous expansion of credit and easy money policies can be maintained through cooperation of all European governments. This Union also merges into the broader movement of political and economic *integration of Europe,* the subject of our inquiry. For the problem of European unification, the Payments Union is of utmost importance, since it allegedly can be developed into a single monetary area with one Central Bank of Europe, thereby providing the first step towards European monetary integration. These two attempts at international cooperation are briefly analyzed in the following.

A. THE AGREEMENTS OF BRETTON WOODS AND THE INTERNATIONAL MONETARY FUND

In April 1943, the American "New Deal" government and the British socialist government [1] advanced a plan for "monetary stabilization" in the postwar period. Newspapers and periodicals in the Allied countries praised it as a "new and fine example of the democratic processes and far-sighted planning of democratic govern-

---

[1] A socialist government is a government conducting socialist policies such as the Churchill government during the war.

ments" now moving toward the adoption of the kind of economic program necessary for world stability and prosperity.[2]

About a year later, in July 1944, representatives of 44 nations met at Bretton Woods, New Hampshire, to deliberate on the proposals submitted by the American and British treasuries. Weeks later, the bulk of experts and representatives approved the proposals and recommended their acceptance. The Congress of the United States accepted the bill on the Agreements on June 7, 1945, and the President approved the Act a few weeks later. The law authorized the President to accept membership in the International Bank for Reconstruction and Development and the International Fund as agreed upon at Bretton Woods.

Objectives of the Fund. In Article I of the Agreements, the purposes of the Fund are listed as follows:[3]

1. To promote international monetary cooperation through a permanent institution which provides the machinery for consultation and collaboration on international monetary problems.

2. To facilitate the expansion and balanced growth of international trade, and to contribute thereby to the promotion and maintenance of high levels of employment and real income and to the development of the productive resources of all members as primary objectives of economic policy.

3. To promote exchange stability, to maintain orderly exchange arrangements among members, and to avoid competitive exchange depreciation.

4. To assist in the establishment of a multilateral system of payments in respect of current transactions between members and in the elimination of foreign exchange restrictions which hamper the growth of world trade.

5. To give confidence to members by making the Fund's resources available to them under adequate safeguards, thus providing them with opportunity to correct maladjustments in their balance of payments without resorting to measures destructive of national or international prosperity.

6. In accordance with the above, to shorten the duration and lessen the degree of disequilibrium in the international balance of payments of members.

Further Provisions of the Fund. Member governments may make use of the facilities of the Fund according to assigned *quotas*, which

[2] See J. H. Williams, "Currency Stabilization: The Keynes and White Plans," in *Foreign Affairs*, An American Quarterly Review, July, 1943, p. 645 *et seq.*

[3] *Yearbook of the United Nations*, 1946/47, p. 772 *et seq.* Also International Monetary Fund, *Articles of Agreement of the International Monetary Fund*, Washington, D.C., 1952.

may be changed by a four-fifths majority of the total voting power of the Fund together with the consent of the member government concerned (Art. III, Sect. 2).

Art. IV, Sect. 3 defines the provisions on *foreign exchange* dealing as follows: "The maximum and the minimum rates for exchange transactions between the currencies of members taking place within their territories shall not differ from parity, (1) in the case of spot transactions, by more than one percent; and (2) in the case of other transactions, by a margin which exceeds the margin for spot exchange transactions by more than the Fund considers reasonable." Sect. 4*b* of the same Article provides that "each member undertakes, through appropriate measures consistent with this Agreement, to permit within its territories exchange transactions between its currencies of other members only within the limits prescribed under Section 3 of this Article. . . ."

The problem of *interest* is solved in Art. V, Sect. 8*c* which reads:

The Fund shall levy charges uniform for all members which shall be payable by any member on the average daily balances of its currency held by the Fund in excess of its quota. These charges shall be at the following rates:

1. On amounts not more than twenty-five percent in excess of the quota: no charge for the first three months; one-half percent per annum for the next nine months; and thereafter an increase in the charge of one-half percent for each subsequent year.

2. On amounts more than twenty-five percent and not more than fifty percent in excess of the quota: an additional one-half percent for the first year; an additional one-half percent for each subsequent year.

3. On each additional bracket of twenty-five percent in excess of the quota: an additional one-half percent for the first year; and an additional one-half percent for each subsequent year.

Article VI, Sect. I, requires the members to employ *controls in capital transfers.* "A member may not make net use of the Fund's resources to meet a large or sustained outflow of capital, and the Fund may request to exercise controls to prevent such use of the resources of the Fund. If, after receiving such a request, a member fails to exercise appropriate controls, the Fund may declare the member ineligible to use the resources of the Fund." And Sect. 3 of the same Article provides that "members may exercise such controls as are necessary to regulate international capital movements."

Further employment of government controls is required by Art. VII, Sect. 3*a*, which reads: "If it becomes evident to the Fund that the demand for member's currency seriously threatens the Fund's ability to supply that currency, the Fund . . . shall formally declare such currency scarce and shall thenceforth apportion its existing and accruing supply of the scarce currency with due regard to the relative needs of members, the general international economic situation, and any other pertinent considerations."

Section 3b adds that "a formal declaration under (a) shall operate as an authorization to any member, after consultation with the Fund, temporarily to impose limitations on the freedom of exchange operations in the scarce currency. . . . The member shall have complete jurisdiction in determining the nature of such limitations, but they shall be no more restrictive than is necessary to limit the demand for the scarce currency to the supply held by, or accruing to, the member in question; and they shall be relaxed and removed as rapidly as conditions permit."

Section 4, finally provides that "any member imposing restrictions in respect of the currency of any other member . . . shall give sympathetic consideration to any representations by the other member regarding the administration of such restrictions."

Article VIII, Sect. 2b, provides for *cooperation of governments* in the execution of exchange controls. It is defined as follows: "Members may, by mutual accord, cooperate in measures for the purpose of making the exchange control regulations of either member more effective, provided that such measures and regulations are consistent with this Agreement."

Article XI speaks of the relations of member states with non-member states and gives member states the express right to impose *restrictions on exchange transactions with non-members.* Section I (iii) says: "Each member undertakes: To cooperate with the Fund with a view to the application in its territories of appropriate measures to prevent transactions with non-members or with persons in their territories which would be contrary to the provisions of this Agreement or the purposes of the Fund." Section 2: "Nothing in this Agreement shall affect the right of any member to impose restrictions on exchange transactions with non-members or with persons in their territories unless the Fund finds that such restrictions prejudice the interests of members and are contrary to the purposes of the Fund."

Article XIV, Sect. 2, provides for maintenance and introduction of exchange restrictions during a transitional period. "In the post-war transitional period," it says, "members may, notwithstanding the provisions of any other articles of this Agreement, maintain and adopt to changing circumstances (and, in the case of members whose territories have been occupied by the enemy, introduce where necessary) restrictions on payments and transfers for current international transactions."

These agreements on the establishment of the Fund were hailed as the adoption of the kind of economic plan and program necessary for world stability and prosperity. Henry Morgenthau, Jr., then Secretary of the Treasury and president of the Bretton Woods Conference, called the agreements a "new beginning." According to him, the great objective of the Fund was to provide the monetary and financial foundation for agreements in all other fields of economic planning and cooperation by governments. Since the monetary foundation had been laid, other needed agreements in the sphere of commercial policy, controls of cartels, the supply of primary commodities, and labor standards could follow.[4] The monetary cooperation was secured, the external monetary pressure which threatened internal government controls and planning was removed, and the real and pure government planning could begin.

SOME CRITICISM

The Background. The fundamental idea of the Agreements of Bretton Woods is the notion that the policy of credit expansion and inflation can be permanently maintained by cooperation of all governments.

When in the nineteenth century and in the decade preceding World War I, individual governments increased the quantity of domestic credit money, the exchange ratio between domestic currency and foreign currencies immediately reflected the new money relation. Before the prices of other commodities were affected by domestic inflation, the foreign exchange dealers anticipated the future rise of domestic prices, and the price of foreign exchange tended to rise to the height corresponding to future domestic prices. Thus, the new exchange rate reflected the future purchasing-power parity of domestic and foreign currencies.

During the nineteenth century and the first decade of the twentieth century the money markets of the world were international. Funds flowed freely from one country to another, and fractions of one per cent of higher interest were often sufficient to induce capitalists and bankers to deposit their funds with the banks in another country. Funds were freely convertible and callable at any time. When an individual government or bank embarked upon credit ex-

---

[4] H. Morgenthau, Jr., "Bretton Woods International Cooperation" published in *Foreign Affairs,* January, 1945, p. 183 *et seq.*

pansion, the foreign exchange relation immediately reflected their
undertaking. The foreign bankers and capitalists who had deposits
in the credit-expanding country became frightened by the aspect
of decreasing value of deposits and began to withdraw their funds.
But through the operation of the gold standard, the fluctuations of
exchange ratios were exceedingly small as compared with the depreciations of today. Fluctuations merely moved between the gold
export and import points. But the aspect of decreasing deposit and
investment value within these narrow limits and the added fear of
an eventual suspension of the gold standard were sufficient reasons
for withdrawal. A sudden withdrawal of considerable funds naturally forced the banks to recall their loans and restrict their lending
and expansionary activities. Interest rates were raised again and a
general tightness of capital resulted.

The advocates of easy money schemes saw the sudden withdrawal
of foreign funds and explained it simply and convincingly. "Foreign capitalists and speculators," they said, "have selfishly raided
the capital resources of the nation and by an unfounded and deliberate withdrawal have plunged the nation into depression and
misery." In order to bring a halt to these "wicked speculation activities," i.e., the recalling of capital funds by the owner, two measures—one domestic, the other international—were advocated. First,
speculation should be prohibited or rendered impossible through
taxation or controls and "freezing" of the accounts of foreigners.
Second, at the same time, all national governments should agree on
simultaneous devaluations and depreciations so that the flight of
capital from one country to another would be rendered unprofitable.
It is evident that capital ceases to flee from one country to another
if all countries offer equally unfavorable conditions to the presence
of capital. This goal of the advocates of easy money schemes is
clearly reflected in the international agreements concluded at Bretton Woods.

Some Misstatements. The stated purposes of the Bretton Woods
Agreements seem praiseworthy at first glance like every other government plan and directive "for the common good." At second
glance, however, the Agreements reveal inevitable consequences
that were neither desired nor foreseen by the planners. Concomitant effects, as, for example, the loss of freedom of the individual
and growing authority of state officials over the individual, render
the policies agreed upon at Bretton Woods undesirable. Furthermore, as shall be shown in the following, the means employed under

the terms of the Fund and Bank do not bring about the results which were the objectives of the Agreements.

Clarity and precision of expression are the first prerequisites of every contract or agreement. In this respect, however, the plans of Bretton Woods reveal serious shortcomings that willfully or negligently misrepresent the objectives of agreement. While the stated objectives are "to promote international monetary cooperation," a more revealing and enlightening description of the objectives would be: promotion of international government cooperation in matters of money management. While it is agreed "to promote international trade, expand employment, and raise incomes" the correct setting of agreement should read: to promote foreign trade by more numerous and efficient controls or government enterprise, to expand employment, and to raise wages by more government spending and investment.

The concluding parties of Bretton Woods are *governments* entering into obligations binding themselves or their citizens. The promotion of "exchange stability," for instance, is an obligation into which governments entered for the individual. His government is to declare an arbitrary exchange rate and he is to sell his media of foreign exchange to his government at the official rate. And he will be prosecuted by his government if he trades at a different rate. This clause is well disguised and erroneously represented as a means to "free" international transactions. That governments should refrain from monetary management and inflationary measures, which alone bring about exchange instability, can neither be inferred from the agreements nor is it congruent with the ideas of Bretton Woods.

Finally, the "assistance in reconstruction and development" is stated as an objective of the agreement. Such purpose is logically based upon the assumption that individual reconstruction and development need government assistance. The means for this assistance would be raised by taxation, inflation, or loans; there are no other means at the government's disposal. When the means are spent as officials see fit, they are logically spent for purposes different from those the individual would have pursued in the absence of taxation or inflation. It is obvious, therefore, that a less ambiguous and more precise definition of agreement would have the following setting: spending for purposes which government officials conceive as reconstruction and development, and which the individual would *not* have pursued in the absence of taxation and inflation. The objective of "assistance" is not only misleading but downright incorrect!

Agreement versus Freedom of the Individual. The fallacies of the Bretton Woods agreements are numerous and far-reaching. The underlying principle of agreement is the notion that governments, through a privileged and controlled bank and stabilization institution must manage *money and banking* and directly handle this part of economic life. This notion is the product of the vast popularity of policies of credit expansion. Public opinion is convinced that good governments lower the rate of interest and that expansion of credit is the suitable means for the attainment of prosperity. It cannot be the task of this work to refute those notions in detail, but a review of the history of the twentieth century thus far cannot fail to impress upon us the disastrous effects of the tremendous inflations that government-controlled banks have brought about. Government interference with the present state of monetary and banking affairs could be justified if it meant the liquidation of the unsatisfactory conditions which former intervention has brought about. This, however, is not the objective of the contract of Bretton Woods.

The government agreements of Bretton Woods sanction and aggravate the *loss of freedom* of the individual. It is obvious that the authority for economic actions cannot rest in two places simultaneously. Either the individual is free to plan and act as he sees fit, in which case government authority does not exist—or the authority for directing economic actions lies with his government. The freedom of the individual thus is limited in direct proportion to the amount of government authority.

The Problem of Allotment Insoluble. The International Fund must be rejected on another important ground: the problem of allotment of the means of the Fund to various governments is not and cannot be solved. Quotas are not based on need—for they are given to countries which need them, and to others which do not; they are not based on the presence of sound monetary policies—for they are given to countries with relatively sound fiscal policies as well as to countries with rapidly deteriorating currencies. The measuring stick of profitability of investment is not considered. Instead, *the height of quota is arbitrarily fixed* by officials whose judgment is difficult to fathom. They may base the quotas on the amount of contribution which obviously favors the industrially advanced and economically stronger nations; or they may base the quotas on the size of population—a mode which would favor the industrially backward nations of the East. It is evident that quotas must be arbitrary.

After long and weary negotiations the member quotas actually were fixed according to population figures, national income, foreign trade, and other factors. The ability to repay, however, was scarcely considered. International loans, in the final analysis, are repaid through export of commodities. Countries without mentionable export industries and without active foreign trade were given quotas that were obviously beyond their ability to repay. China, for instance, was given a quota which is nearly 40 per cent larger than that of India, although her foreign trade before World War II was only one-half as large; and her quota is double that of Belgium, although her foreign trade and ability to repay are considerably smaller.[5]

If we compare the quotas with "lines of credit" in private enterprise, we can immediately see the enormous differences between private and government lending. A bank does not grant credit on the basis of certain groups of industry, but on a specific evaluation of the ability and individual position of a specific borrower. If the borrower's financial position changes essentially, the line of credit may be cancelled.

Quotas a Reward for Inflationary Practices. The quotas of the Fund are rigidly fixed and *constitute a reward for inflationary practices.* For the most part, central bank and stabilization funds are used in the transactions of the Fund—neither investor's nor taxpayer's money is generally employed. But this means that the more central bank or reserve money a government was willing to "create" and contribute, the higher could be its quota. The system of quotas thus constitutes a clever trick to swap self-created and deteriorating currency for foreign exchange—especially United States dollars.

Under the terms of agreement, each member government of the Fund contributes in gold 25 per cent of its subscription *or* 10 per cent of its "net gold holdings and United States dollars"—whichever is smaller. (Art. III, Sect. 3b.) Only one-half of the gold subscription need be delivered to the Fund; the other half must be "earmarked." The remaining 75 per cent of each subscription is to consist of paper currencies and non-negotiable, non-interest bearing notes.

It can easily be assumed that most of the member governments chose to submit to the second term of subscription, i.e., to the contribution of 10 per cent of their "net gold holdings and United States dollars." Let us assume, for the sake of illustration, that a government has subscribed to the equivalent of one billion dollars.

[5] See V. O. Watts, The Bretton Woods Agreements, in *The Economic Sentinel,* Vol. 3, No. 1, March 1945, p. 7.

Because of its inflationary policies, confiscatory taxation, nationalization and control policies, the total gold and dollar holdings of
her central bank amount to only one hundred million dollars. This
is a fair assumption since very few central banks actually hold more
than this amount. Under the terms of the Fund, this government
is to contribute 10 per cent of gold or dollar holdings, i.e., ten million dollars or one per cent of the subscription, of which five million
dollars or one-half per cent must be delivered. Ninety-nine per cent
of the total subscription may consist of paper currency and non-
negotiable, non-interest bearing government notes fresh from the
treasury.

The Interest Rate Insures Cheap Money. The *rate of interest*
charged for advances from the Fund insures an *inflationary* "cheap
money" policy. According to Art. V, Sect. 8, a service charge of ¾
per cent is to be levied on a member's exchanges of foreign currencies. No interest is to be charged on advances up to 25 per cent of
a member's quota. All of a nation's gold subscription, including
the gold earmarked at home—and in many cases more than this—
may be borrowed back without charge of interest. Double the
amount of gold and dollars may be borrowed, interest-free, for a
period of three months. One-half per cent interest is paid for each
additional 25 per cent of a nation's quota.[6]

In the clauses on interest we find no reference whatever to the
fact that the rate of interest is a market phenomenon which is subject to the laws of the market. Gross rates of interest encountered
on the market are neither uniform nor unchanging. They depend on
the constantly changing magnitudes of originary interest, of the risk
component of each specific transaction, and of a price premium
which is the outcome of an understanding of present and future
money relations. These fundamental principles of the market phenomenon of interest are either ignored or denied by the Agreements
of Bretton Woods. But if market laws of interest do not exist, why
do the Fund and Bank charge any interest at all? Even the smallest
rate conceivable would then be unfounded.

Debtors in Control of Lending. The Bretton Woods Agreements
provide no proper restraints upon the use of funds. Under the system of free enterprise the creditor does the lending, which seems
natural. But the International Fund puts the *debtors* in control of
the lending. It is true there are provisions for restricting or with-
holding credits within the quotas, but they are inadequate and
vague. The Board of Governors, a majority of which necessarily

[6] See also V. O. Watts, *Ibid.*, p. 5 *et seq.*

represents borrowing governments, does the lending. A representative of a borrowing government cannot be expected to cast his vote against another government similarly situated, unless he is prepared to meet retaliation when his own government is concerned. Thus, the borrowing governments will always act in concert and counteract any restraint that representatives of lending governments should endeavor to impose.[7]

The United States actually appoints only one out of the 44 members of the Board of Governors and only one out of the 12 Executive Directors of the Fund. In addition to being outnumbered 12 to 1, one must remember that the American appointees were usually advocates of free money, easy spending, or some other brand of "Fair-Dealing" and did not necessarily assume the normal role of a representative of a creditor.[8]

"Scarce Currencies" Rationed by Governments. Another clause with even worse effects is the authorization of the Fund to declare a currency scarce and of member governments to ration and control the scarce currency (Art. VII). Rationing currency means the control and distribution of foreign means of payment by government officials as they see fit. They select purposes of payments for which scarce currencies are rationed; they select the individuals who may receive the foreign currency and with whom it may be exchanged. That such authority for arbitrary judgments must ultimately result in corruption, oppression, loss of freedom of the individual, and disruption of foreign trade relations is evident. The businessman and investor must constantly be on guard for a declaration of scarce currency and the resulting blockage of his funds. It is absurd to assume that the flight of capital may be avoided, or that confidence may be increased and foreign investments encouraged.

Cooperation in Exchange Controls. The Fund sanctions and brings about exchange restrictions. Under the Bretton Woods Agreements each member government undertakes to force its citizens to exchange foreign currency at a rate fixed in collaboration with the Fund. "Appropriate measures" of coercion are to be taken to prevent any individual from exchanging at any other price (Art. IV, Sect. 4). An execution of this provision, of course, is very difficult as long as individuals are free to trade and exchange foreign

[7] See Benjamin M. Anderson, *Economics and the Public Welfare*, D. Van Nostrand Co., New York, 1949, p. 585.

[8] The American key appointee, H. D. White, was not only a "Fair-Dealer" but proved to be a traitor to his country and in the service of the government of Soviet Russia.

currency with each other. How is a government to enforce its arbitrary official price of foreign exchange? Even the most rigorous measures of coercion will hardly induce the citizen to exchange his foreign funds at an arbitrary price. In order, therefore, to enforce its official exchange rates, a government is bound to monopolize foreign exchange dealings. That is to say, only government institutions and their representatives are authorized to buy from and sell to individuals. Only through government monopolization of foreign exchange dealings can this provision of the Agreement be realized.

The Agreement also provides for a pledge of cooperation among the governments in the execution of exchange controls. That is to say, governments will cooperate in prosecuting individuals who may dare to attempt to avoid the monopoly and deal with other individuals in their own or in a foreign country. They also agreed that they would cooperate "to control international capital movements." The objective of this article is the avoidance of the flight of liquid capital from countries with deteriorating currencies, confiscatory taxation, or policies leading towards nationalization or economic controls. In the nineteenth century, when the central banks were losing their deposits of gold and foreign exchange, they raised the interest rate one-half to one per cent, and deposits began to flow back. Naturally, in modern times when the total capital is in danger of being devalued, nationalized, or blocked, a one per cent rise in the interest rate becomes insignificant—only direct controls and direct government compulsion may still hinder an extensive outflow of liquid capital. The member nations of the Fund agreed to cooperate in this control of the movement of capital. Thus, the effects of unsound monetary and fiscal policies are sheltered under a series of new and more stringent controls by all member governments.[9]

Foreign Exchange Control Leads to Tyranny. Several provisions of the Agreement requiring the member states to apply government controls and restrictions have an enormous significance for industries that largely depend on imports of raw materials and other vital materials from abroad. A government that fixes the parity of its domestic money against gold or foreign exchange and continues to depreciate its own money through policies of inflation and credit expansion will bring about the effects described by Gresham's Law.

---

[9] Confusion of modern economic thought is such that the Fund is often represented as "eliminating foreign exchange restrictions." Neither the underlying ideas of Bretton Woods based on Keynesian economics, nor their actual effects as they appear to us, can justify such a statement. As shall be shown below, foreign exchange restrictions and regulations have actually increased and the monetary chaos has grown.

That is to say, people will prefer to use the bad domestic money and hoard the better foreign money or ship it abroad. Thus a "scarcity" of foreign exchange will result. According to the Bretton Woods Agreement, this government-created "scarcity" entitles the member states to ration and allocate the scarce supply of foreign exchange. But this control over the media of foreign exchange by government officials invites government arbitrariness and tyranny.

Many important industries in Europe depend entirely on the importation of raw materials, capital goods, and other vital materials from abroad. Their operation and their prosperity or depression depend on the prompt allocation of media of foreign exchange for their vital imports. If, for any reason, the foreign exchange official should fail to allocate the desired supply of foreign exchange, the industry must curtail its operation to the level of foreign exchange allocation. Inasmuch as foreign exchange is inevitably scarce in case of government inflation of domestic currency and arbitrary government-enforced exchange rates, the foreign exchange official always thereby curtails the operation of industries dependent on imports. But what does he use as his yardstick for this curtailment? It is called "essentiality" and "national interest." But how is this yardstick applied? Which is more important—the textile industry or the truck manufacturing industry, the news or hosiery business, the manufacture of bicycles or airplanes, typewriters, washing machines, textbooks, or thousands of other commodities? Of course, the foreign exchange official pretends to know, and his wisdom spells prosperity or doom to the multiplicity of importing industries. He also pretends to know how each single industry is to be "fairly" curtailed, whether or not the enterprises are to be curtailed equally according to the "scarcity" of the media of foreign exchange or whether only certain "unessential" enterprises are to be curtailed while other enterprises of the same industry are to receive the desired quantity of foreign exchange supply. It is obvious that each single decision of the foreign exchange official must be arbitrary.

Consider the following example. Many European textile industries vitally depend upon the import of cotton since there is no cotton grown in Western Europe; and they depend on allocations of foreign exchange for these purchases from their respective foreign exchange authorities. The same is true of the gasoline, kerosene, and paraffin industries which, because little petroleum is found in Western Europe, are largely dependent upon imports of petroleum from abroad. Let us assume that the Central Bank of Italy, because of its monetary policies, suffers from foreign exchange shortage. Now, which industry is the Italian foreign exchange official to curtail, the textile industry or petroleum industry? To what extent? We do not know. But let us assume he decides to curtail the textile industry because of "its lesser importance." Which enterprise within the industry is to be curtailed? An old and established company or a young and growing enterprise? Should he curtail them equally? Or should he distinguish between enterprises in unemployment and full-employment areas? What should be the yardstick for curtailment?

The lack of such a yardstick and the tragic importance of foreign exchange allocation invite arbitrariness, bribery, and tyranny of public officials. In the name of "national interest" a public official may refuse to allocate foreign exchange to a businessman who failed to "pay him off." The businessman may belong to a different party, nationality, religion, social group, etc. He or his employees may have failed to contribute sufficiently to the election fund of the foreign exchange official or his party. He or his employees may have voted for or advocated the "wrong" party ticket. His plant may be located in an area whose greater part of population may be opposed to the policies of the party in power which appointed the foreign exchange official. Or, in the case of publication industries, a businessman may want to import newsprint, magazines, periodicals, and books in order to explode the fallacies of the doctrines and policies of the party in power. Will he obtain the necessary supply of foreign exchange from the foreign exchange official in power?

A businessman may want to import books that explode the fallacy of foreign exchange control. Will the foreign exchange official allocate media of foreign exchange for this purpose, i.e., the abolition of his own office? If he does not, he is curtailing the freedom of publications and the press. At any rate, he will decide on the "essentiality" of each book, magazine, and newspaper imported. As small countries largely depend on imported textbooks and other information, the foreign exchange official may decide what the nation may read, what may be published, printed, and what information may be distributed. The individual is no longer free to inform himself and to study what he himself sees fit. The foreign exchange official insures his information and education.

These are the effects of the foreign exchange provisions of the International Fund. To whatever extent they are applied by the governments of member states, to that extent do they curtail the liberty of the individual and subjugate him to the tyranny of foreign exchange officials.[10]

Policies of Devaluation Permissible. According to the Agreements of Bretton Woods, a devaluation of a currency as to its gold content is permissible. The member governments may devalue their currencies 10 per cent without interference, and another 10 per cent to which the Fund may object within 72 hours. Of course, there is no reason to expect that further devaluations, under "extraordinary conditions of grave national emergency," may meet effective resistance by the Fund. As Anderson pointed out, the permanent threat of future devaluation sanctioned by the Fund "will create 'hot' money which would not otherwise exist." [11] Investors must be ready at all times to shift their funds to safer places where they need not fear the loss of 20 per cent or more of their capital. It is obvious that every investor gladly foregoes a moderately higher interest rate obtainable abroad, to avoid risking the loss of 20 per cent or more of his capital without notice.

Black Markets Created. If present-day conditions were proof to assertions won by reasoning, we could cite the chaotic state of foreign exchange of the major currencies as proof that the ideas expressed in the Bretton Woods Agreements are fallacious. Although one objective allegedly is "monetary stability," currencies have steadily depreciated; whereas another goal allegedly is to avoid discriminatory exchange practices, competitive currency depreciation, and exchange control, these practices have been condoned or even brought about by Bretton Woods policies. Wherever a law fixes a ratio of exchange at a height other than the market rate, or attempts to prescribe values which are fictional and do not exist, "illegal" transactions always spring into existence. In 1952, for instance, more than 12 billion dollars' worth of trading in currency and precious metals took place on the "black" markets of the world.[12] Of the total transactions in gold amounting to approximately 1.17 billion dollars in 1952, more than 75 per cent were illegal—legal offenses or crimes on the part of either the buyer or the seller, or both.[13]

Depreciation of Currencies Continues. Sanctioned by the provisions of the Bretton Woods Agreements, the depreciation of cur-

---

[10] For attempts to justify the provisions and their effects, see International Monetary Fund Publications: *Annual Reports, Reports on Exchange Restrictions, International Financial Statistics, Staff Papers, Balance of Payments Yearbooks, International Financial News Survey*, all published in Washington, D.C.

[11] B. Anderson, *Ibid.*, p. 585.

[12] Franz Pick, *Black Market Year Book*, N. Y., 1953, p. 3.

[13] *Ibid.*, p. 107.

rencies due to governmental inflationary and expansionary measures continued. "During the last 27 months," says F. Pick, "under the increasing pressure of international rearmament, at least 55 currencies have undergone legal devaluation." [14] If 55 currencies have been legally devaluated, it is permissible to assume that even more have depreciated *de facto,* although the fictional official values have remained. The 55 legal devaluations naturally do *not* represent changes from a fictional level to the true ratio of free exchange and purchasing power. Such devaluations would be contrary to the ideas expressed in the Bretton Woods Agreements. They are mere changes from one fictional official level to another. It is not surprising, then, that 69 kinds of pound sterling with 69 ratios of exchange and foreign prices are traded all over the world.[15] Some of these transactions are legal and sanctioned by the law, but a significant number are illegal.

Wherever official rates of exchange become more and more fictional and less enforceable, the government exchange market dwindles and finally ceases to exist altogether. Modern government itself then embarks upon vast black market operations reaffirming the validity of the market laws of exchange. But the individual is not allowed to trade on the free market under penalty of crime.

Government Control Over Capital Movements Includes Control Over All Foreign Transactions. The Agreements of Bretton Woods make a distinction between "current transactions," the freedom of which is an alleged objective, and "capital movements," which are to be controlled. Such a distinction, however, is impossible in practice. The devices developed for transferring funds from one country to another without exchange transactions are many. Goods can be shipped out of the country and the proceeds left abroad. A businessman or a company may do business in two or more countries and slowly shift funds by lending and borrowing from one country to another. Thus, control of capital movements must not only include control of all foreign exchange transactions, but also "control of all borrowing and lending transactions by companies doing business in several countries and of all export and import movements, not to mention the searching of pockets and traveling bags of every traveler, and censorship of the mails." [16] It is obvious that there is no room for freedom, either in "capital movements" or in "current transactions."

[14] *Ibid.,* 1951 edition, p. 4.
[15] *Ibid.,* 1953 edition, p. 15.
[16] B. M. Anderson, *Ibid.,* p. 586.

A Misrepresentation of History. Those responsible for and in favor of the Agreements often point to the period of wild currency disorder after World War I as a justification for their agreements. We have learned the lesson, they say, that external monetary stability means sacrificing internal stability. We have the choice between stable exchanges or stable internal prices, incomes, and employment, without the tyrannical interference of the gold standard and its strait-jacket.

Inasmuch as historical phenomena in their complexity can never constitute proof for a reasonable and logical assertion, the following is offered, not as proof for or against any previous statements, but as an elucidation of economic laws and principles applied to recent history.

After World War I there was much waste and misuse of loans granted to stabilize exchange rates which were not accompanied by a stabilization of currencies. From the Armistice in November 1918 through September 1920, the United States government provided 3 billion dollars in direct loans to European governments to stabilize and support the exchange rates of Europe. Private investors financed another 3½ billion. Within less than two years, these funds were spent on imports from the United States and other parts of the world.[17]

The European governments, with the exception of Great Britain, did nothing to return to sounder principles of government financing, balancing the budget, or refraining from inflationary measures. It was so convenient—politically and socially—to spend and not to tax or borrow from their own people. Besides, speculating businessmen, who anticipated the deterioration of currencies by government inflation, could be blamed for the rising prices.[18] Under those conditions the exchange rates could not be stabilized regardless of how many billions of dollars the United States government spent.

In the fall of 1920, America had learned its lesson. If exchange rates were to be stabilized, European currencies would have to be stabilized first. During the next two years the problem of stabilization was approached quite differently. Small loans were given to

[17] B. M. Anderson, *Ibid.*, p. 582 *et seq.*
[18] The notion that it is the speculator who, by buying and selling currencies, wrecks one currency after another is as popular as it is fallacious. Governments, at all times, have needed individuals on whom they could lay the blame for their own misdeeds or for situations which they did not understand. In medieval Europe it was the witch, in Hitler-Germany the Jew, in communist Russia the capitalist, and to the progressive Western government the speculator, whose misfortune consists mostly of his ability to foresee and anticipate future government actions and their effects.

European governments with the express condition that internal government finances were to be stabilized. In 1923, Austria, whose crown had dropped to 14,000 to 1 in terms of gold, under the auspices of the League of Nations, received a loan of about $113,-000,000. The conditions accompanying the loan were drastic curtailments of government expenditures, increases in taxes, a balancing of the budget and a stabilization of the currency on a gold basis. Thus, the conditions requested for the attainment of the loan, and not the loan itself, really did the stabilizing.

The same thing was done for Hungary in 1924. The conditions of a loan of about $50,000,000 effected a drastic reform in government policies, and the stabilization succeeded.

In 1924, America did the same thing for Germany. A loan of $200,000,000 was provided under the condition that expenses be curtailed, the budget be balanced, there be a definite stabilization of currency on gold, and that there be a foreign representative in the Reichsbank and a foreign commissioner in Germany for the purpose of supervising certain taxes. These controls over the policies of an étatist government brought about the stabilization. The enormous difference between this approach and that of Bretton Woods lies in this control *over* the government instead of *by* the government.

Poland, too, received a loan of $72,000,000, the conditions of which brought about an improvement in monetary and fiscal practices in the Polish government. The stabilization of foreign exchange rates inevitably followed.

Great Britain, Belgium, France, and Italy also had experienced a deterioration of their currencies by inflationary spending under wartime conditions. Great Britain went back to the gold standard and brought the pound back to the prewar par in April 1925. The actual purchasing power of the pound, as prevailing in 1925, however, lay at about 90 per cent of the old par. To avoid the ill effects of a deflation, a stabilization at about 90 per cent of the old par would have been suitable. But the government of Great Britain decided to embark upon the necessary readjustment of prices and costs of about 10 per cent in order to achieve the prewar par. Under the conditions of free enterprise such as prevailed in the nineteenth century this readjustment would have been taken in stride. But under the twentieth-century conditions of nation-wide union bargaining, rigidity of labor costs, and price-fixing combinations of industries organized behind highly protective walls of tariffs, such a readjustment was impossible. Many marginal enterprises were closed and Britain's unemployment soared and remained high until the beginning of World War II.

In July 1926, the deterioration of the French franc had progressed to a new low of less than 2¢ in foreign exchange markets. Within a few weeks during the spring of 1926 alone, the franc had dropped from 5¢ to 2¢. Prices were rising continuously. When nearly all the European governments had completed their drastic reforms and had stabilized their currencies, sentiment among French politicians and statesmen finally demanded financial reforms also. In the fall of 1926, under Poincaré, the French government embarked upon a policy of cutting expenditures, cutting pensions, dismissing needless civil servants, raising taxes, and even creating a fiscal surplus.[19] The franc rallied dramatically. Within a short time the French franc rose from 2¢ to approximately 4¢ on the foreign exchanges. France then stabilized the franc at nearly 4¢ *de facto* at the end of 1926 and *de jure* in 1928.

In all the above-mentioned cases exchange stabilization was brought about through stabilization of the currency, which was brought about by curtailing government expenditures, balancing the budget, and refraining from inflationary government measures. An International Fund and an International Bank were not necessary, nor could they have yielded those results.

Fund's Resources Spent. Since the establishment of the Fund in 1946, several years have elapsed. Its inevitable failure has become evident even to the most ardent defenders of the Agreements and the institution. Within a few months after operations began, the convertible currencies—mainly the American contributions—had been spent for the stabilization of currencies which the respective governments were busily depreciating through credit expansion, inflation, deficit spending, etc. After the first flurry of operations in 1947, the Fund practically had to suspend its exchange transactions because of lack of exchangeable currencies. Although the Fund was established to stabilize the exchange rates of the national currencies, the member countries continued freely to manage their rates of exchange, flouting the Fund's advices and proceeding with their own plans of exchange restrictions and devaluations which the Fund was supposed to eliminate. Only five members, out of more than 40 member governments, did not invoke Article XIV which denies the Fund's jurisdiction over exchange relations during the "transition period." Their national currencies are still in a "state of transition,"

[19] See B. M. Anderson, *Ibid.*, p. 156.

that is to say, in the transition to further depreciation and planned monetary chaos.

Proposals for Revision. Nevertheless, it would be erroneous to assume that the advocates of easy money schemes and international monetary cooperation have learned the lesson. On the contrary, numerous plans for a revision of the Fund statutes have been brought forward. The Monetary Fund is supposed to have more and broader responsibilities and, above all, new American contributions. It lies in the nature of omnipotent governments and their institutions to extend continuously their sphere of authority. Once it has been accepted by popular belief that government or its institutions know how to manage the affairs of the individual better than he does, limitation of authority becomes vague and arbitrary. No valid reason remains, for instance, why government should not regulate the domestic exchange of goods if it is to manage the field of foreign exchange. There is no reason whatever stated for the defense of foreign exchange regulation which could not be cited for the advocation of domestic government regulations.

The Fund is a government institution born and provided with power and authority that tend to expand. It is growing in its usefulness as a tool of an ideology aiming at and bringing about the destruction of freedom and free enterprise, in the soil of which Western civilization has grown and without which this civilization must vanish.

B. THE EUROPEAN PAYMENTS UNION

The Economic Background. At the end of World War II, Europe suffered from acute shortages of all sorts—food, clothing, raw materials, machinery, equipment, etc. In many cases these things could not be produced within the boundaries of a state and so had to be imported. But imports require media of foreign payment which can be obtained only through foreign trade or through grants and loans from foreign lenders. Since foreign businessmen could hardly be expected to loan their funds to Europeans in countries having exchange restrictions and practicing monetary depreciations and government blocking of accounts, the European governments applied for and received large grants and loans from the country which was willing to supply them—the United States of America. Attempts were also made to revive foreign trade in order to acquire the media of foreign exchange so urgently needed for the payment of essential imports.

In accordance with modern ideas on government and its transactions, these attempts at revival of foreign trade were handled in the following way: strict foreign exchange controls by governments over exchange transactions of the individual were introduced; the media of foreign exchange were carefully rationed as to purpose of use and recipient country; and foreign trade transactions of the individual were carefully scrutinized by government officials as to their importance and congruence with the over-all government planning. In general, the fundamental policy was such that exports to countries with "convertible" currencies [20] were encouraged through numerous government measures in order to earn "hard currencies." Imports from these countries, however, were either prohibited or rendered difficult if they did not concur with the government's plan of essential imports. On the other hand, imports of essential goods from countries with weaker and more rapidly depreciating currencies—whose supply was often abundant—were allowed. But exportation of goods to these countries was disapproved because the central bank would hesitate to accept the weaker currencies of doubtful convertibility. At the same time, governments with still weaker currencies would prohibit the importation on grounds of "unessentiality" or scarcity of the necessary media of exchange which were "hard currencies" for them.

The inevitable consequence of this careful planning for trade revival by European governments was a marked decline in inter-European trade. The government planners deliberated and inferred. Our exchange plans and foreign trade controls do not work satisfactorily, they said, because an Inter-European system of settlement is needed which would keep account of the foreign trade of the nations. Foreign exchange controls lack an international supplement, that it to say, an international institution of control over the national systems of control over the foreign transactions of individual. And so this institution was set up.

An Intra-European Payments Agreement. In October 1948, the First Intra-European Payments Agreement [21] was concluded by the European countries which participated in and benefited from the American program for European Recovery. This payment agreement linked intra-European trade with American aid. Through bilateral negotiations between governments the volume of trade between the citizens of the various ERP countries was to be deter-

[20] A "convertible" currency, in this connection, is a currency which can freely be converted into other currencies. Convertibility into gold is another matter.

[21] See also William Diebold, Jr., *Trade and Payments in Western Europe,* Harper & Brothers, New York, 1952, p. 34 *et seq.*

mined. The anticipated balance of payments between national central banks was to be calculated and determined in advance. In cases where a government anticipated that exports of its citizens to a certain country would exceed their imports from it, thus causing the incoming payments to exceed those going to the foreign country, the governments agreed that the difference should constitute a gift, called "drawing right," to the central bank owing the balance. In return, the central bank providing the gift, in order to pay its own citizens for the surplus exports, was to be compensated generously out of dollar aid funds provided by the United States.

Drawing Rights Illustrated. To illustrate, let us assume that the total export volume of German businessmen to French buyers is expected to amount to one billion dollars during the coming year. At the same time, let us assume that the French businessmen are expected to export only 750 million dollars' worth of goods to German customers. Thus it is anticipated that the payment agent for the French businessmen—the Bank of France—will pay one billion dollars to the payment agent of the exporters in Germany—the Bank Deutscher Länder. And the latter central bank will pay the Bank of France $750 million for exports of goods to Germany. The difference of $250 million represents an amount in German currency, or gold, or acceptable currency which the Bank of France probably does not have, even though it receives full payment in French francs from French importers.

The modern solution to this problem is government prohibition of the excess of imports over exports. But the First Intra-European Payments Agreement was designed to discontinue this curtailment of foreign trade. In our example, the German government, as the manager of the Bank Deutscher Länder, would now renounce its claim against the Bank of France, that is to say, it would grant 250 million dollars' worth of "drawing rights." Of course, the Bank of France would collect the full indebtedness from the French importers. It would even encourage them to import fully one billion dollars' worth of goods, since the last $250 million would constitute a clear profit. Of course, since the Bank of France is a "non-profit" government-owned and regulated institution, it would then lend these funds out at low interest rates—preferably to the government to cover deficits or to nationalized industries with deficits. The Bank Deutscher Länder, on the other hand, would pay the full amount to the German exporters, but would be compensated generously out of aid funds provided by the United States. Thus the interpayment relations of citizens of different countries could be settled via two central banks and one superbank without resort to gold or other "hard" currencies based on gold. Government exchange control supplemented by an international institution of settlement could thus be substituted for individual freedom of payment relations.

Agreement Promotes Disequilibrium. The sad part of this intergovernmental agreement was that it did not work. Some governments complained about the interference of the agreement with foreign trade and exchange control programs of their own; others complained about errors of anticipation of deficits on which the drawing rights were based—some had granted too many and received too little and complained that others had granted so little and received so many; others even complained about their own businessmen leaving drawing rights unused. In June 1949, at the expiration of the agreement, 15 per cent of the rights were unused,[22] which means that the central banks had foregone 15 per cent of the total profits because importers, who had to pay their central banks for foreign purchases in full, simply abstained from importing. Governments thereupon began encouraging imports. They even discouraged exports because the amount of drawing right aid was based on the amount of prospective surplus of imports over exports. The larger the export deficit, the larger the amount of aid which constituted lucrative profit to the central bank. But this government trade policy was diametrically opposed to the objective of agreement, which was balance and equilibrium of inter-European economic relations. Finally, many European governments concurred in the complaint that American compensation out of aid funds was insufficient.

A Revised Payments Agreement. Another system of inter-European payment control and settlement had to be designed and established. In September 1949, the European governments signed a Revised Payments Agreement. In its essentials, this new agreement constituted a development of the preceding agreement. But again the governments endeavored to forecast the next year's balance of payments between the national central banks. The anticipated "creditor" central banks then granted drawing rights to the "debtor" central banks in the amount of expected excess payments. But the major shortcoming of the drawing rights, as granted under the preceding agreement, was corrected—that is to say, the central banks were assured of better utilization of the drawing rights in that 25 per cent of them were made "multilateral."

[22] W. Diebold, *Ibid.,* p. 49.

In order to illustrate this new feature, let us return to our preceding example. Let us assume that French businessmen imported goods from Germany in the amount of $750 million and that the Bank of France received drawing rights for an additional 250 million dollars' worth of imports from Germany. If no additional imports are made by French businessmen, the drawing rights obviously are worthless and no drawing right profit can be made. The transferability of 25 per cent of drawing rights granted was supposed to correct this shortcoming. The new agreement provided therefore that the multilateral drawing rights could be used to cover the recipients' payment obligations with any country signing the agreement. Let us assume that our French importers preferred to import goods from Italy instead of from Germany. They paid the purchase price in French francs to the Bank of France in full. The Bank of France, which may have more payment obligations towards the Banco d'Italia than it has claims for French exports against it, may now use its multilateral drawing rights granted by the German central bank or any other bank to discharge its Italian obligation. The Banco d'Italia is obliged to accept "payment" for its claims by honoring these rights and in return it is to be compensated generously out of American aid funds.

Its Failure. But this revised system of inter-European payment control and settlement did not bring about the desired result—the revival of inter-European trade. Foreign trade by thousands of European businessmen simply did not conform to the careful forecasts of the government planners. But the whole system rested upon the correct anticipation of future trade. The inter-European flow of goods was changing constantly and rapidly in direction, quantity, and composition. A central bank which had anticipated being a "creditor" bank and granted drawing right aid might become a "debtor" bank during the current year, and vice versa. In no case did the actual volume of trade conform with the anticipated volume —a fact which resulted in numerous "injustices" and undesired effects. A central bank which had granted a certain amount of drawing rights may have found that more drawing rights were used against it than it had established. The central bank of Portugal, for example, established only $800,000 in rights, but it was obliged to honor $8.3 million.[23] Or, the drawing rights which a central bank provided were not sufficient to cover the actual surplus in export trade. This resulted in new trade barriers which other European governments erected against goods from this "creditor" country.

[23] W. Diebold, *Ibid.*, p. 74 *et seq.*

Belgium, for instance, whose government did not indulge in excessively inflationary practices, experienced an export surplus throughout the postwar period. The drawing right aid which the Belgian central bank granted was not sufficient to cover the deficits which other European central banks had with the former. The Belgian government therefore agreed to establish further drawing rights and lend out the anticipated balance in the form of inter-central bank loans. The Belgian central bank, on the other hand, received dollar aid from the United States by an equal amount.

None of these measures of national exchange control and international settlement had the desired effects. The inter-European trade, during this period, increased only slightly and for reasons other than the Payments Agreement. European governments, therefore, came to the conclusion that a new approach to the problem of inter-European payment settlement had to be found. This new approach was the European Payments Union the agreement of which was formally signed by the OEEC governments in September 1950.

The Payments Union. Under the terms of the Union, each central bank's foreign exchange surplus or deficit with every other member central bank are set off against one another.[24] The balances are reduced to a single net surplus or deficit with the Payments Union. Foreign exchange deficits up to a certain amount are automatically covered by a grant of credit by the Union to the debtor central bank. If the deficits exceed the automatic credit, part of this deficit is covered by further credits and part by payment of gold or other convertible currencies. A central bank's position is thus determined by its debt to or from all the other member central banks in the Union.

The clearing agent for the EPU is the Bank for International Settlements in Basle, Switzerland. It calculates and determines each central bank's position with the other banks every month. During the periods between settlement, the central banks grant the necessary credits for the continuation of foreign trade.

Quotas Assigned. Each central bank was assigned a "quota" which is equal to about 15 per cent of the foreign trade of a country's citizenry with those of other member countries during the year

---

[24] OEEC, *A European Payments Union and Use Rules of Commercial Policy to be followed by Member Countries,* Paris, 1950. See also OEEC, "Agreement for the Establishment of a European Payments Union," in ECA, 9th Report, Supplement, 6-34; R. F. Kahn, "The European Payments Union," *Economica,* August, 1950, pp. 306-316; R. Triffin, *Monetary Reconstruction in Europe,* Carnegie Endowment for International Peace, New York, p. 282 *et seq.;* W. Diebold, Jr., *Ibid.,* p. 87 *et seq.*

1949. The British quota was based on and is used to facilitate foreign trade between European exporters and importers and businessmen in the whole sterling area, with the exception of Iceland. If the net debt of a central bank amounts to only one-fifth of its quota, or less, the EPU will grant it credit for the full amount. If a central bank's credit position amounts to one-fifth of its quota, or less, the EPU receives credit from this bank for the full amount. If the credit or debit position of a central bank exceeds one-fifth of its quota, some part of the balance is settled by further extension of credit and the rest is covered by gold or other convertible currencies. Creditor central banks receive half the sum due them by the EPU in gold once the first 20 per cent of the quota is exceeded. Debtor national banks pay gold for debit balances at an accelerating rate of percentage (20 per cent gold from 20 to 40 per cent of the quota, 40 per cent gold between 40 and 60 per cent of the quota, 60 per cent gold between 60 and 80 per cent of the quota, 80 per cent gold between 80 and 100 per cent of the quota). Since the divergence between the ratio of gold payment by debtor banks to the Union and that of gold payment by the Union to creditor banks could cause the Union to pay out more gold than it would take in, the United States of America supplied a EPU working fund in the amount of $350 million.[25]

The Payments Union Does Not Affect the Individual. The individual businessman still needs his license to operate his export or import business. He still must deal with a buyer or seller abroad. If he wants to conclude a transaction, he must apply for an export or import license for the specific transaction planned. He must apply for an allocation of the necessary media of foreign exchange. He must comply with his government's foreign exchange control rules and with the government's bilateral trade agreements on volume and essentiality of imports. He must conform with his government's general regulation of imports and tariff duties. And, finally, he must comply with the rules and restrictions of the government in which his foreign buyer or seller resides. Having succeeded in fulfilling all requirements and having received all government licenses, for which he naturally is charged, the buyer must deposit the purchase price with his commercial bank well in advance. The commerical bank then transfers the deposit to the central bank which reports it to the Bank for International Settlements. At the same time, if and when the foreign contract party is equally successful in fulfilling all requirements and has received all licenses from its government, the

25 R. Triffin, *Ibid.,* p. 287. See also W. Diebold, *Ibid.,* p. 87 *et seq.*

import or export transaction may proceed. Naturally, when goods cross borders, they are thoroughly checked by other government officials of both countries as to value and conformance with declaration papers and licenses. If everything is found in full agreement with the latest government requirements, the tariff duties may be paid.

Equilibrium Through Restrictions and Inflation. The European Payments Union Agreement, in anticipation of difficulties in case a central bank's quota becomes exhausted, included special provisions. If a central bank's *credit* position exceeds 75 per cent of its quota, a change in government policy should be considered to restore the balance of trade with the Union. If the position is about to reach the member bank's quota, definite arrangements should be made for the restoration of the balance. Four means for attaining this objective, the first three of which have been successfully used, are as follows:

1. A central bank may extend additional credits to the Union. These may be temporary or constitute an enlargement of its quota.
2. Other member governments may be permitted to restrict importation from the country whose central bank has exhausted its quota.
3. A member government may inflate its currency to such an extent that the depreciation of currency exceeds the rate of depreciation of the other European currencies. The depreciation then results in an increase of imports and a decrease of exports.
4. A government is free to withdraw from the Union once its central bank has exhausted its quota.

In order to relieve the payments position of an extreme *debtor*, a government is allowed to limit importation of goods from certain countries or unilaterally from all other countries. Furthermore, the debtor country may ask for a recommendation for more American aid in the form of grants or loans.

Sterling Area Included. The inclusion of the Sterling Area in the European Payments Union created many difficulties. Prior to the Union, in numerous bilateral agreements between Great Britain and a number of Continental countries, the pound sterling was used as the calculating unit and the generally accepted medium of intergovernmental payments. Consequently, British officials fearing that the automatic settlement of inter-European payments in the EPU unit of account would curtail the demand for and threaten the position of sterling in international trade, asked that a provision be inserted in the agreement which made it possible for the member central banks to use sterling payments whenever it seems desirable to them.

Amortization of Unfunded Debts. Another major difficulty in the conclusion of the Payments Union Agreement was the risk that the Union would drain gold and convertible currencies from central banks with large bilateral debit balances. Continental banks, for example, were holding large sterling balances which—as the British government feared—they would throw into the Union clearing. As the total amount would probably exceed the automatic credit of the British quota, the Bank of England would be called upon to pay the balance in gold or convertible currencies. But this had to be avoided. Another special provision was therefore inserted into the Agreement, providing for amortization of the unfunded debts between the member central banks in case the debtor and creditor banks might not agree on the terms of repayment.

Other Provisions. These were the basic provisions of the European Payments Union Agreement which was first concluded for an initial period of two years and successively extended annually after long and laborious discussions. A great deal of effort was required for the simple objective of settling payments between European central banks. Governments often balked at the suggestion of allowing an automatic procedure in international transactions to replace the numerous government controls as employed in bilateral settlement. The gold standard had been abolished for this very reason, for it kept governments from controlling money and credit and international trade. Similarly, "automatic" provisions of the Union Agreement ran counter to the very nature of government control. They were accepted, nevertheless, because of the great pressure for "cooperation" which the United States government exerted on the European governments. Of course, the fact that the United States put up the necessary working capital and that it pledged to assist weak debtor banks made the agreement acceptable to European governments. And the final bit of persuasion was the addition of the clauses on an easy termination and liquidation of the Union.

SOME CRITICISM

Government and Foreign Exchange Control. It is one of the fundamental theorems of economic theory that an artificial scarcity is created wherever a government fixes a price at a point lower than that determined by the market. Whenever a government fixes the parity of gold or foreign exchange against its own money at a point lower than the free market, i.e. whenever it undervalues gold or foreign exchange, a state of affairs results which can be described by Gresham's law. The demand for foreign exchange at the price arbitrarily fixed by the government exceeds supply. The foreign money disappears and the domestic money remains. In order to remove this undesirable state of affairs, interventionist governments then nationalize all foreign exchange transactions. Buying and selling of foreign exchange thus become the privilege of government authorities. Finally, when the discrepancies of official foreign exchange rates and market rates result in complete destruction of foreign trade, governments resort to barter and bilateral clearing agreements with foreign governments. When also these agreements fail because the domestic currency loses its usefulness as a calculating unit in international trade, governments endeavor to conclude multilateral payment and settlement agreements which are to eliminate the shortcomings of preceding price and foreign exchange policies. The European Payments Union is the work of such an agreement and is the logical outcome of government endeavors to eliminate the price laws of the market and establish government supremacy in the field of foreign exchange.

E.P.U. Analyzed. Our following critique is based on this fundamental concept of government activity in the field of foreign trade and exchange. It hinges upon the following contentions which we shall endeavor to prove:

1. The European Payments Union is a supplement to national policies of inflation and exchange controls and endeavors to make exchange controls work.

2. The fundamental provisions of the European Payments Union further credit expansion and. perpetuate European imbalance of trade and payment.

3. The Payments Union condones and advocates inflationary policies by member governments and exerts pressure on creditor banks to inflate their currencies.

4. The Payments Union condones and advocates exchange and trade restrictions. It perpetuates controls inasmuch as it depends on controls. A sound money policy by any member state of the Union would cause its collapse.

5. The Payments Union reverses all principles of credit by granting credit to central banks which are inflating their currencies and

to governments which are running large budget deficits. Such extension of credit tends to encourage and perpetuate such policies.

6. The European Payments Union is financed and upheld by the United States of America and would collapse without American financial aid.

7. The European Payments Union is an institution organized by governments in disregard of the individual, of his freedom, planning and choices.

EPU a Supplement to National Controls. The European Payments Union is a supplement to national policies of inflation and exchange control and seeks to make exchange controls work. Wherever individuals are free to base their economic relations on gold, they will do so without hesitation and shun the media of exchange that are subject to large-scale depreciation by governments. Inasmuch as the purchasing power of gold is independent of government wishes and plans, in order to be able to regulate the monetary affairs of the individual, governments nationalize the trade in gold and "retire" the individual's gold holdings. Government paper money, provided with a court-enforced property of legal tender, then replaces the kind of money which the individual preferred in his payment relations. Having succeeded in destroying the gold standard, governments may now embark upon a manipulation of prices and wage rates. Credit may be expanded at a vast rate, and governments may spend lavishly on public works and social programs.

A policy of inflation and credit expansion, however, brings about an external drain of the media of exchange which finally results in "unfavorable" balances of payment. The increasing depreciation of domestic money, together with the inevitable phenomenon of rising prices, induces importers to import more goods than they would have otherwise. Exporters, on the other hand, find it increasingly difficult to sell to countries where prices did not rise. This process continues until the reserves in gold and foreign exchange of the central bank—the only institution endowed by law to trade in gold and foreign exchange—are exhausted. At this stage governments resort to foreign exchange controls, i.e., controls over purpose of spending, allocation, and regulation of prices of foreign currencies.[26]

In the meantime, however, the policy of inflation, credit expansion, and government spending continues, and the purchasing power

[26] On foreign exchange control see also L. von Mises, *Human Action*, Yale University Press, 1949, pp. 795 *et seq.*

of the domestic money against gold and foreign exchange continues to fall. No control and no government coercion can alter the fact that the purchasing power of the inflated currency is bound to decline as long as other officials are busily employed in increasing its quantity. The external drain of gold and foreign exchange reserves of the central bank continues at an accelerated rate. As the discrepancy between foreign exchange control prices and market prices increases, the profit of those importers who obtain allocations of foreign exchange against inflated domestic money increases accordingly. Governments then resort to further makeshifts which are to encourage exports and discourage imports.

The final attempt at making the increasing number of government controls over the actions of individuals work is the resort to international monetary cooperation—a kind of concerted government action for the continuation of a policy of inflation and credit expansion. It is based on the belief that it is the external drain of foreign exchange that frustrates domestic policies. There is no need to bring again to the reader's attention the fallacy of this notion.

Differences in Monetary Depreciation Must Destroy the Union. The European Payments Union is an institution of international monetary cooperation whose aim is not to check but to facilitate inflation and credit expansion policies. But monetary depreciation and imbalanced trade and payment are inseparable phenomena. Since the sovereignty for national monetary policies has not been limited and member governments are free to inflate according to their own plans and liking, the differences in degree of national monetary depreciation must sooner or later destroy the Union and its "cooperation" and "integration." Even if we were to assume a uniformity of action on the part of member governments, the Payments Union would still be plagued by the problems of *European* unfavorable balances of payment and decreasing purchasing power of the European media of exchange against gold and outer-European media of exchange. Only a complete autarky of the European Union would eliminate the inflation-created problems of international payment and foreign exchange.

EPU Based on Credit Expansion by Member Banks. The fundamental provisions of the Payments Union facilitate continuous credit expansion by the central banks. Under the terms of the Union each central bank's foreign exchange surplus or deficit is set off against every other central bank. Each bank thus remains with one credit or debit balance with the Union. Interbank deficits, amounting to less than a certain percentage of a bank's quota, are covered by a

228 STEPS TOWARD UNION

grant of credit from the Union to the debtor central bank. If the debit balance exceeds this amount, further credits up to a bank's quota are granted. On the other hand, if a central bank is a "creditor bank," it is obliged to grant credit to the Union up to its quota. This credit to the Union or by the Union, under present-day government policies, is extended through credit expansion. The creditor banks of the Union grant credit to the Union and, in order to facilitate the foreign trade of their citizens, pay their exporters for the goods exported in full. This payment to exporters, in addition to the extension of credit to the Payments Union, is achieved through credit expansion. Of course, it is conceivable that a creditor central bank refrains from expanding credit by not paying its exporters or, provided it chooses to pay exporters, through contraction of loans to others. Contemporary credit policies, however, do not conform with this sound money principle which constitutes the essence of the gold standard and is the very reason for its destruction by governments all over the world.[27]

We may illustrate the expansionist policies of the central banks as follows. Let us assume that the central bank of Germany, the Bank Deutscher Länder, has a claim of one-half billion dollars against the Payments Union for exports by German businessmen to other countries in the Union. According to the provisions of the Payments Union Agreement, the Bank Deutscher Länder grants full credit to the Union which then extends it to debtor central banks (let us say, the Bank of France) for approximately the same amount. The Bank of France then, in spite of its credit from the Union, continues to collect the full purchase price for goods imported. When all imports have been paid for by the French businessmen, the Bank of France has on hand one-half billion dollars more funds than it had before the extension of credit by the Union. On the other hand, the Bank Deutscher Länder, having given credit to the Union in an amount of one-half billion dollars, proceeds to pay German exporters for goods exported in full, or one-half billion dollars. Credit in this amount has thus been created by the Bank Deutscher Länder and granted to the Union which extended it to the Bank of France. The Bank of France is thus enabled to lend funds in the amount of one-half billion dollars, which undoubtedly will be utilized to cover government deficits or assist nationalized industries. The inescapa-

[27] It is also conceivable that a central bank may extend credit, without expanding, out of original deposits by commercial and savings banks or individuals having accounts with the former. All central bank credit exceeding these deposit funds is "created" and constitutes credit expansion.

ble consequence of this new lending is a further enhancing of prices in France. A rise of prices, however, makes it profitable for French businessmen to import from foreign countries. And, again, the Bank of France faces the danger of an increasing external drain upon its gold and foreign exchange reserves. Consequently it stays a "debtor bank" and depends upon further extension of credit by the Union. It is in this respect that the European Payments Union is an institution for the perpetuation of the imbalance of European trade and payment.

EPU Compared with the Gold Standard. The significance of the European Payments Union is most clearly illustrated in a contrast with the functioning of the gold standard. Under the operation of the gold standard, the French importers of our example would have had to pay for goods in gold and foreign exchange. This means that an equivalent amount of gold and foreign exchange would leave the country, and immediately the money markets in Germany as well as in France would reflect the new supply situation. In Germany the inflow of funds would tend to lower the money rates; in France interest rates would tend to rise. The difference in rates on French and German money markets would immediately induce some German bankers to deposit funds in the French money market in order to profit from the higher money rate. Or, they would begin to buy French commercial paper. Also French bankers would tend to recall funds deposited in Germany and invest them at a higher rate in France. That is to say, an outflow of gold or foreign exchange would, within a matter of hours, bring about effects that cause a return of funds. Only if the outflow would exceed this return, the volume of money in France would contract. This contraction then would tend to lower prices in France, which in turn would decrease the profitability of imports. On the other hand, the inflow of money and foreign exchange in the exporting country would tend to enhance prices which would constitute a check on further exports and an incentive for more imports. Thus, through the operation of the gold standard, exports and imports would always be in balance and the contemporary phenomenon of "unfavorable" or "favorable" balances of trade and payment would cease to exist.

EPU Advocates Inflation. It is our contention that the Payments Union condones and advocates inflationary policies by the governments of the member nations and that it exerts pressure on creditor banks to inflate their currencies. It is one of the provisions of the agreement that a change in policy is to be considered as soon as a bank's surplus exceeds 75 per cent of its quota. If the surplus is about to exhaust the central bank's quota, definite arrangements are to be made for the restoration of the balance of the creditor bank to all other central banks. To work off a surplus position with the Union, a central bank must aim at a temporarily unfavorable balance of payment—that is to say, at an external drain of gold and foreign exchange. Such an objective can be achieved only through a monetary policy which is relatively more inflationary than that of the other central banks of the Union. The central bank which inflates its currency most quickly and expands its credit most widely cannot fail to bring about an outflow of foreign exchange. Another makeshift solution to this problem is for the creditor government to apply stringent export controls and the importing country to apply stringent import controls against the country having the surplus position. Through the combined efforts of the border police forces of both countries a temporary change in the payment position may be enforced. A permanent change in the payment position, however, can be brought about only through government policies affecting money and credit.

The member governments of the European Payments Union have successfully employed both means to change a payment position. Towards the end of 1950, the Portuguese central bank, for example, was about to exhaust its quota of 70 million dollars as creditor bank when the Managing Board of the OEEC began to reprimand the Portuguese government for its "tight credit policies" and lack of measures to check the inflow of capital seeking refuge from depreciation.[28] It is obvious that the criticism of "tight credit policies" is identical with advocation of credit expansion policies. When the Portuguese government then embarked upon "easier" money and credit policies while other central banks of the Union temporarily refrained from expanding and inflating at an even greater degree, the Portuguese central bank began to run deficits with the Union. The balance of trade and payment between Portugal and the European Union was thus restored through credit expansion on the part of Portugal and the attainment of an approximate uniformity of expansion by all member governments of the Union.

Also, the Belgian central bank's surplus repeatedly reached its quota limit because the Belgian government frequently refrained from policies of inflation and credit expansion while other European governments indulged in easy money policies. The Belgian government was then coerced to extend further credit to the Union by reason of the provision which permits debtor member banks to re-

[28] W. Diebold, Jr., *Ibid.*, p. 134.

strict importation of goods from countries having exhausted their quota. The Belgian central bank preferred to expand credit rather than to allow its exporters to be discriminated against by all other governments of the Union.

EPU Advocates Exchange and Trade Restrictions. This illustration also leads us to the inference that the European Payments Union condones and advocates exchange and trade restrictions. It perpetuates controls because its existence depends on controls. A sound monetary policy by any member country would cause its collapse. Let us assume that a member central bank would decide, in order to facilitate a monetary and economic reconstruction, to refrain from any further inflation and credit expansion. We may even assume that it decides to go back to the gold standard. Within a few weeks time, this central bank would become a "creditor" bank and would exhaust its quota with the Union. According to certain provisions of the Payments Union Agreement,[29] debtor governments are permitted to limit imports from a country whose central bank has exhausted its quota as "creditor bank." Such a country would soon be surrounded by a wall of trade and payment restrictions by the Union members. It would then have the choice of abandoning its sound money policy or withdrawing from what is commonly believed to be the initial step toward European monetary "cooperation" and "European integration." Before all the world this government would assume responsibility for having caused the downfall of the Union and its attempt at European unification. But no democratic government can risk being blamed for this consequence. It is understandable that it rather prefers to continue to inflate its currency in order to be united with other governments in monetary depreciation.

The Union's attitude toward government exchange and trade restrictions is also manifest in its position towards European trade with the dollar area. Not only has it left intact the discriminatory trade policies with respect to American goods, but it has even increased that discrimination. Of course, the policies of the governments of the EPU system are in full agreement with the scarce currency provisions of the Monetary Fund Agreement. The scarcity of the United States dollar which led to additional restrictions of imports from the United States is the inevitable consequence of its relatively stable purchasing power compared with that of European currencies. The fact that the purchasing power of the American dollar decreased by a mere 25 per cent (from 77¢ to 52¢ of the

[29] OEEC, *Code of Liberalization,* Paris, July, 1951, Art. 3 and 31, pp. 14, 15.

1940 dollar) during postwar years, while the European currencies depreciated at a much faster rate, caused a scarcity of dollar exchange. The inference drawn by contemporary European governments was that additional restrictions and controls over the individual's trade with America were needed. The European Payments Union aids and encourages this belief.

EPU Reverses All Principles of Credit. As has been pointed out, the Payments Union also reverses all principles of credit in that it grants immediate credit to central banks which are inflating their currencies. The central banks then extend this credit to governments which are running large budget deficits. Such an extension of credit by the Payments Union naturally tends to encourage deficits and perpetuates inflationary policies. Under provision of the Union Agreement a central bank that inflates its own currency and enforces a fictitious foreign exchange rate—and consequently suffers from foreign currency scarcity—receives immediate credit up to its quota for the amount of foreign exchange it owes to other central banks in the Union.

A government may adopt a policy of inflation for two reasons: to bring about a great business boom, the after-effects of which are recession and depression; or to offset expenditures which it has been unable to pay for through taxation and borrowing. Often a government hesitates to present to its citizens the full and true bill for its spending. It then simply resorts to the old practice of inflation. In order to make its policy of money depreciation as unnoticed as possible, it may even accuse its businessmen of "price violations," "greediness," etc.

It was for the latter reason that a policy of inflation was pursued in postwar Europe. Almost every government was running large deficits. They hesitated or were unable to raise an equivalent amount for their spending through taxation and, inasmuch as they were unable to find enough investors for floating loans to cover the deficits, they resorted to printing. But also a new source of funds was welcome that never inquired into the credit status of debtor central banks; this was the European Payments Union. The higher the government deficit and the greater the government inflation, the sooner would it extend credit to the inflator. From an interventionist point of view, it is indeed an ideal institution, supplementing and facilitating policies of easy money and credit.

Union Financed by the United States. The European Payments Union is financed and upheld by the government of the United States, without whose financial aid, we contend, the Union would collapse. As has been stated, the initial working fund of $350 million, without which the Union could not have been established, was not put up by the member states of the Union, but by the government of the United States. Furthermore, the United States government is making full or partial payment to the Union on behalf of certain countries whose central banks have exhausted their quota with the Union. If a member government of the Union has depreciated its national currency through easy money and credit operations at a rate faster than the depreciation of the currencies of other member nations, the central bank of this government is bound to suffer a deficit with the Union. As soon as its credit quota is exhausted and further deficits must be met with gold and foreign exchange in full, its government may resort to additional import restrictions. The Payments Union finally loses all significance to the debtor member because it is excluded from the automatic credit operations by the Union. At this moment, however, the United States government steps in and makes full or partial payments on behalf of the debtor central banks that must either leave or be dropped from the Union, thus allowing them to be reinstated as a participating member.

During the operation of the EPU the United States, for example, made full payments for deficits to the Union on behalf of Greece and Iceland and made substantial payments on behalf of Austria and Turkey.[30] Altogether it spent several hundred million dollars to uphold the function and organization of the European monetary system. With the United States government standing ready to replenish the quota of a debtor central bank, no matter how great the rate of monetary depreciation, the European Payments Union can and must be temporarily successful in its inflationary objectives. But there cannot be any doubt that one debtor bank after another, *de facto* and *de jure*, would drop from the Union if the government of the United States would cease to foot the bills for deficits. And there cannot be any doubt that the European Payments Union would instantly collapse if the American government would proceed to call its loans or the initial working fund without which the Union would never have been constituted.

The European Payments Union is an international institution conceived and organized by governments united in disregard of the

[30] R. Triffin, *Monetary Reconstruction in Europe,* Carnegie Endowment for International Peace, New York 27, New York, p. 289; see also "Unveränderte Tendenzen in der EZU," *Deutsche Zeitung und Wirtschaftszeitung,* 4/25/53, 8th year, #33, p. 10.

individual, of his planning, freedom and purpose. It is the logical outcome of an ideology that advocates the substitution of government planning for individual freedom and private enterprise. The Payments Union is a supplementary instrument of control over the payment relations of individuals. It is no isolated phenomenon, no coincidental realization of an objective of the ideology of planning, but merely one of its numerous aspects. When the fundamental freedom of the individual in his monetary and foreign exchange affairs fell, other economic freedoms could easily be abolished. When economic freedoms fall, all political liberties and bills of individual rights, sooner or later, become empty and meaningless. This is the significance of the European Payments Union in the struggle between the ideology of control and that of individual freedom.

VII

The European Coal
and Steel Community

Unification As Seen by Robert Schuman. The revolutionary idea
of European unification "has taken shape so fast and without the
violence that usually accompanies revolution." These are the words
of Robert Schuman, father of the European Coal and Steel Community, expressing his feeling of gratification about the conclusion
of the Treaty. Previous attempts at European unification have
failed, according to Schuman, because "no European country was
ready for the concept of a supranational authority." Aristide Briand,
who was the first to raise officially the question of unity, had proposed a "European Association" that excluded any infringement
upon national sovereignty. He had confined himself mainly "to outlining a legal structure, in particular a system of arbitration." His
attempt to settle the Franco-German problem by signing the Locarno Pact in October 1925 also failed, because certain provisions
of the Treaty of Versailles held Germany in an inferior status, while
France clung to her legal rights of reparation payment for war damages. "German nationalism, nourished by incessant but futile scold-
ings, grew until its supporters at length felt strong enough to deny
that Germany had suffered any military defeat or bore any political
responsibility. Banking on the fact that an alliance with Russia was
possible, they moved rapidly to split Europe. Hitler completed the
break when he came to power in January 1933. . . . In such an
atmosphere," says Schuman, "there was no possibility of cooperation." [1]

After World War II, the situation was different. Germany had

[1] Robert Schuman, "France and Europe," in *Foreign Affairs,* An American Quarterly Review, April 1953, Vol. 31, No. 3, p. 350.

suffered a crushing military defeat by the Allied armies which occupied the whole country. It was in a state of disorganization,
without either an army or a central government. Furthermore, the
occupation of the Eastern Zone of Germany by the Russians made
the German people thoroughly hostile to the thought of any Ger-
man-Russian alliance. Now, the political prerequisites for Western
European cooperation were present.

When, in 1947, the Western Allies became aware of Russia's menace towards the free world, they soon began to counteract Russian
moves. In 1948, the first permanent pan-European organization, the
Organization for European Economic Cooperation, was set up and
entrusted with the task of allocating and putting to work the funds
contributed by the United States government under the Marshall
Plan. Thus, "under the threat of danger, and prompted and encouraged by generous assistance from America, Europeans began to
acquire a consciousness of 'Europe'." The basis for European cooperation was broadened by the Brussels Treaty of March 1948 and
the London Agreement of June 1948 which inaugurated a construc-
tive policy toward Germany.

In May 1949, because of the initiative of France and Belgium, the
governments of twelve European countries signed the Constitution
of the Council of Europe, which constitutes a permanent assembly.
Its delegates vote individually on recommendations to member governments without being instructed by their own governments.
Western Germany joined this organization a few months later. In
initiating this move towards integration, the French government,
according to Robert Schuman, followed two primary purposes.
First, the French government endeavored to "strengthen the European countries, which if left to fend for themselves would be condemned to political and economic dissolution; and second, to bring
Germany into the common endeavors so that she would not repeat
her former errors." [2]

Participation in the Council of Europe was the first step in this
direction, but it was not enough and France did not hesitate to
take another. She envisaged the creation of such strong organic
bonds among the European nations—Germany, in particular, included—that no German government could break them, and the establishment of a living and permanent community that would put
an end to old antagonisms and usher in an era of profitable collaboration. Such a community must be based on mutual good faith and

[2] *Ibid.*, p. 352.

confidence—and that is possible only if all members find it to their interest to keep faith with the others, recognizing that what promotes the common advantage will promote their individual welfare.

"In a solemn declaration on May 9, 1950, France proposed to Germany and the other European countries that they put their production of coal and steel under an authority independent both of governments and private interests. For the first time in history there was to be an agency above national parliaments and private business which would reach its decisions in consultation with producers, workers and political bodies and which would be responsible only to an assembly representing the participating Powers. Thus we hoped that considerations of narrow national interest would be replaced by regard for the common interest, that national antagonisms would be transcended, and that, since none of the partners had control of its own coal and steel, war among them would be unthinkable. The objective was to remove the danger of war between rival nations and to develop a community spirit which would not weaken national attachments but provide a wider basis for new activities and new goals. Such a community would also be able to solve problems which arise from the uneven distribution of natural resources and technical skills." [3]

"The unification of Europe is irrevocably under way," says Robert Schuman rejoicingly. The political union, it is true, should have come first. However, the "functional" approach was chosen "for the practical reason that it seemed wiser to begin with integration in a restricted technical sector of national life: the important thing was to go ahead quickly so as to catch the public imagination and win over doubters and scoffers. Also, though the fields in which unification was achieved are of the first importance, they lie somewhat outside the areas of sharpest political controversy. As we have noted, the coal and steel plan has now become a symbol of European political unity. It has created an atmosphere in which integration can develop further and it also represents a concrete and lasting step in the program of Franco-German reconciliation." [4] The European faith in the future, according to Schuman, rests "on a cooperation which, since it derives from a fusion of economic interests and the growth of common institutions, ought to be permanent. The idea of a united Europe will no longer be a theme for poets, a utopian vision; it will be a living reality, because the conscience

[3] *Ibid.*, pp. 352, 353.
[4] *Ibid.*, p. 358.

of the European people will have recognized it as their chance of salvation." [5]

The Objectives of the Coal and Steel Community. The Treaty of the European Coal and Steel Community, concluded by the governments of Germany, Belgium, France, Italy, Luxembourg, and The Netherlands, was signed at Paris on April 18, 1951 and ratified by the respective parliaments of the six countries during the following fourteen months. It went into effect on July 25, 1952. According to Article 2 of the Treaty, it is the mission of the European Coal and Steel Community:

"to contribute to economic expansion, the development of employment and the improvement of the standard of living in the participating countries through the institution, in harmony with the general economy of the member States, of a common market as defined in Article 4. The Community must progressively establish conditions which will in themselves assure the most rational distribution of production at the highest possible level of productivity, while safeguarding the continuity of employment of the member states." [6]

It is the function of the Community:

"(a) to see that the common market is regularly supplied, taking account of the needs of third countries; (b) to assure to all consumers in comparable positions within the common market equal access to the sources of production; (c) to seek the establishment of the lowest prices which are possible without requiring any corresponding rise either in the prices charged by the same enterprises in other transactions or in the price-level as a whole in another period, while at the same time permitting necessary amortization and providing normal possibilities of remuneration for capital invested; (d) to see that conditions are maintained which will encourage enterprises to expand and improve their ability to produce and to promote a policy of rational development of natural resources, avoiding inconsiderate exhaustion of such resources; (e) to promote the improvement of the living and working conditions of the labor force in each of the industries under its jurisdiction so as to make possible the equalization of such conditions in an upward direction; (f) to further the development of international trade and see that equitable limits are observed in prices charged on external markets; (g) to promote the regular expansion and the modernization of production as well as the improvement of its quality, under conditions which preclude any protection against

[5] *Ibid.*, p. 360.

[6] This and the following quotes referring to the Treaty constituting the European Coal and Steel Community are taken from its text as distributed by the Press and Information Division of the French Embassy in New York, N. Y.

competing industries except where justified by illegitimate action on the part of such industries or in their favor."

The Establishment of the Common Market. According to Article 4 of the Treaty, the following policies and practices are conceived to be incompatible with the common market and are, therefore, abolished and prohibited within the Community:

"(a) import and export duties, or charges with an equivalent effect, and quantitative restrictions on the movement of coal and steel; (b) measures or practices discriminating among producers, among buyers or among consumers, specifically as concerns prices, delivery terms and transportation rates, as well as measures or practices which hamper the buyer in the free choice of his supplier; (c) subsidies or state assistance, or special charges imposed by the state, in any form whatever; (d) restrictive practices tending towards the division of markets or the exploitation of the consumer."

The Community is to accomplish its mission with limited directed intervention.

"To this end, the Community will: enlighten and facilitate the action of the interested parties by collecting information, organizing consultations and defining general objectives; place financial means at the disposal of enterprises for their investments and participate in the expenses of readaptation; assure the establishment, the maintenance and the observance of normal conditions of competition and take direct action with respect to production and the operation of the market only when circumstances make it absolutely necessary; publish the justifications for its action and take the necessary measures to ensure observance of the rules set forth in the present Treaty. The institutions of the Community shall carry out these activities with as little administrative machinery as possible and in close cooperation with the interested parties." (Art. 5)

In order to facilitate the exercise of its functions and the attainment of its ends, the Community shall enjoy

"the most extensive juridical capacity which is recognized for legal persons of the nationality of the country in question." (Art. 6)

The Institutions of the Community. The institutions of the Community, in charge of implementing the plan, are: a High Authority, assisted by a Consultative Committee; a Common Assembly; a Special Council, composed of Ministers; and a Court of Justice.

The *High Authority,* composed of nine members, eight of whom are designated by agreement among the member governments and one elected by the others, is the executive of the Coal and Steel

Community. It was set up with headquarters at Luxembourg and has been functioning since August 10, 1952. The High Authority, whose members are to act in the interest of the Community and completely independent of their national governments, has the right to make decisions which are binding in all their details. It can formulate recommendations which are binding in their stated objective, but leave the way of execution to those to whom they are directed. And, finally, it can formulate opinions which are not binding (Art. 8-17).

Attached to the High Authority is the *Consultative Committee* which is composed of an equal number of producers, workers, consumers, or dealers from the Community. Its members are appointed by the Council of Ministers. It is a kind of technical committee which the High Authority may consult each time it deems such action to be useful, and which it must consult in important cases where prescribed by the Treaty. It is through the intermediary of this Committee that the High Authority keeps itself constantly informed of market conditions. This Committee also meets in Luxembourg.

The *Assembly*, composed of 78 parliamentary representatives of the Community states, exercises the supervisory powers which are granted to it by the Treaty (Art. 20-25). The High Authority is responsible to it; by a vote of censure on the annual report, which must be presented by the High Authority, the Common Assembly can force the latter to resign in a body. The number of members is apportioned among the six member nations as follows: France and the Saar 18, Italy 18, German Federal Republic 18, Belgium 10, The Netherlands 10, and Luxembourg 4. The Assembly holds its annual session at Strasbourg, France.

The *Special Council of Ministers*, composed of representatives of the member states, was created for the purpose of coordinating the actions of the High Authority with the general economic policies in each of the six countries. To this end, the Council and the High Authority consult and exchange information on the national coal industries, the iron mines, and the steel mills placed under European authority. The Council may request the High Authority to examine all proposals and measures which it deems necessary for the realization of common objectives. The Council of Ministers makes its decisions by a qualified majority or unanimous vote without any right of veto (Art. 26-30).

The *Court of Justice* with its seat in Luxembourg is to interpret and apply the law of the Treaty and its implementing regulations

(Art. 31). The Court has jurisdiction over appeals by a member state or by the Council for annulment of decisions and recommendations made by the High Authority on the grounds of lack of legal competence, substantial procedural violations, violation of the Treaty or of any rule of law relating to its application, or abuse of power. The judgments of the Court, like the decisions of the High Authority, are binding throughout the territory of the member states (Art. 32-45).

Economic and Social Provisions. According to the economic and social provisions of the Treaty, the High Authority is to carry on a permanent study of markets and price tendencies, publish program forecasts dealing with production, consumption, exports and imports, and work out general programs with respect to modernization, the long-term orientation of manufacturing, and the expansion of productive capacity. The High Authority may raise funds necessary to accomplish its mission by placing levies on the production of coal and steel and by borrowing. Funds attained through levies, which may not exceed one per cent of the average value of production, are to cover administrative expenses. The funds obtained by borrowing may be used by the High Authority to grant loans. The member states must assure a free transfer of funds derived from levies and loans, to the extent necessary to their use for the purposes set forth in the Treaty.

The High Authority may facilitate investment programs by granting loans to enterprises or by giving its guarantee to loans which may be obtained elsewhere. In order to encourage a coordination of investments, the High Authority may require enterprises to submit their individual investment programs in advance. The High Authority may then issue an opinion on such programs, accompanied by a justification which must be brought to the attention of the government concerned. An unfavorable opinion by the Authority has the force of a decision and the effect of prohibiting the enterprise concerned from using resources other than its own funds. The High Authority may impose fines on unapproved programs put into effect by enterprises violating this investment provision (Art. 54). Another objective of the Authority is to encourage technical and economic research which is expected to lead to an exceptional reduction in labor requirements in the coal or steel industries. In order to meet unemployment problems thus created, the High Authority may provide other activities in order to assure employment to released workers. Or it may pay indemnities to workers until they can obtain new employment. It may also grant allowances for reinstallation expenses and finance the technical retraining of workers who have to change their employment.

Consumption and Production Regulated. The High Authority is to cooperate with governments in the regulation or influencing of general consumption, particularly that of public services (Art. 57). In the event of a decline in demand, the High Authority, after conferring with the Consultative Committee and obtaining the concurrence of the Council, must establish a system of production quotas. If the High Authority fails to act, one of the member states may bring the matter to the attention of the Council which, acting by unanimous vote, may require the High Authority to establish a system of production quotas. In particular, the High Authority may regulate the production rate of enterprises by appropriate levies on overproduction. The sums thus obtained are to be earmarked for the support of those enterprises which produce even less than the official rate, in order that the continued employment of their workers is insured. Enterprises violating the quota decisions are levied with fines not in excess of a sum equal to the value of overproduction (Art. 58).

Consumption Priorities and Allocation Quotas. If the Community is faced with a serious shortage of coal and steel, the High Authority may establish consumption priorities and determine the allocation of the Community's resources among all industries, exports, and other consumption. If the High Authority fails to take these steps, the Council, acting by unanimous vote after consultation with the High Authority, shall determine the priorities and allocation quotas, which are to be carried out under the responsibility of the member governments. In situations of serious shortages the High Authority may also decide on the establishment of export restrictions to third countries. If the High Authority should fail to act, the Council may impose such restrictions. Enterprises violating these decisions may be fined at a maximum of twice the value of the illegitimate trade (Art. 59).

Maximum and Minimum Prices. As to the price policies of the Community, the following practices are declared to be contrary to the objectives of the Treaty and are therefore prohibited: unfair competitive practices—in particular, purely temporary or purely local price reductions in order to acquire a monopoly position within the common market; and discriminatory practices based on the nationality of the buyer. However, the High Authority, after due consultation with the Consultative Committee and the Council, may fix for one or more products: (a) maximum prices and minimum prices within the market and (b) minimum or maximum export prices. If the High Authority should fail to act, the Council, by unanimous vote, may invite the High Authority to fix such prices. In order to prevent the price of coal from being established at the level of production costs of the most costly mine, the High Authority, after conferring with the Consultative Committee, may authorize subsidies to high-cost mines. The High Authority may impose fines not to exceed twice the value of the illegitimate sales upon enterprises violating these provisions. In the event of second offense, the fine maximum may be doubled (Art. 60-64).

Equilibrium Through Subsidies. All enterprises and associations of enterprises are forbidden to prevent, restrict, or impede competition within the common market, and in particular: (a) to fix or influence prices; (b) to restrict or control production, technical development, or investments; (c) to allocate markets, products, customers, or sources of supply. If any action of a member state should impede competition and if such an action is likely to create a disequilibrium by increasing the costs of production, the High Authority may ask that state either to remove such effects or to grant assistance to such enterprises. This provision is also applicable in case a similar disequilibrium is caused by variations in wages and working conditions. Even if such variations are not the result of a government act, the High Authority may authorize a state to grant assistance to enterprises whose wage costs impede the competitive position (Art. 65-67).

Double Control of Wages and Benefits. The methods of fixing wages and social benefits in various member states remain unaffected, provided the following situations do not exist: (a) abnormally low wages fixed by enterprises or member governments which entitle the High Authority to make recommendations for raising wage rates; (b) a lower standard of living for labor caused by wage reductions and used by enterprise for permanent improvement of its competitive position, which entitles the High Authority to make recommendations to assure compensatory benefits to the labor force. If an enterprise should fail to conform to a recommendation made to it, the High Authority may impose fines and daily penalty payments not to exceed twice the amount of unfair savings in labor costs. As to the movement of labor, the member states renounce any restriction on employment of workers from other member states, provided they conform with standards of qualification. This commitment, however, is subject to the limitation imposed by the fundamental needs of health and public order. In order to assure

agreement on "qualification," the member states are to work out
common definitions and standards. Where an expansion of production in the coal and steel industries might be hampered by a shortage of qualified labor, the member states agree to adapt their
immigration regulations to the extent necessary to eliminate that
situation. In particular, the member states agree to collaborate in
the reemployment of workers from coal and steel industries of other
member states. Also government arrangements are to be made so
that social security measures do not stand in the way of the movement of labor (Art. 68, 69).

Uniform Transportation Rates. The member states agree to abolish all discriminations in transport rates of the nationalized railroads.
Different rate scales, different prices, and transport provisions for
coal and steel, originating in or destined for another country of the
Community, are prohibited (Art. 70-74).

Protection Through Tariffs. The competence of member governments concerning commercial policies remains unaffected. With
respect to customs duties on coal and steel toward third countries,
however, the High Authority or the Council by unanimous decision
may fix minimum rates below which the member states are bound
not to lower their duties and maximum rates above which they are
bound not to raise such duties. Between these limits the member
governments are free to set their tariff rates. The administration of
import and export licensing toward third countries is the responsibility of the governments in question which, however, are subject
to supervision by the High Authority.

Where non-member countries, or enterprises situated in such
countries, are engaging in dumping operations or other practices
condemned by the Havana Charter, the High Authority is empowered to take all measures necessary to meet these practices. If a
difference between outside prices and inside prices is due only to
competitive conditions contrary to the provisions of the Treaty, the
High Authority, with the concurrence of the Council, may also make
recommendations to member governments on restrictive policies to
which they are free to resort under the international agreements.
Finally, the High Authority may recommend restrictions if coal or
steel is imported in relatively increased quantities, and if such imports inflict or threaten to inflict serious damage on production
within the common market (Art. 71-75).

Two Preliminary Stages to the Common Market. Finally, the
member governments agreed that the Community shall remain in
effect for fifty years from the date of its entry into force. In a by-law

to the Treaty, the contracting parties resolved that the common market is to be established after two preliminary stages: a preparatory period of six months from the time of the establishment of the High Authority, or from August 10, 1952 to February 10, 1953; a transitional period to last five years from the time of the establishment of the common market, that is to say, from February 10, 1953 to February 9, 1958. This period may be prolonged for a maximum of two years, or until February 9, 1960 (Art. 97).

International Position of the Community. The existence of the Community as a sovereign body alongside states has been recognized by several states since the Community was established. Great Britain, Sweden, the United States, Norway, Denmark, Switzerland, and Austria have accredited to the High Authority special representatives of a diplomatic status. In addition, the governments of Great Britain and the United States have established a close and lasting association with the Community through the creation of a "Joint Committee" which includes the President and several members of the High Authority, the Head and the members of the British delegation and a staff of experts.

Close relations were also established between the Community and the Council of Europe. The High Authority not only communicates its reports to the Consultative Assembly of the Council of Europe, but it also has agreed to participate in certain meetings of its organs and follows with interest its work in economic and social fields. Furthermore, the parliaments of the six member states have, in most cases, elected to the Common Assembly of the Community those of their members who were already delegated to the Consultative Assembly of the Council of Europe.

Towards Political Unification. As the Coal and Steel Community is believed to constitute an essential step towards European unification, further progress is expected to result from an extension of the scope and method of the Coal and Steel Community. With this in mind, the Council of Ministers empowered the Common Assembly, on December 10, 1952, to draw up a Treaty of European Political Community. Only five days later, the Common Assembly constituted itself an "Ad Hoc Assembly," composed of the 87 delegates of the Common Assembly and 9 members chosen by the Consultative Assembly of the Council of Europe. In addition, 13 observers represented the countries of the Council of Europe that do not belong to the Coal and Steel Community. The Ad Hoc Assembly then set up an "Ad Hoc Commission" which it entrusted with drawing up the draft treaty. During the following weeks, this Commission adopted a preliminary draft of a constitution for a European Political Community which it presented to the Ad Hoc Assembly in January 1953, in Strasbourg. The Commission also prepared a draft treaty comprising a Statute for the European Community which was accepted by the Assembly and immediately sent to the Foreign Ministers of the member countries.[7]

Community in Operation. In the first General Report of the High Authority on the activities of the Community, published in April 1953, its first decisions regarding the establishment of the common market for coal, iron ore, and scrap were given. The price policies of the member states before the establishment of the Community are reviewed and its first decisions are presented. In Germany, according to the report (No. 63) maximum prices for coal were fixed for the coal fields and the lignite mines by the German government. In Belgium, prices for coal were fixed by the Belgian government, but there was no official price control in the case of coke. In France, the government determined the general level of prices, and on this basis the "Charbonnages de France" calculated average prices for the various coal fields; on this basis the prices for the different grades were fixed in each coal field. In the Netherlands, the government fixed the "delivered" prices for the consumers; these prices were identical in every part of the country for each grade of coal, whether imported or home-produced. In Italy, coal prices were government-fixed, both for home-produced and imported coal. Lastly, in Luxembourg, the government fixed import prices and transport charges, and laid down uniform prices for the various grades of coal. This was the situation before the Community was established. Now, having sought the opinion of the Consultative Committee and having consulted the Council of Ministers, the High Authority itself decided to fix maximum prices for coal. Absolute maximum prices were fixed for each category, and the price of any grade of coal within each category was decreed not to exceed the maximum price. Furthermore, as it is the chief responsibility of the High Authority to determine the level of coal prices, the High Authority, at the outset, fixed average prices for each category of coal which must not be exceeded. Finally, for certain grades in short supply, for which prices were very firm, the High Authority fixed maximum prices. Consequently, the High Authority, in its first weeks of operation, fixed average maximum prices, a maximum price

[7] European Coal and Steel Community, *First General Report of the High Authority,* August 10, 1952 to April 12, 1953. See also, French Embassy, Press and Information Division, *European Affairs,* Document No. 2, June 1953.

per category for each coalfield, and special maximum prices for particular grades which were deemed to be in short supply.

Other activities of the European Community, during the first half-year of its existence, were still in the formative stage. In particular, with respect to problems arising from the operation of the Common Market, such as turnover taxes, depreciation and price-scales, agreements and concentrations, the manpower situation, free movement of labor, wages and working conditions, occupational training, construction of workers' houses and related problems, the High Authority was waiting for statistical information and the results of inquiries before determining the direction of its future action.

SOME CRITICISM

The European Coal and Steel Community has raised more widespread interest and stimulated more public discussion in the field of European integration than all other projects and attempts at unification. Its relative success is acknowledged without reserve and scarcely a dissenting voice doubts its significance for European progress toward peace and unity. Since its inauguration many similar plans have been developed for communities in other economic sectors, such as the project of a European agricultural community and of a Transport Pool which would invest the power of controls in new High Authorities. The "functional approach" to integration has proved feasible—at least this is the belief of most contemporary writers and experts in the field of foreign affairs.

Indeed, it is surprising and fascinating to observe how six European nations, which fought and quarreled with each other for many decades, have suddenly decided to establish a European economic community. What has happened to persuade the governments to embark on a road of integration and unity? Was it the last war, this dreadful and gruesome experience of nations? No, this cannot be, for history shows that wars were fought and followed by other wars. Was it a change of economic outlook and political ideology which made the European nations despise conflict and prefer peace and cooperation? No, for we fail to find evidence of a change in political, social, and economic ideologies. The same ideas which influenced and determined past policies still prevail in the minds of men and determine national and party policies. Is there any valid argument for peace and cooperation which was not valid before? No! What then has caused the European governments to pool their coal and steel production within less than a year after Robert Schuman called upon them to unite? What has caused the respective parliaments to ratify the Treaty by large majorities? The answer lies in the realm of politics—in the opportunity for numerous European parties to realize an old and essential point in their party platforms through participation in the "functional approach" towards unification. This point is the *socialization of basic industries*. And the European Coal and Steel Community is the realization of this point.

Socialization of the Coal and Steel Industries. It is the essence of socialism that all the means of production are in the control of society. It does not matter in what level of organized society the power to economic control is vested—whether in a community, state, or national government, or in a supranational organization. Nor is the fundamental character of socialization altered if the coal and steel industries are socialized through transfer of legal ownership from individuals to government, or the government merely conducts the planning and exercises executive controls. The institution of private property is then preserved in a formal legalistic sense, while in fact there is only public ownership, i.e., government control over the employment of the factors of production of the coal and steel industries. In an unhampered market society the profit-seeking producer and proprietor employ the factors of production for the satisfaction of consumers' wants. In order to derive the benefits from his property, the proprietor must unconditionally submit to the wishes of the public. For it is the public—the consumers—who, through buying and abstention from buying, daily decide anew what shall be produced and who shall manage the production process.

The European Coal and Steel Community reverses the production structure and abolishes the social function of ownership, i.e., its employment in the best possible way for the consumers' benefit. It is the institutions of the Community that are defining the general objectives of production (Art. 5). They decide on the financing of production programs and on construction and operation of production facilities. They control investments and financial assistance and may prohibit enterprises to resort to capital and money markets to finance their expansion programs (Art. 54-56). Having decided what shall be produced and who shall produce it, the institutions of the Community are to regulate or influence general consumption (Art. 57). The High Authority not only may establish a system of production quotas but also consumption priorities, and it may determine the allocation of the coal and steel resources among consumers

(Art. 58-59). It may fix maximum and minimum prices for goods consumed in the territory of the Community as well as for goods exported to other countries (Art. 60-64). It may restrict the importation of coal and steel and thus decrease the supply for consumers (Art. 71-75). Finally, having regulated production, fixed prices, and allocated quotas of consumption, the institutions of the Community may determine the costs of production by deciding wage rates and other benefits to labor employed in the coal and steel industries (Art. 68). In all these economic decisions it is the High Authority or other institutions of the Community that are sovereign. The public, the consumers, no longer control the production process. Through buying or abstention from buying they no longer determine the price and market structure. The Treaty constituting the European Coal and Steel Community has put the consumers in the care of supranational trustees.

Politicians and Union Secretaries in Control. The institutions of trusteeship, according to provisions of the Treaty, are made up of politicians and laymen in the coal and steel business. The members of the High Authority are government-appointed and "may not exercise any business or professional activities, paid or unpaid, nor acquire or hold, directly or indirectly, any interest in any business related to coal and steel during their term of office or for a period of three years thereafter" (Art. 9). The Assembly is composed of parliamentarians whom the parliaments of each of the member states designate once a year from among their own membership (Art. 21). The Council is composed of representatives designated by the member states from among members of their administration, (Art. 27). The judges of the Court "may not acquire or hold, directly or indirectly, any interest in any business related to coal or steel during their term of office and during a period of three years thereafter" (Art. 4 of the Code of the Court of Justice). Thus it is fair and reasonable to assume that the members of the institutions of the Community are politicians, parliamentarians, party and union secretaries, who are entrusted with the administration of two vast industrial combines. At any rate, it is undeniable that the *legal owners* do not and cannot play any decisive role in the institutions of the European Coal and Steel Community.

The socialization of the factors of production employed in the coal and steel industries has been well anchored and entrenched by the Treaty constituting the Community. It is true these industries had been subject to extensive government controls and regulations prior to the Treaty. However, in most member states the controls and regulations were established through government decree and could be abolished through a simple countermanding decree by the same or a following administration. The Treaty, however, sealed the socialization for half a century to come when the parties agreed that the Community shall remain in effect for fifty years from the date of its entry into force. Is it surprising, then, that numerous European parties, whose platforms have long demanded "socialization of basic industries," approved this "functional approach" towards European unification? Is it surprising, then, that the Treaty which comprised the realization of old and essential hopes of millions of Europeans was ratified by large majorities of the respective parliaments? There cannot be any doubt as to the answer to these questions.

Does the Community Render War Unthinkable? Robert Schuman, the author of the Treaty constituting the Coal and Steel Community, gave expression to another hope connected with the realization of the Community. According to Schuman, France "envisaged the creation of such strong organic bonds among the European nations—Germany in particular included—that no German government could break them, and the establishment of a living and permanent community that would put an end to old antagonisms and usher in an era of profitable collaboration. . . . Thus we hoped," says Schuman, "that considerations of narrow national interest would be replaced by regard for the common interest, that national antagonism would be transcended, and that, since none of the partners had control of its own coal and steel, war among them would be unthinkable." [8]

These hopes and objectives of the Treaty are undoubtedly praiseworthy. But we must raise the question whether the Community with its control over steel and coal production and consumption really can render war among member states unfeasible and whether the creation of economic bonds among the European nations really ends old antagonisms and leads to collaboration. We indeed doubt the correctness of both contentions, and we maintain that the European Coal and Steel Community is not the slightest check on a member state's ability to wage war on its neighbor if it so decides. Moreover, it is our conviction that the Coal and Steel Community will be the *source of new conflicts and additional antagonisms.*

The assertion that war is unthinkable among the member states of the Community because the national governments lack control over coal and steel industries is incompatible with past experience

[8] Robert Schuman, *Ibid.*, p. 353.

THE EUROPEAN COAL AND STEEL COMMUNITY 251

and, especially, with the European history of the last fifty years. It also reveals an astonishing degree of naïveté and superficiality.

Our age is an age of total state and total war. Long ago, governments, in the name of the majority, began to put the individual under public tutelage. Governments began to control the means of production, to regulate the foreign relations of their citizens, and to resort to discrimination and coercion against the citizens of other states. Such policies inevitably led and are still leading to war because they are based on national discrimination and protection of one group against another. Where there is no freedom of trade and no freedom for the individual, there is conflict and strife. The final resort to war logically presupposes all other forms of international conflict. It presupposes, in particular, the removal of all obstacles that confront a government determined to seek solution of its grievances by war. The least of all worries is the breaking of treaties.

World War II could never have broken out if the numerous international treaties to which Germany was a party had been observed and fulfilled. In 1899 the German government voluntarily and unconditionally signed the Convention of The Hague which purports that a government, before resorting to mobilization and war, has to appeal to neutral powers for mediation of the conflict.[9] In 1907, similar provisions were included in the International Convention for peaceful mediation of conflicts in which the contracting parties also agreed that armed hostilities should not begin without preceding information and formal declaration of war. In 1919, the Treaty of Versailles prohibited German rearmament (Part V) and the occupation and fortification of the Rhineland by German armed forces (Art. 42-44). It determined that Austria should stay independent (Art. 80). Germany also acknowledged the independence of Czechoslovakia (Art. 81) and the secession of certain German territories. In 1925, at Locarno, the German government signed treaties of mutual guarantees and mediation with Belgium, France, Great Britain, Italy, Czechoslovakia, and Poland. In 1926, Germany signed similar treaties with the Netherlands and Denmark, and in 1929 with Luxembourg. The Kellogg-Briand Pact, which outlawed wars of aggression, was signed by the German government in 1928. When Hitler came to power in 1933, he signed a series of treaties of non-aggression and friendship of which the Treaty with Poland, in January 1934, and that with Soviet Russia, in August 1939, are most significant. All these conventions and treaties, solemnly concluded

[9] *Das Urteil von Nürnberg* (The Verdict of Nurnberg), Munich, 1946, pp. 56-58.

by a German government, were broken and disregarded by Hitler. And we may also infer that another "Hitler," animated by similar ideas of power and government omnipotence, would not be hindered in the least from invading and conquering other states by the existence of new and additional treaties. But the problem of world peace is just this: to make the world safe from aggression by dictators and governments of the Hitler type. We need not fear men who believe in man's liberty and in our civilization, even if there were no peace treaties.

A Source of New Conflicts. But not only is the Treaty unlikely to avoid war among the member states—it will also be the source of new conflicts. The governing bodies of the Community hold the power to define the general objectives of production. They decide on the financing of production programs and on construction and operation of production facilities. They control investments and financial assistance and may prohibit enterprises to resort to capital and money markets for financing their expansion programs. Having decided what shall be produced and who shall produce it, they may regulate or influence everybody's consumption. Having established a system of production quotas, they may order consumption priorities and determine the allocation of the coal and steel resources among consumers. They may fix maximum and minimum prices and restrict the importation of coal and steel. Finally, they may determine the costs of production by increasing wage rates and other benefits to workers employed in the coal and steel industries. But the use of any one of these powers inevitably leads to national conflicts.

Let us look at Article 61, for example. This article gives the High Authority and the Council the right to fix maximum and minimum prices. Now, if they really fix maximum prices that are lower than free market prices, certain coal mines and steel mills are run at a loss. Their production costs exceed the revenue obtained under the maximum prices. Consequently, production in those mines and mills is restricted or even stopped. Unemployment arises, and output in coal and steel decreases. Consumers then no longer can buy the quantities which they used to buy and which they would like to buy. In such a situation the authorities of the Community are empowered to set up consumption priorities and determine the distribution of coal and steel. So far, this example contains two sources for national conflicts. First, a conflict will arise if most of those coal mines and steel mills whose operation is connected with high costs are located in one state only, say, in Belgium. The losses and unemployment caused by the official price ceilings will be concentrated in the coal and steel industries in Belgium, and managements as well as workers naturally will complain about the policies of the Community. A conflict between Belgium and the other member states, whose mines and mills operate at lower costs, has thus come into existence. The second course of conflict is the power of the Community to allocate and distribute coal and steel products. What should be the principle of "fair distribution"? Let us assume we live in a period of great scarcity. The order books of mines and mills are filled for many months in advance, and coal consumers are pressing for early delivery. Let us assume that a few French coal consumers succeed in convincing the High Authority that their demand is most urgent. The High Authority then allocates to them an extra and immediate supply of coal, and orders German producers to ship a certain quantity to France. Immediately thousands of German coal consumers will protest against the delivery of "German coal" which is so urgently needed in their own country. German building construction is retarded, other reconstruction is delayed, all because "German coal is shipped to France." Or the example can be reversed. The High Authority orders French steel producers to sell their products to German consumers who succeeded in proving an extraordinarily urgent demand. Then thousands of French consumers will complain about "French steel" being shipped to Germany and their own needs being neglected in favor of the Germans.

The use of regulatory powers by institutions of the Community leads to national conflicts. Fixing maximum prices, determining production quotas and consumption priorities, allocating products, controlling investments and financial assistance, and exercising the power to prohibit expansion programs inevitably lead to national conflicts. Can you imagine German enterprises being prohibited from expanding while competing French enterprises are allowed to grow, perhaps even by use of German capital and money or with financial assistance to which the German enterprises are forced to contribute? But this is precisely what Articles 54-56 of the Treaty mean. Or can you imagine cheap German coal being imported into France while there are depression and unemployment in the French coal industry? Hardly—the French will not allow it. Or can you imagine German coal being imported to France while there is great scarcity in Germany? The Germans would not allow it. Or can you imagine Italian coal and steel workers being allowed to immigrate into Germany, competing with German workers, and causing German wage rates to drop? The German coal and steel labor unions would oppose it. "But the governing bodies of the Community will not conduct such policies," the retort might be. "They will leave German coal in Germany, French steel in France, Belgian capital in Belgium, and Italian workers in Italy." We agree. For if they conduct Community policies, they will inevitably bring about national conflicts and the destruction of the Community.

A Supranational Monopoly. With the vast powers given to the High Authority—and especially the power to assign production quotas and regulate capital investments—the High Authority becomes in effect a supranational monopoly, which substitutes concerted action for competition and constriction for expansion. The Community is a monopoly of coal and steel supply. The whole Western European supply is controlled by the governing bodies of the Community. They are in the position to restrict the supply in order to raise the price for their products. And they need not fear outer-Community competition as Articles 71-75 give them the right to limit imports. These are the characteristics of a monopoly.

But can the Community make use of its position to charge monopolistic prices? It undoubtedly can because the demand for coal and steel, which are essential for many other industries, is such that a moderate restriction in the supply causes prices to rise considerably. Millions of consumers depend on coal and steel. Now, whether the High Authority will employ its powers and really embark upon restricting output in order to raise prices depends entirely on the men who formulate the policies of the Community. If they really exercise the powers, they will make an old-fashioned national cartel look innocuous, because their policy would rest not merely upon the protective policies of one member state, but will have the backing of the courts and police of all member states. "There are already a few uneasy signs of this," says the *Wall Street Journal.* "The prices of many steel products in Europe have been declining; some steel bars formerly selling at $150 a ton have been offered at $84 a ton. As a result, there are reports that the High Authority will set minimum prices to 'bolster' the market. One dispatch from Luxembourg hints that the whole steel price level will be raised by decree." [10]

A monopolistic restriction of production, however, inevitably leads to national conflicts and disruption of the common market. While differences among Community producers are unlikely to result, the conflict of interests will be limited, on the one hand, to producers and, on the other, to consumers. The restriction of pro-

[10] *The Wall Street Journal,* February 13, 1953, p. 6, in "Review and Outlook."

duction by producers makes prices rise. The consumers, however, clamor for lower prices. "But how does this producer-consumer antagonism lead to national conflicts?" it might be asked. Well, it is a matter of fact that three member nations of the Community (Holland, Luxembourg, and Italy) are mainly coal- and steel-consuming nations, while Germany, France, and Belgium produce more than they consume. They sell the surplus to Holland, Luxembourg, and Italy and other consumers outside the Community. It thus becomes clear that a restriction in output and the following rise in prices will favor the three exporting nations while the consuming nations are bound to be hurt. Thus, national interests conflict with each other. If the High Authority then does not abandon its monopolistic policies, it will cause the consuming member nations to leave the Community and the common market to collapse. If they should hesitate to abandon the Community because of their pledge to uphold the Treaty for a period of fifty years, they undoubtedly will retaliate against the monopolistic prices with other restrictive measures against the coal-exporting countries.

Monopoly and Free Market. The Coal and Steel Community is of a peculiar nature. One face of this gigantic supranational structure is clearly monopolistic and is directed at constriction of production and at monopolistic prices. Another face is pointed at the objective of freeing Europe's coal and steel industry from the imprisonment of national boundaries. It is directed at an increase of production and at making steel available at lower prices. At least, this is what the fathers and advocates of the Community assure us and want us to believe. But there is a contradiction. At first they set up a monopoly and provide it with ample power of compulsion. Then they say: "Go ahead, be free and compete with each other. We'll watch you!" This is like building a formidable penitentiary, appointing the warden and other officials, and inviting free people to live in it with the freedom to come and go as they wish. If the member governments really wanted freedom of trade and competition, why did they not merely take down the barriers of boundaries and other government restrictions? Why don't they merely leave business alone? Where there is government regulation and control, there is no freedom. And where there is freedom, there is no government control.

We do not know in what direction the Community train will finally roll. But we do know that a large majority of politicians and statesmen embrace the ideology of control, advocate protection and regulation, and oppose individual freedom and free enterprise. We may thus fairly assume that the politician-engineers will soon head the Community train towards monopoly and restriction.

Community versus "Social Justice." Prior to the establishment of the common market, coal and steel industries were controlled extensively by the governments of member states. Prices were fixed that were considered "fair" and suitable to the national economy. Wages were determined that were believed to do justice to coal and steel workers. Naturally each government exercised its controls according to its own concept of fairness and justice, which differed more or less from that of other governments. Consequently, wide price and wage discrepancies developed. But the common market, on which the European Coal and Steel Community is based, would inevitably wipe out national discrepancies in coal and steel prices. This means that common market prices would replace the "fair" prices fixed by national governments.

The substitution of uniform market prices for national prices which conform with the conception of justice necessarily creates dissention and conflict. Even a compromise between the various national prices must be unjust, as justice is not open to compromise.

Consider the example of Belgian coal prices. Because of previous government restriction and protection many Belgian coal mines work with higher production costs than other mines in the Community. Without this protection, which the Belgian government granted for reasons of social justice and "national interest," mines with high costs of production would have been undersold by domestic and foreign competitors. As a result, only mines with low production costs would have remained in operation. Government protection and restriction, however, made Belgian coal prices rise until mines with high production costs could stay in business. In addition, the Belgian government even paid subsidies in the amount of 200 million Belgian francs per year to the most costly mines to keep them in operation.[11]

Now, assume that the High Authority would really establish a common market with a uniform market price. The Belgian mines with high production costs would close their gates immediately. They would be undersold by efficient Belgian, German, Dutch, and French competition. But do you think the Belgian government, thousands of coal miners who would lose their jobs, and the coal miner's unions and their representatives in the Belgian parliament would accept such effects of the market price? Or do you believe that the market price would be just and fair in the eyes of those Bel-

[11] European Coal and Steel Community, *Ibid.*, p. 83.

gians who are adversely affected? What do you think the unions and political groups that have worked and fought for "fair" national prices will do about those lower Community prices? Will they not protest, strike, slow down, pressure the Belgian parliament, and attempt to influence the institutions of the Community to abandon their policy? There cannot be any doubt that the pressure groups who are responsible for national prices will fight market prices; and they are well organized and powerful, to which the height of national prices clearly attests.

The High Authority fully recognizes the situation. It pays the Belgian mines a subsidy in the amount of 1350 million francs of which the Belgian government is ordered to provide one half and the German and Dutch mines the other half.[12] Now the mines with high production costs can charge the common market price and yet stay in business. "But what will happen at the end of the transition period when all subsidies must cease?" you will ask. All the effects that subsidies avert for the time being will then appear. Subsidies only postpone the inevitable conflict between the adherents of common market prices with those of "fair" national prices. In no way do they solve the conflict.

The Denial of Economics. Economics is the science of the regularity of the means-and-effect relations in human economic action. It is a science that deals with means for the attainment of ends, the choice and preference of which, however, stay outside of its sphere. An important task of economics, under present-day conditions, is the analysis of the means-and-effect relations of economic actions of the state, and in particular, the effects of government interference with prices, wages, and other economic phenomena.

Let us take the example of government interference with prices. An economic analysis shows that market prices equalize supply and demand, that is to say, the volume of demand coincides with the volume of supply. If the government fixes prices that differ from market prices, this equilibrium of demand and supply is abandoned. Maximum prices, for example, prevent potential buyers from buying, although they are willing to pay the maximum price. Minimum prices keep potential sellers from selling, although they are willing to accept the minimum price or even less. Thus the fixed prices lose their significance for the allocation of goods. Governments then resort to rationing. Production or consumption quotas are determined.

But the most important feature of the market price is that it directs the employment of the factors of production into those fields

[12] *Ibid.*, p. 84.

where they are most urgently needed. A government's price ceiling, however, stops the inflow of additional factors of production and keeps output lower than it would be with higher prices. Minimum prices, on the other hand, keep output higher than it would be with lower prices.

The same holds true of government regulation of wages. A "wage stop" below the height of the market causes a scarcity of labor. On the other hand, minimum wages above the height of the market bring about unemployment. This knowledge is the result of irrefutable economic reasoning.[13]

Now let us compare this knowledge with the price and wage provisions of the Treaty constituting the European Coal and Steel Community. The inevitable outcome of those provisions is manifestly contrary to the intentions of the fathers of the Community. Article 61 gives the High Authority the right to fix maximum prices within the common market, if it deems that such a decision is necessary for the establishment of the lowest prices possible. At the same time, it is the objective of the Community to produce at the highest possible level of productivity. But this is nonsense. The objective asserted stands in outright contradiction to the means applied. At first the Authority is to make coal and steel more easily accessible to the consumer through the highest possible level of productivity. But then it is to resort to means, that is to say, maximum prices, which can only restrict the level of productivity and the volume of coal and steel for consumers.

The same contradiction is apparent in the provisions concerning minimum prices and wages. Article 68 gives the High Authority the right to assure workers "compensatory benefits." This means that it can interfere if it deems wages too low. The objective of this provision is the protection of the worker from exploitation by the employer. The result of minimum wage decrees, however, is unemployment. Thus, while it is the objective to further the interest of the worker, they are injured instead.

Numerous contradictions of this kind could be cited. In order to enumerate and analyze them all, a comprehensive treatise on economics would probably have to be written. Here, however, we may limit ourselves to raising the question whether the founders of the Community earnestly wanted a realization of the stated objectives and merely mis-selected the means, or whether they wanted and needed the means for the realization of other objectives. We are

---

[13] For detailed analysis of the market's reaction to government interference, see L. v. Mises, *Human Action*, p. 756 *et seq.*

inclined to assume the former. If we deny the existence of a regularity of the means-and-effect relations in human economic action, or, if we apply some simple notions of kindergarten-economics, we may begin to understand the reasoning of the founders of the Community. It might have run like this: "To contribute to economic expansion and common prosperity we shall assure the highest possible level of productivity. If prices should rise 'too high' we shall resort to maximum prices. If prices should fall 'too low' we shall resort to minimum prices. If the workers' compensation is unsatisfactory to us, we shall assure him minimum wages." How wonderful it sounds! And what a nonsense it is! It denies the existence of economics and rejects two hundred years of economic thought.

A Common Market Without Convertible Currencies. When a coal dealer in New York has received a car-load of coal from Pennsylvania, he signs a check drawn against his own bank in New York and mails it to the seller in Pennsylvania. Thus the whole transaction is completed. In the common market of the European Coal and Steel Community transactions proceed in a different way. When a coal dealer in Paris, France, intends to order a car-load of coal in Duisburg, Germany, he must apply with the Bank of France through mediation of his own commercial bank for allocation of the necessary media of foreign exchange, i.e., German marks. If the proper bank authority approves his transaction and allocates the needed quantity of marks to him, our dealer may put in his order. When he finally receives his car-load of coal, his own bank will charge his account and pay the purchase price to the Bank of France, which in turn reports the transaction to the European Payments Union, which in turn then attempts to balance out this transaction against others.[14] This is how the common market operates. The Community is to assure free movement of coal and steel without assurance of the freedom to make and receive payment. But how common is a market where you can deliver goods without the freedom to receive payment, or where you can receive goods but cannot pay?

It is true that the Treaty constituting the Community contains two provisions dealing with this matter. Article 86, Par. 3, reads as follows: "To the extent of the competence, the member States will take all appropriate measures to assure the international payments arising out of trade in coal and steel within the common market; they will lend assistance to each other to facilitate such payments." You will note the ambiguity of the term "all appropriate measures." What is appropriate? Is it appropriate for a member state to allo-

[14] For more details, see section on "European Payments Union," p. 221 *et seq.*

cate $10 million in foreign exchange for purchases of coal and iron
if its total exchange reserves amount to only $10 million? Is it ap-
propriate to make payment while its reserves are $20 million or $30
million? That even the authors of the Treaty were in doubt on the
meaning and limit of "appropriate measures" can be inferred from
the provision that the member states are "to lend assistance to each
other to facilitate such measures." It is obvious that certain appropriate measures are not expected from a single member state without assistance by others.

Article 52, which refers to funds at the disposal of the High
Authority, contains a similar provision that leaves the decision on
their transferability with member states. It reads as follows: "The
member States shall take all necessary measures to assure the free
transfer . . . of funds . . . to the extent necessary to their use for the
purposes set forth in the present Treaty. The methods of transfer
among member States, as well as to third countries, . . . shall be
subject of agreements concluded by the High Authority with the
interested governments or the competent bodies; no member State
which applies controls shall be obliged to assure any such transfers
to which it has not explicitly agreed." Can this provision be any
clearer? What will happen if a member state does not agree? It
may have many reasons for its refusal.

Community or Planning: An Alternative. The member nations
have a choice: Either they may have a Community, or they may adhere to their systems of government planning. One choice is incompatible with the other. Assume that a member state, France, for
example, inflates her currency to a greater degree than her neighbor, Germany. French businessmen will then import more coal
and steel from Germany than they would have without inflation.
Or assume that the French government decrees a rise in social costs
as, for example, wages and fringe benefits. This will put the French
industry at a serious disadvantage toward its German competition.
French production will decrease and more coal and steel will be imported from Germany. Or assume that the French government
increases its taxes on business for reasons of social or national necessity. Again French importers will find it more advantageous to import coal and steel from Germany. The more the French government
inflates, or taxes, or increases production costs, the more will French
importers buy in Germany. And the High Authority will ask the
Bank of France "to assure the international payments arising out of
these imports of coal and steel." Undoubtedly, the Bank of France
at first pays. But its foreign exchange reserves fall lower and lower.

At the same time, the French coal and steel industries begin to complain about the effects of inflation, the higher costs of business, and increasing German competition. Finally, many French coal mines and steel mills suffer losses (or greater losses than they otherwise would suffer), and unemployment of capital and labor arises. At this time the foreign exchange reserves of the Bank of France are exhausted or near exhaustion. Something must be done. The French government then has the following alternative: It may cease to make payments for imports of coal and steel because of lack of foreign exchange funds. Without payment, imports stop immediately. And without imports, French production at the old rate is resumed and unemployment disappears. Indeed, a simple and common solution!

The other choice open to the French government is the following: It may refrain from inflating its currency, it may lower its taxes, or decrease the social costs. Thus with lower business costs French coal mining and steel production become profitable again and production in France rises again.

Which road will the government choose? Will it turn against the Coal and Steel Community and refuse foreign exchange payments—in other words, allocate only "fair amounts"—or will it turn its critique at its own policy? Will it shoulder its responsibility for the undesirable state of affairs and henceforth refrain from inflation? Will it lower taxes and social costs even though they are believed to be identical with "social progress"? There cannot be any doubt that it will prefer to declare the Community guilty and cease to allocate foreign exchange payments.

This example is by no means of theoretical interest alone. If nations do not want to return to a gold standard, the depreciation of national currencies through inflation and credit expansion by governments necessarily proceeds at various rates. Similarly, national tax burdens and "social progress" costs will differ from state to state and according to the policy of the governments in power. A free flow of coal and steel within the territory of the Community, however, limits the scope of the monetary, fiscal, and social policies of member states since it forces them to assimilate their policies. Any special burden on an industry by its own government causes it to suffer from higher production costs and favors unburdened competitors in other states of the Community. Subsequently, a government must limit the scope of its own policies or the scope of the Community. And this inescapable alternative for each member government will be with us every day as long as the Community is in existence.

Turnover Taxes versus Community. Goods that move from one country of the Community to another are exposed to different national systems of taxation. The power to tax lies with the national governments. As the Treaty did not limit the sovereignty of the national states to tax, they are free to impose levies wherever they deem fit. One of the many taxes to which modern government may freely resort is the Turnover Tax. It is an efficient tool for government interference with the operation of the common market.

Turnover taxes are sales taxes on transactions that affect a change in ownership on goods in the process of production. Every time goods change hands before they reach the ultimate consumer, they are taxed at a percentage rate of their market value. In the process of steel production, for example, the sale of iron ore by a mine to a steel mill is taxed. When iron scrap is sold to a scrap merchant, it is taxed. When he sells it to a wholesale dealer, it is taxed. When the wholesale dealer sells it to a steel mill, it is taxed. The same is true with respect to transactions in coal needed for steel production. When the steel mill sells the finished product to a steel wholesale dealer, the sale is taxed. When he sells it to a retail merchant, it is taxed. And finally, when he sells it to a consumer, it is taxed again.

This turnover tax can be—and actually is—used for government direction of the inflow and outflow of goods of the common market. A government may tax, it may refund the total tax levied in the process of production, it may refund a certain percentage, and it may levy an "equalization tax" on goods imported from other member states in which taxes are lower.

Consider the following example which actually has led to differences of opinion between Germany and France. When the customs barriers between the member states of the Community were abolished on May 1, 1953, the German price for steel was quoted at 410 German marks per ton (approximately 97.62 U.S. dollars). When steel was exported from Germany, the German government granted a refund of sales taxed at a rate of 4% of the sales price—that means it paid 16.40 marks per ton to the exporter. When the steel was sold in France a turnover tax of 20%, or the equivalent of 78.72 marks, was levied by the French government. German steel offered in France was thus quoted at the equivalent of 472.32 German marks. On the other hand, the French government refunded 16%, or the equivalent of 65.60 German marks, on French steel exported to Germany. The German government then imposed a "tax equalization levy" of 6%, or 20.664 marks, on French steel sold in Germany. The price of French steel consumed in Germany thus was quoted at 365.064 German marks.

Because of differences in taxes, refunds, and "equivalization levies," the following steel prices, quoted in marks, existed in the two countries of the Community: German steel in Germany, 410 marks; French steel in France, 410 marks; German steel in France, 472.32 marks; and French steel in Germany, 365.064 marks. As the Community consists of six member states with diverging taxation systems, 6 different steel prices were calculated in each member state. "But don't prices tend to equalize in a common market?" you will ask. Yes, they do to a certain degree. The differences in prices are brought about through government planning and interference with the market; under the pressure of the common market, governments will be eager to equalize prices through new and additional planning and interference. In the foregoing example of steel prices in Germany and France, the essential difference in prices was finally leveled out in this manner.

In Germany, complaints became loud about the low prices of French steel offered to German consumers. They were charged "too little." Representatives of the steel industry and secretaries of the steel unions protested vigorously against such an "unfair" state of the market. The German press attacked the High Authority for allowing such "unfair" practices which, as they said, would ruin the German steel industry. The *Deutsche Zeitung*, a leading economic periodical in Germany, even came to the conclusion that "it becomes evident again that the main goal of the Community, above all others, is the opening of the larger German market to the French steel industry." [15] Thereafter, the German members of the High Authority proposed that steel exporters should be forced to charge their foreign customers the price of steel *plus* the amount of tax which their own government would refund to them. Consequently, the price of French steel in Germany should thus be raised by 16%, or 65.60 marks. This proposal was rejected by the majority of the members of the High Authority as being incompatible with the application of the Treaty.[16]

But then the German government acted. It was simply intolerable that 50 million Germans should enjoy cheap steel produced in

[15] *Deutsche Zeitung und Wirtschaftszeitung*, May 2, 1953, No. 35, p. 5, in "Die Autokratie der Hohen Behörde."

[16] Haute Autorité, *Rapport Spécial sur l'établissement du marché commun de l'acier*, May, 1953, p. 47, sect. 35.

France. It would raise the German standard of living! What should
happen to those German steel mills which were unable to lower
their prices and meet French competition? Or what should happen
to a few thousand German steel workers who might be forced to
change their jobs? No, those cheap steel prices were intolerable.
In order to equalize French and German prices, the German government had an alternative. Either it could lower its own turnover
taxes which caused the German steel industry to be at a disadvantage towards the French industry, or it could raise its "equalization
tax" on steel imported from France. In the first case, the price for
German steel could be lowered to the point of French prices. In
the second case, the price for French steel would be raised approximately to the height of German prices. You probably have guessed
which of the two ways the German government preferred. It raised
the "equalization tax," of course.[17] Thus, the prices for steel were
high all around, and, in addition, the German Treasury enjoyed
higher tax revenues. The national danger arising from cheap steel
prices was averted and the scope and effect of the common market
corrected. But what happened to the common market and the Community?

Foreign exchange control and the unlimited power to tax are
efficient means of government planning and government intervention. It is true the Treaty constituting the European Coal and Steel
Community abolished the customs barriers within the territory of
the Community. But you probably will raise the question: "What
does the elimination of customs barriers mean for the establishment
of a common market? What is the significance of such a step?" Indeed, it means very little, for customs barriers merely are insignificant tools in the hands of modern government. Controls and the
power to tax are entirely sufficient to direct the individual as governments see fit.

National Controls, Supercontrols, and the Citizen. The common
market established by the Treaty of the six European nations should
not be mistaken for a free market in which the individual is free to
pursue his own purpose as producer or consumer. On the contrary,
it is a market which is controlled and directed by six national governments whose policies are coordinated and supervised by one
supranational authority. As has been pointed out, the power of
member governments to tax has been left unrestrained by the Community Treaty. Some provisions of the Treaty even emphasize the

[17] *Deutsche Zeitung und Wirtschaftszeitung,* May 6, 1953, No. 36, p. 5, in "Aus-
serdeutsche Stahlpreise werden steigen."

freedom of the member state to regulate the economic affairs of its citizens. Article 68, for example, explicitly states that "the method of fixing wages and social benefits in force in the various member States shall not be affected." Of course, this freedom of the state is subject to certain limiting provisions as agreed upon in the Treaty. The power of the national states to enact "social legislation," as, for example, social security laws, industrial supervision and sanitary acts, is not infringed upon by the Treaty. Moreover, collective bargaining acts, workers' codetermination and nationalization laws affecting the coal and steel industries can freely be enacted by national governments. And finally, as has been illustrated before, the payment relations of coal and steel industries in the Community can be regulated through monetary and foreign exchange policies of the member states.

The institutions of the European Coal and Steel Community are entrusted with additional and supplementary powers of control over the actions of the Community citizen. The governing institutions define the general objectives of production. They decide on the financing of production programs and on construction and operation of production facilities. They control investments and decide on the question of financing assistance. Having decided what shall be produced and who shall produce it, the institutions of the Community can regulate the coal and steel consumption of more than 150 million citizens of the Community. They may order production quotas and consumption priorities; they may allocate the goods of the market and fix maximum and minimum prices; they may restrict the importation of coal and steel from third countries; and may determine wage rates and other production costs. These are a few of the many powers of the Community institutions over citizens.

The center point of this eager activity of national and supranational authorities is the citizen. We admit, his well-being is probably the objective of all controls, whether national or supranational. Many adherents of this welfare philosophy cling to the old belief that a planned economy would produce a larger output than the free enterprise system. A well-managed national economy supervised by a neutral supranational authority they say, can increase production and abolish poverty. That this hope is false has been proven repeatedly by the fiasco which every central planner in history experienced within a short time of his planning. Other adherents of this philosophy have long since abandoned this false belief in the superior productivity of a managed economy. But they advocate planning because "it enables us to secure a fairer distribution of wealth and income." We readily admit that such an objective of planning, the realization of someone's ideal of fairness and justice, can be secured only through central management by the group or individual whose ideal is to be realized. But then two questions arise: First, does the planner's ideal concur with all others' ideal of fairness and justice? If it does not, the realization of the planner's ideal will be "unfair" and "unjust" to others. Second, is the realization of someone's ideal of fairness and justice worth the price which all others have to pay? Or does this price lead to more discontent and more injustice than existed before?

It is our belief that a government or supranational authority cannot manage the fields of human welfare with the justice and economy that are possible when these same fields are the direct responsibility of morally sensitive human beings. According to Clarence Manion, "The loss of justice, economy, and effectiveness is increased in the proportion that such governmental management is centralized. . . . Government cannot make men good; neither can it make them prosperous and happy. The evils in society are directly traceable to the vices of individual human beings. It must be remembered that 95 per cent of the peace, order, and welfare existing in human society is always produced by the conscientious practice of man-to-man justice and person-to-person charity. When any part of this important domain of personal virtue is transferred to government, that part is automatically released from the restraints of morality and put into the area of conscienceless coercion. The field of personal responsibility is thus reduced at the same time and to the same extent that the boundaries of irresponsibility are enlarged." [18]

Community and Integration. The European Coal and Steel Community is said to be the first and an essential step towards European unification. It is hoped that further progress toward a united Europe will come from an extension of the scope and method of the Coal and Steel Community. Its "Ad Hoc Assembly" was constituted to draft a treaty of European Political Community. Two final steps remain to be done, say these adherents of unification: first, the European governments have to transform the draft into a treaty; and second, the parliaments have to ratify the treaty. Once these final steps have been achieved, Europe will be united. "A Chamber of Nations" elected by direct universal suffrage from Hamburg to

[18] Clarence Manion, "Legalized Immorality," in *Essays on Liberty,* published by The Foundation for Economic Education, Inc., Irvington-on-Hudson, New York, 1952, p. 23.

Bordeaux and from Antwerp to Brindisi and even to Dakar in French West Africa, will constitute the legislature. An Executive of nine members—formed like the High Authority of the Coal and Steel Community—will execute the European laws. And a Council of Ministers will coordinate the actions of the institutions of the Political Community with those of the governments of the member states. Thus the evolution toward political unity, as well as economic unity, is reaching its last and final stage. United and as an integral part of the free world, Europe can and will survive culturally, economically, and politically.

The difficulties confronting the realization of the plans and hopes of European unity cannot be overestimated. European unification is not merely a process of removing the existing governmental controls or the coordination of such controls by supranational authorities. The crux of the unification problem lies in the nature of ideologies prevailing in the minds of men. Doctrines that advocate and commit governments to policies of economic regulation and development, full employment, inflation and protection, parity and social welfare, have led and still are leading to wide divergencies in the structure of economies. They are the product of willful and central planning and are identical with social welfare and progress. Nations having a desire to unite have a choice: Either they adhere to ideas and policies of planned divergencies and abandon the hope of unification or they abandon the ideas of central planning and render unification possible. There is no other alternative.

The European Coal and Steel Community, seen in the light of this knowledge, merely constitutes an arduous though futile attempt on a road to nowhere. At its best, it can only enjoy a sham existence for half a century to come, a unification *ad hoc et non ultra,* meaningless to all and beneficial to none.

VIII

The Brussels Treaty
and the Western Union

DURING the year 1947 it became evident that Communist Russia showed little signs of being satisfied with the limits of her tremendous postwar expansion. In the Balkans the Communists had extended their influence without regard for the peoples' right to choose freely their government and institutions. In Germany, Russia refused to cooperate in the shaping of a democratic Germany capable of peaceful international cooperation. In Greece and Turkey, Soviet Russia attempted to broaden her influence and draw those countries into the communist orbit. And the communist rule of Poland, Czechoslovakia, and other countries behind the Iron Curtain alarmed the free nations throughout the world.

On January 22 of the following year, Ernest Bevin, the British Foreign Minister, in a major foreign policy address to the House of Commons, called attention to the danger of continuous Soviet expansion and appealed for consolidation of Western Europe. Following his initiative, the *Brussels Treaty* establishing the "Western Union" was concluded on March 17, 1948, by Belgium, France, Luxembourg, the Netherlands, and the United Kingdom. The stated purpose of the Treaty was closer collaboration in economic, social and cultural matters and collective self-defense.[1]

Functions. The principal function of the Western Union was to provide permanent consultive machinery for joint defense against armed aggression. But it also set up a goal to collaborate in economic, social and cultural matters. Automatic military and other assistance in case of armed attack, no matter from what source, was

[1] Department of State, *Bulletin*, May 9, 1948, pp. 600-602.

268

provided for in its Article 4 in which no mention was made of a definite aggressor. It provided simply that "an armed attack in Europe" shall bring the mutual obligation into effect. The Brussels Pact also provided for consultation on a wide range of problems, including "a threat to peace, in whatever area this threat should arise." In agreement with Article 51 of the Charter of the United Nations, Article 5 of the Brussels Pact provided for immediate reporting to the Security Council of all measures taken and for their termination as soon as that body "has taken the measures necessary to maintain international peace and security."

Organization. The Treaty set up a "Consultative Council" composed of the five foreign ministers which was so organized "as to be able to exercise its functions continuously." This Council was a top-level political organ composed of the foreign ministers on a basis of equality. At the first meeting of the Council in Paris in April 1948 it decided:

1. To set up a permanent Commission in London that would meet monthly and act in behalf of the Council. It was to be assisted by a permanent Secretariat;

2. To bring together periodically the ministers responsible for economic and military matters;

3. To set up a permanent Military Committee under the direct authority of the Consultative Council.

In addition, several subordinate committees, boards, and subcommittees of ministers or experts on military, economic, social, and cultural questions were established, all being responsible to the Consultative Council.

One Year of Operation. During their first year of operation the several committees and commissions immediately got to work planning the defense of the West, sharing responsibilities, studying problems of logistics, working towards standardization of arms and equipment, and coordinating production of war materials.

In the social and cultural fields, the Brussels Treaty Organization has taken credit for several achievements by its various commissions, the most important of which are: multilateral conventions on social security, agreements on the exchange of student employees, on government regulation of wages and conditions of frontier workers living on one side of a national boundary and working on the other, on social and medical matters, and on public health. Furthermore, its commissions have also taken credit for the fact that visas have been abolished among the five member countries and "cultural identity cards" have been substituted. Agreements have been reached on the exchange of students, young laborers, and university professors. All these measures are said to build up good will step by step and thus contribute to the establishment of a solid foundation on which it will be easier to build a permanent structure of a European union.[2]

Inactivation of the Western Union. The Western Union has served as a forerunner of other European organizations and of the North Atlantic Treaty Organization which are now pursuing its purposes on a broader basis. With the signing of the North Atlantic Treaty and the activation of the Supreme Headquarters Allied Powers, Europe (SHAPE), the military importance of the Brussels Treaty Organization temporarily passed into the background. The members of the commissions and committees were assigned to other missions. As a result of the formation of the "Organization for European Economic Cooperation" (OEEC) embracing all the Brussels powers only one month after the Brussels Pact was signed, the economic provisions of the Western Union Treaty lost their significance and never became a major concern of Western Union. In addition, the Council of Europe assumed its social and cultural functions on a much broader basis.

A Treaty on a European Defense Community. For more than four years following the establishment of the Western Union, the imagination of world public opinion was caught by another defense treaty—the treaty constituting a European Defense Community. This Community was envisaged as another link in the chain of European integration. In the opinion of the French government, which advanced the plan, the creation of a European army was desirable for the common defense of a unified Europe. It was the French government's answer to the request by the United States government that Germany participate in Atlantic defense. The rearmament of Germany, unpopular as it is in Europe and especially in France, was to be made acceptable to the European countries. It was with the hope of accomplishing this that the French government proposed a European formula, which was to make it possible to include German army units in a common army and to bind Germany to common duties and interests to European solidarity.[3]

[2] John Goormagthigh, *European Integration,* International Conciliation, Carnegie Endowment for International Peace, New York, 1953, pp. 88-90. See also Jane Perry Clark Carey, "Western European Union and the Atlantic Community," *Foreign Policy Reports,* June 15, 1950.
[3] Réné Pleven's declaration of October 24, 1950, to the French National Assembly. Service de Press et Information, Embassade de France, New York, N. Y., *Document No. 23,* p. 5.

The fundamental principle of the Defense Community plan was the creation of an army that was to be common to the six participating countries—France, Germany, Italy, Belgium, the Netherlands, and Luxembourg. In this European army the manpower and material resources from the member states were to be merged into a homogeneous whole in which all commands, all staffs, and all the attached services were to be integrated, i.e., composed of officers and men of various member states.

The finishing work on the draft treaty was done by experts from the member countries at a Paris Conference which opened in February 1951. Then followed meetings between the Foreign Ministers of these countries in November and December 1951 and in January 1952, which contributed to the elaboration of the Treaty finally accepted and signed by representatives of the six governments concerned on May 27, 1952.[4]

In the following two years the parliaments of Western Germany, the Netherlands, Belgium, and Luxembourg ratified the Treaty. The parliaments of Italy and France continued to discuss all aspects of the Defense Community. In September 1954, finally, in the French Assembly, EDC came to an early end. The French representatives voted down their own project. The European Defense Community proved not to be the answer to the problem of the defense of Europe and its civilization.

Towards a "Western European Union." After the sudden death of EDC, the governments of the free nations in Europe and of the United States made another attempt at the common goal of unity and security. On October 23, 1954, in Paris, they signed a set of agreements which brought West Germany into the Western Union and the North Atlantic Treaty Organization. Also Italy, being already a member of NATO, was invited to join the expanded Brussels pact organization officially called "Western European Union."

Thus the Western nations tentatively agreed to a new approach to rearm West Germany under the joint control of the Brussels powers and of NATO. The Western European Union received authority to set *ceilings* on all armed forces maintained by the member states. It also was given authority to control the manufacture of armaments by its members—especially West Germany—within agreed limits. The NATO powers then invited West Germany to raise a 500,000-man national army and join the North Atlantic Community. To prevent an independent deployment of the German

---

[4] La Documentation Française, Ministère des Affaires Etrangères, *Traité Instituant la communauté européenne de defense*, Paris, 1952.

forces, or even their employment against the Western democracies, increased powers were given to the supreme NATO commander over the German and all other NATO continental forces and over their placement, logistic provisions, and supplies.[5]

Mutual Security or Economic Nationalism? The endless negotiations on common European defense and the multiplicity of apparently insurmountable difficulties on the road to European unity induce us here to refrain from analyzing them in detail. However, we would like to present a short condensation of essential defense problems of the West.

First, the preservation of peace, security, and freedom of Western nations from potential *outside* aggression is of pre-eminent importance. Through mutual defense they must seek to remove the danger of attack by any outside aggressor who might otherwise hope to succeed in overcoming them one by one. A mutual defense treaty makes it clear, in advance, that any armed attack affecting the security of one member state will be met immediately by the collective defense of all member states. It is hoped that a war can thus be prevented. The problem, therefore, is the achievement of alliances and military preparedness in order to repel outside aggression. Second, Western civilization may also perish by reason of destructive forces *within* the Western nations themselves. The keystone of our civilization is the freedom of the individual and the safety of his property. Both factors have enabled Western man to achieve great industrial productivity which has raised the standard of living to a level heretofore unknown. If these fundamental factors are greatly curtailed or destroyed, through internal forces based on collective ideologies, this civilization will vanish by its own hand.

The nineteenth century witnessed an irresistible advance of the civilization of capitalist nations into all parts of the world. A healthy civilization was firmly founded on individual liberty and property, bringing law and order to nations to whom these concepts were unknown. The economic and military strength of European nations was by far superior to that of any other nation; and outside aggression against one or several of the European powers was suicidal and usually resulted in the aggressor state being incorporated into the empire of the European nation. During this period it was evident that a capitalist nation is a formidable match to any would-be aggressor.

For many decades the European nations have traveled the road to self-destruction—individual liberty is greatly curtailed and indi-

[5] *The New York Times,* October 24, 1954, p. E1.

vidual property is superseded by the rights of the state and society. The keystones of our civilization have been removed and replaced by the doctrines of collectivism. Since the beginning of the twentieth century, the standard of living of European nations has not only remained stagnant, but in some states it has even declined materially with the reduction of productivity. In addition, the sagging strength of European nations was freely used in wars and dissipated in economic policies against each other. The final, inevitable outcome of this road to collectivism must be the downfall of Europe.

Economic nationalism is the international aspect of collectivism. It is a government policy that discriminates in favor of its own citizens to the detriment of citizens of other states. As has been demonstrated repeatedly, governments, aiming at national welfare and other collectivist schemes which bring about socialism, necessarily conduct a policy of economic nationalism. The European governments on their road to national and social welfare inevitably must wage economic wars upon each other. It is inherent in the system. The domestic regulation of prices necessitates the regulation of imports and exports; the manipulation of interest rates presupposes foreign exchange control; and the manipulation of wage rates requires migration barriers. Whatever economic policy we may analyze, European governments are committed to a policy of economic nationalism, which sooner or later must result in self-destruction.

The two concepts, "survival through mutual security" and "self-destruction through economic nationalism," are diametrically opposed to each other. It is obvious that there cannot be survival where there is self-destruction. And the degree of self-destruction determines the point at which the security from outside aggression is lost. The nations of Europe undoubtedly have passed this point; without an alliance with the United States and other nations of the West, Europe would be an easy prey to communist Russia and her satellites. With the assistance and protection of capitalist America, Europe, at the present, may still enjoy security. But as long as the process of self-destruction continues, Europe's value as an ally to the capitalist nations continues to decline correspondingly.

The preservation of Western civilization depends upon the Western nations themselves. If the keystones of our civilization—the freedom of the individual and the safety of his property—are safeguarded, there is no reason for fear, no mentionable threat from outside aggressors. If the Western nations choose to destroy this foundation, there is no hope for survival, whether or not there are outside aggressors.

IX

The North Atlantic Treaty Organization

Background and Purpose. In November 1949, the North Atlantic Treaty Organization (NATO) was established in accordance with the articles of the North Atlantic Treaty, for which the negotiations were concluded on March 15, 1949 and which became effective in August 1949. The sole purpose of the treaty, as indicated in the Preamble, is to safeguard peace and security through combined efforts of the member states. "The Parties to this Treaty," reads the Preamble, "reaffirm their faith in the purposes and principles of the Charter of the United Nations and their desire to live in peace with all peoples and all governments. They are determined to safeguard the freedom, common heritage, and civilization of their peoples, founded on the principles of democracy, individual liberty, and the rule of law. They seek to promote stability and well-being in the North Atlantic area. They are resolved to unite their efforts for collective defense and for the preservation of peace and security." [1] In Article 1 the Parties indicate their desire to settle international disputes in which they may be involved according to the provisions of the United Nations Charter, and to refrain in their international relations from the threat or use of force in any manner inconsistent with the purposes of the United Nations. Article 2 reflects the desire of the member states to contribute toward peaceful and friendly relations "by strengthening their free institutions, by bringing about a better understanding of the principles upon which these institutions are founded, and by promoting conditions of stability and well-being." The Parties also pledge to seek "to eliminate conflict

[1] Department of State, *Bulletin,* March 20, 1949, pp. 339-342.

in their international economic policies and to encourage economic collaboration between any or all of them."

In Europe the way was prepared for the Treaty by the Brussels Pact of March 1948 which provided automatic military and other assistance in the event of armed attack upon the member states Britain, France, and the Benelux nations. In the United States the way was prepared by the Senate's adoption on June 11, 1948, of a resolution proposed by Senator Arthur Vandenberg favoring the development of regional and other collective arrangements for individual and collective self-defense. After the passage of this resolution, discussions were held in Washington between the United States, Canada, and the members of the Western Union on a treaty of collective security for the North Atlantic area. In addition to these seven states, Portugal, Italy, Ireland, Denmark, and Norway were later invited to the formal negotiations leading up to the Atlantic Pact. The treaty was signed on April 4, 1949.

Mutual Aid. Article 3 provides that "the Parties, separately and jointly, by means of continuous and effective self-help and mutual aid, will maintain and develop their individual and collective capacity to resist armed attack." According to the interpretation of Dean Acheson, who then was U. S. Secretary of State, this article means that "no party can rely on others for its defense unless it does its utmost for its own defense as well as for collective defense." This provision includes the general obligation of determined self-defense and mutual aid wherever it is deemed feasible. According to this official interpretation, mutual aid is defined as such aid by each party "as it reasonably can give, consistent with its geographic location and resources and with due regard to the requirements of basic economic health. . . ." [2] This provision does not create any obligation to make specific contributions. Each party gives what it can.

Consultation in Case of Threat. According to Article 4 of the Treaty, "the Parties will consult together whenever, in the opinion of any of them, the territorial integrity, political independence or security of any of the Parties is threatened." Let us especially note the use of the word "threat" in this connection. The provision is not confined to threats arising from foreign aggression, but may be interpreted to include threats to political independence or domestic security arising from *internal* uprisings and attempts to overthrow

[2] Report of the Secretary of State to the President, April 7, 1949, Department of State *Bulletin*, April 24, 1949, p. 532.

a member government. There is to be consultation in the event of domestic as well as foreign "threats."

Collective Defense in the Event of Armed Attack. In Article 5 "the Parties agree that an armed attack against one or more of them in Europe or North America shall be considered an attack against them all; and consequently they agree that, if such an armed attack occurs, each of them, in exercise of the right of individual or collective self-defense recognized by Article 51 of the Charter of the United Nations, will assist the Party or Parties so attacked by taking forthwith, individually and in concert with the other Parties, such action as it deems necessary, including the use of armed force, to restore and maintain the security of the North Atlantic area. Any such armed attack and all measures taken as a result thereof shall immediately be reported to the Security Council. Such measures shall be terminated when the Security Council has taken the measures necessary to restore and maintain international peace and security." This provision approaches the problem of armed attack very simply. It does not enter into a complicated definition of provocation and responsibility. The simple fact of armed attack— provoked or unprovoked—suffices to bring the defense provision into effect.

No Time Limit. The North Atlantic Treaty has no time limit. However, it does provide that after twenty years any member state may withdraw after one year's notice. After ten years the parties may consult together for the purpose of reviewing it (Art. 12).

Organization. The North Atlantic Treaty Organization was founded by the governments of twelve countries: Belgium, Canada, Denmark, France, Iceland, Italy, Luxembourg, the Netherlands, Norway, Portugal, the United Kingdom, and the United States. In February 1952, two other countries, Greece and Turkey, acceded after having been invited to sign the treaty.

NATO's principal body is the North Atlantic *Council*, which is responsible for the execution of the provisions of the Treaty and is in permanent session in Paris, France. Its permanent delegates are representatives of the member governments on the Council, and its chairmanship is rotated annually among the Foreign Ministers of the member governments. Special assistance to the Council is provided by an integral international secretariat whose chairman is also the vice chairman of the NATO Council and who presides in the absence of the chairman. Other functions of the Council are concerned with defense expenditures, economic and financial resources, and financial arrangements for transferred military equipment, supplies, and production tools. The Council has also been charged with the duty of stimulating the production and facilitating the distribution of military equipment and supplies. Finally, permanent or temporary committees have been established to assist the Council in fulfilling its broad responsibilities.

The military supreme command of NATO consists of the "*Military Committee*" and the two groups directly responsible to it, a "Standing Group" and a "Military Representatives Committee." The Military Committee consists of the Chiefs of Staff of the NATO members, meets periodically, and is responsible for directing military measures and efforts for the defense of the North Atlantic area. It also provides general policy guidance to the Standing Group which is composed of one military representative from each of the United States, United Kingdom, and France. This Standing Group is the executive arm of the Military Committee and is in permanent session in Washington, D. C. It is authorized to instruct and guide the various NATO commands on military matters. The Military Representatives Committee is also in permanent session in Washington and may provide general policy guidance to the Standing Group when the Military Committee is not in session.

There are two major NATO commands presently in existence. One covers Europe, and the other the Atlantic Ocean area. Furthermore, a planning group for Canada and the United States, as well as a Channel and Southern North Sea Command, was set up. The European Command (SHAPE), the supreme headquarters of which are in Paris, France, acts under the general direction of the Standing Group and directs the defense of the Allied countries in continental Europe. The Supreme Allied Commander in Europe would, in case of war, direct all land, sea, and air operations in Europe. In particular, he would direct three subordinate commands: Central Europe, Northern Europe, and Southern Europe. The Supreme Allied Commander, Atlantic, acting under the general direction of the Standing Group, is responsible for the defense of the Atlantic Ocean area. His headquarters presently are at Norfolk, Virginia.[3]

Mind and Peace. To protect us from armed attack and armed revolution and to promote the peace and security of the North Atlantic area are the purposes of the Pact. Through an advance proclamation of a common intent to resist aggression the signatories of the Treaty hope to preserve peace and security. This, of course, presumes that there are armed might and strength with which an ag-

[3] U. S. Government Printing Office, O-1953, *Regional Organizations,* pp. 21 etc.

gressor can be repelled. It also presumes that collective defense leads to an increase of common strength. Inasmuch as these presumptions are not yet fact, but need to be realized, the North Atlantic Treaty Organization undertakes to enhance the common strength through rearmament and industrial mobilization and preparedness. In essence, then, the Pact deals with the problem of the extent to which defensive forces should and can be raised. It deals with armed might—with material and manpower, tanks and airplanes, ammunition and firepower, etc. Let us not underestimate the importance of such preparedness.

But there is still another aspect of American and European security that is far more important than the preparedness expressed in the number of men and horsepowers. This is the strength of spirit and ideas which cause us to act. Armed might cannot ultimately be depended upon if our minds disdain the spirit and ideas of self-defense. Rulers and nations who have rejected this fundamental principle of human action have fallen before the assault of their enemies. And we, as well as they, must finally fall if our minds embrace the spirit and ideas of weakness and self-destruction.

The communist menace to world peace stems from the aggressive character of its ideology which animates the minds of many millions of people throughout the world. As men act according to their political and social ideas, hundreds of millions submit their actions to plans and orders of communist leaders for the realization of communism without hesitation and of their own accord. On the other hand, the free world is determined to safeguard its freedom because it rejects the ideology of communism and Soviet socialism as leading to the enslavement and poverty of the individual. As the world's public opinion is thus ideologically divided, anarchy emerges, bringing with it the danger of revolutions and war. The only conceivable solution to this state of ideological anarchy and danger to world peace lies in the conversion of the adherents of communism to the ideology of individual freedom and democracy. There can and will be peace if the communists should abandon their ideas of central planning, public ownership of the means of production, and government of the proletariat ruled by the central planners in Moscow. On the other hand, if all the world were communist, numerous causes for world conflict would continue to exist. The ideology of individual liberty is the only conceivable road to lasting peace and security. Whoever desires and strives for their realization must ultimately strive for conversion of human minds to the love of and respect for liberty.

If the free world with its way of life is to be conserved, its ideas and ideologies must be conserved. The foundations of our civilization, the freedom and dignity of the individual and his right to property, must be preserved through steadfastly living and promoting the world view and ideology that further such freedoms. Perhaps then we can win the followers of communism to an understanding and acceptance of our ideas and in that way win the freedom and peace we all strive for. A most important aid in this conversion is a thorough exposure of the ideological fallacies of communism and its inevitable ultimate effects as well as a clear and logical presentation of the free world's ideology. This is not a task for our armies, but for our philosophers and economists.

This brings us to some crucial questions. Are our philosophers and economists in the position to meet the ideological challenge of communism? Are they prepared to explode the fallacies of communist doctrines and defend the liberal principles of liberty and peace? Are they in the position to spread the ideology of freedom and dignity of the individual and his freedom to pursue happiness? Sadly but truthfully we must answer this question in the negative. Most of our thinkers and leaders have long since discarded liberal philosophy and substituted the socialist ideology of central planning, public ownership or control of the means of production, and government omnipotence of the majority over the individual. They are supported by a great number of poets, novelists, and writers who in turn enjoy enormous popularity with most of our intellectuals. But how can we meet the ideological challenge of communism if our own philosophers and economists and the public opinion of the "free world" embrace the fundamental ideas of communism? Whoever accepts the ideological foundations of communism as the standard of his own thought and action is not in a position to refute the Soviet Russian contentions as to the nature of the political and economic world.

So we see the ideology of this civilization in retreat. Certain fundamental freedoms of the individual have fallen, numerous economic freedoms have been abolished, and in some countries of the "free world" political liberties and bills of individual rights have become empty and meaningless. The ideology of control has been substituted for that of individual freedom.

The hopeless position of the free world in the realm of ideological communication leaves us with one dubious means of defense. The only way open to us for the repulse of Russian communism is to defeat Soviet Russia in war in the event she attacks. And yet, even

victories on battlefields may become belatedly lost to the van-
quished through the superior force of his ideology. Unprepared as
we are in spirit and mind, we must thus ready our arms for the
defense of our civilization which our prevailing ideas are unable
to defend.

Mind and Armed Might. The defense of our civilization on fields
of battle is subject to the same supposition as its defense in the
clash of ideas. The value of an army depends on arms and equipment and, *above all,* on the readiness of the thousands of soldiers
comprising the army to fight and risk their lives for its cause, whatever it may be. Brilliant and heroic fighting is the outcome of an
attitude of the soldiers animated with the will to stake their lives
rather than to surrender. Poor fighting, on the other hand, or the
refusal to fight stem from the soldiers' conviction of the uselessness
of the fight or its unworthiness. Man's ways of fighting, like all
other ways of human action, are determined by the set of ideas
that animate him.

This brings us to the most important question: Are the millions
of soldiers who comprise the armies of the North Atlantic Treaty
Organization animated with the will to fight for the defense of our
civilization from communist onslaught? I ask the reader to form
his answer to this question after the following consideration. The
armies of several member states of NATO consist of millions of men
who are professed members of communist party organizations, who
vote communist party tickets, and who strive for the realization of
communism in their own countries. It is fair to assume that 30 to
40 per cent of all soldiers of the French and Italian armies are
communists. Several more millions are communist sympathizers or
radical socialists who might, at any time, find conversion to communism agreeable and convenient. Now can you imagine these men
risking their lives on the day of decision on the battlefield for the
defense of a system which they themselves despise? Can you imagine these men repulsing the onslaught of communist soldiers whom
they consider class comrades and liberators? Or will they rather
surrender than fight?

Europe and Its Own Defense. In the event of war between Russia and the Allied Nations, Russia in all likelihood will launch a
major offensive in Central Europe in order to avoid facing a serious
attack from the West. The choice open to the leaders of Soviet
Russia is simple—either Russian armies attack and attempt to occupy the European continent, or Russia must be prepared to face
an offensive by Allied armies. In any case, Central Europe will be

the theater of major operations in the event of war between East and West. This has even been so in the past. Not less than three times in modern history has Russia been invaded by enemy armies coming from Central Europe. Napoleon, in 1813, reached Moscow with his French and allied armies, but was finally defeated by a malicious Russian climate. In 1917, German and Austrian-Hungarian armies penetrated deep into Russia, defeating the Russian armies and forcing her government to surrender. In 1941, German armies again invaded Russia and probably would have defeated her if it had not been for the help of the United States and the opening of the second front in the west. All three invasions show that Russia is vulnerable to invasions coming from Central Europe.

But not only will these considerations of defense lead Soviet Russia to wage a major war in Central Europe, but also the economic and military advantages connected with a Russian occupation of the European continent will probably induce the Russian government to launch a major offensive in Central Europe. This is the strategic situation which the European nations will be facing in case of war.

Now, what are European governments presently doing to maintain and develop their individual and collective capacity to resist armed attack? It is interesting to observe the European preparations of self-defense in this perhaps gravest crisis of Europe and its civilization.

Henry Hazlitt gives an excellent description of European defense preparations in a comparison of European defense efforts with those of the United States.[4] "The United States," says Hazlitt, "is spending on national defense more than four times as much *absolutely* as ten of its European beneficiaries combined (some $53,200,000,000 against a total of $11,800,000,000). It is also spending much more *relatively*—15 percent of its gross national product (total value of goods and services produced) against an average of 7 percent for the ten beneficiaries."

Hazlitt then offers the following table on the 1953 armament expenditures of the NATO member states as compared with their total central-government expenditures and their gross national product.

While the government of the United States is spending some 70% of its total budget on defense, the European governments are spending on the average some 30% of the budgets on defense and some 70% on non-defense items such as deficits on their nationalized

DEFENSE EXPENDITURES

Country	Percentage of Total Central-Government Expenditures	Percentage of Gross National Product
Belgium-Luxembourg	23.6	6.3
Denmark	24.2	3.5
France	37.6	11.2
Greece	39.0	8.5
Italy	26.4	5.8
Netherlands	23.3	6.2
Norway	26.5	5.0
Portugal	35.5	5.0
Turkey	40.8	6.5
United Kingdom	37.2	12.0
United States	71.3	15.0

industries, overexpanded social-security programs, subsidies to government-controlled industries, and other "welfare programs." It would be logical to assume that the 30% of expenditures for defense are considered sufficient to repel the eventual Russian onslaught on the European continent and that the high percentage of non-defense items can be maintained because of an indubitable safety of Europe. However, when all the facts are analyzed, such an assumption must be seen to be fallacious. The truth is that the European governments consider their domestic "welfare" and nationalization programs more urgent and important than their defense from Soviet Russian dangers. The insufficiency of European defense preparations is openly admitted by the European governments; they do not even hesitate to ask the United States, which is spending some 71% of total expenditures on defense, to contribute generously to European defense. The United States indeed is contributing some $4,200,000,000 a year to their defense. "Why can't they, instead, take this out of their nondefense expenditures?" asks H. Hazlitt. The ten NATO countries "spend altogether a modest $11,800,000,000 on defense and some $34,200,000,000 on nondefense." The answer is obvious. "Social successes" and "progress" are considered more important than self-defense. As to the ultimate effect of the European preference of "welfare" and socialism over defense, no further comment is necessary.

But this picture of European willingness and preparedness for self-defense as described by Henry Hazlitt is even darker in reality. Only total *central*-government expenditures are compared with expenditures for defense. It would be fair to take into consideration total government expenditures which include not only those by the central government, but also those of state and local governments and other public authorities. A comparison of total government spending on all levels of government with total defense spending would reveal an even larger ratio being spent in favor of welfare and socialist programs.

As has been pointed out repeatedly at other places, the European nations as well as all other nations have a choice: either they may choose the libertarian road of freedom or they may take the welfare or socialist road which will lead them to ultimate self-destruction. The defense and welfare expenditures by the European governments are irrefutable proof that the nations of Europe prefer and have chosen the latter.

An Alliance of Freemen

I

The Liberation of Man

THE market economy is a world economy of peaceful cooperation. It perishes when governments deny their citizens the liberty to do whatever they desire, according to their own plan and purpose. It distintegrates into heterogeneous national units when governments, in the name of national necessity and social justice, interfere with the operation of the market economy to bring about national divergencies in market and production structures. When the market economy perishes, both in domestic affairs and in international relations, peace among nations comes to an end. For only in a world without trade barriers and restrictions upon the liberty of man are there no incentives for war and aggression.

Individual liberty constitutes the only basis for international peace and cooperation. While the system of individual liberty and laissez-faire is the only system in which peaceful coexistence of sovereign nations is possible, the systems of socialism and interventionism always create international conflicts. The government that prohibits importation of foreign goods in order to raise the price of domestic goods discriminates against and harms foreign producers; it creates a conflict. A government that nationalizes foreign investments, that blocks, depreciates, or destroys them in any way, creates international discord. A government that conducts policies of inflation and credit expansion, foreign exchange restrictions and allocations, import quotas and protective tariffs, creates international conflicts. The same is true with respect to trade and migration barriers which separate comparatively overpopulated countries from underpopulated countries, and richer nations from "have-not" nations. Policies of interventionism and socialism tend to immobilize the population and capital of the world, thus bringing about or maintaining the world divergencies of productivity, of wealth and income. A government that nationalizes efficient industries producing for the world market and then mismanages them not only hurts the interests of its own people but also those of other nations living in a world community.

These international conflicts are inherent in the systems of interventionism and socialism and cannot be solved unless the systems themselves are abolished. The principles of national welfare as conceived by our progressive planners conflict with the principles of international cooperation and division of production. If international cooperation is to be restored, the policies of government interventionism and socialism must be abandoned. If the policies of interventionism and socialism are to be continued, the disintegration of the world market and world cooperation with all its ill consequences must be accepted. There is no other alternative—no middle road.

The various movements for international unification of states want us to believe that the nations are free to travel both roads simultaneously. They maintain that policies of planned welfare and planned production can be conducted and, simultaneously, the diverging national units can be unified. It is obvious that this contention contains a serious contradiction.

There follows an outline, offered by this writer, of the path to international peace and cooperation. It is an outline that conscientiously follows the only road to peace and unity. It uncompromisingly rejects the principles of government interventionism and socialism because of their inherent quality of international disunity and conflict.

The preservation of individual liberty is a requisite to international peace and cooperation. Only free people can deal with each other willingly and cooperate to their mutual advantage. He who desires peace and international cooperation must logically desire recovery of lost individual liberty. In his excellent work on "Liberty: A Path to Its Recovery" [1] F. A. Harper sets forth three distinct areas of liberty: (1) beliefs—thoughts, ideas, faiths; (2) physical relationships; (3) economic affairs. In all three spheres of human life and action the individual must be free to plan and act according to his own choice and liking.

Beliefs, according to Harper, are always inalienable so far as liberty is concerned. Like the famous "four freedoms"—freedom of speech, and worship, from want and fear—the freedom of beliefs is

[1] The Foundation for Economic Education, Irvington-on-Hudson, New York, 1949.

even enjoyed by the inmates of penitentiaries. So far as the individual's beliefs are concerned, liberty is not in danger. "It is the expressions of belief," says Harper, "not the beliefs themselves, that are threatened with loss of liberty. The danger is in connection with those devices by which one reveals his beliefs to others, such as printing and distributing evidences of them through the mails, using the radio, or meeting with others in a church for purposes of overt expressions of religious belief. These are the things attacked by those who would destroy liberty. Tools for the expression of beliefs are mainly economic matters. If they are not directly economic matters, they at least employ economic devices for carrying out the exchange of information or for the demonstration of beliefs. The newspaper or the radio, or some land and a building where a meeting is to be held, all involve physical act or economic considerations. The problem of liberty arises only in these spheres." [2]

The *liberty of physical relationship,* according to Harper, is the individual liberty of selection of associates. "Under liberty, the right to select associates is sacred." [3] The relationship among associates is based on voluntary agreement and contract. Under liberty, contractual obligations based on agreement and contract and on the freedom of choice by the parties must be made binding by the law, for contracts do not violate the tenets of liberty but rather constitute a vital means of interhuman communication and civilized relationship. The concept of contract on which the idea of law is built has facilitated the development of the exchange economy. Agreement and contract transcend the problems of ownership and embrace most of our economic relations.[4]

Economic liberty is the most important of all individual liberties. It touches the production, distribution, and consumption of goods, the ownership of property, contractual arrangements involving economic affairs, and all other economic matters. Economic liberty is the liberty of the individual to use his talents and his property to produce whatever he pleases. It is the liberty to sell or exchange his goods and services to whomever he wishes at whatever price he desires. If the individual is prohibited from doing this, his liberty is thereby transgressed. As to the liberty lost, it does not matter by whom his liberty is infringed upon, whether by another individual, a group of individuals, the community, the government, a

---

[2] *Ibid.,* pp. 20, 21.
[3] *Ibid.,* p. 24.
[4] On the problems of ownership and contract, see L. von Mises, *Socialism,* Yale University Press, 1951, p. 37 *et seq.*

labor union, a professional organization, or whomever. A government that owns all the tools of production and prohibits its citizens to acquire them thereby denies its citizens the liberty to produce. An economic stabilizer who "regulates," i.e., interferes with and overrules the plans and intentions of individuals, thereby infringes upon their liberty. A government that restricts imports, controls and allocates media of foreign exchange, fixes commodity prices and rates, and regulates the cost of money and its supply infringes upon the economic liberty of individuals.

The right of a person to the product of his own labor is what F. A. Harper calls the *foundation of economic liberty*. This principle of ownership and distribution is diametrically opposed to two other conceivable methods: each person may either seize by way of violence whatever he desires, or some authority may distribute the goods and services which individuals produce.

Distribution by way of violence rests upon the principle that might makes right, a principle which is identical with the "law of the jungle." "This method makes ownership hazardous and highly unstable," says Harper. "Under such a system, the one who produces anything faces the immediate danger that it will be taken from him against his will. It may then be stolen from the thief, and stolen again from the second thief—again and again until it has been consumed. An economy conducted in this manner will remain primitive, or will return to the primitive state, living largely on the 'natural products' of the forests and the streams.

"The law of the jungle discourages production and encourages consumption of even the little that is available; there is every urge to squander, and little or no incentive to thrift. He who would be enterprising, and who would create and use the tools of progress, is discouraged from doing so because of the likelihood that they will be taken from him by robbers. Wolves live in this manner; members of the pack subsist on what they can grab from the carcass of a sheep that has been pillaged from the farmer who reared it. An economy of this design will never build a Detroit, or a Radio City, or a great institution of research and learning." [5]

If some *authority distributes* what each person has produced we speak of an authoritarian society in which someone other than the producer is entitled to decree who shall have whatever is produced. Like the principle of distribution by violence it is based on the right of a non-producer to take from the producer the product of his labor. However, two basic differences between these systems of

[5] F. A. Harper, *Ibid.*, pp. 28, 29.

ownership and distribution are advanced by the numerous adherents of this popular authoritative principle. They maintain that authoritative distribution is a "public matter." The liberty of the individual is infringed upon in the "public interest;" his goods and services are taken from him for "public use" and "public welfare." On the other hand, they maintain, distribution by violence is a private matter, and as such is objectionable and detestable.

The utter emptiness of this contention becomes apparent as soon as we reflect upon the meaning and contents of the concept "public." Let us assume a small society, say of three individuals. If the majority of this society, i.e., if two individuals, resolve to take by force all or part of the product of the labor of the third individual, either to consume it or to employ it to their future advantage, this appropriation of the person's property or income is called a "public matter." Consumption of his property by the majority is in the "public interest" and for the "public welfare." Now I ask you to find the difference between this "public" distribution by the majority of this small society and the robbery by two men holding up a third. Also, if you may, what is the difference between the public distribution in a small society of three persons and that in a larger society comprising three million persons?

The numerous adherents of this authoritative principle of distribution claim that the taking by violence is for selfish purposes and the "public taking" for unselfish purposes. They maintain that robbers take for their own consumption and the improvement of their living conditions. Public taking is said to be beneficial to the majority of the public. If we apply this difference to our small society, the two individuals comprising the public majority are said to act unselfishly and in the public interest by taking the property and income from the third individual. It is obvious that this is a flagrant misstatement. In both cases non-producers selfishly take from the producer the product of his labor; in both cases the liberty of an individual is transgressed. Robin Hood is said to have helped poor people with the fruits of his robberies. Did he rob unselfishly and in the public interest? Some thieves are known to have contributed to "worthy causes." Did they steal unselfishly and to the benefit of the public? Leading politicians, government regulators, and economic stabilizers holding vast economic powers have often thickly feathered their private nests with the proceeds from extortions from private enterprise, with "gifts" and "contributions" from individuals whose economic well-being they were in a position to regulate, or with enormous salaries from taxes "soaked" from the rich. Is their taking motivated by unselfish purposes? Do they act in the public interest? As far as the producer is concerned, his property and income have been taken from him against his wishes in both instances.

"The only method consistent with liberty," says Harper, "is the one that distinguishes between mine and thine according to the rule that the producer shall have the right to the product of his own labor. This foundation of economic liberty is important above all other considerations. By this concept, the right of ownership arises simultaneously with the production of anything; and ownership resides there until the producer-owner chooses to consume the product or to transfer its ownership to another person through exchange, gift, or inheritance. The right to produce a thing thereby becomes the right to own it; and to deny one right is, in effect, to deny both." [6]

The Road to Liberty and International Peace. If international cooperation is to be restored and peace is to return to mankind, the ideologies and policies of government interventionism and socialism must be abandoned. The individual must be freed from the multiplicity of infringements upon his liberty by the public, i.e., the majority of his fellow men, and the individual must regain the right to the product of his own labor. Special privileges to any person or groups of persons must be denied because they are identical with infringements on the rights of others. The granting of benefits by government violates the principle of liberty in that it limits the liberty of others. Special privileges in the form of income or of position in the market for goods and services and special protection of certain producers and professions should be abolished. Special protection in the form of sanctioned monopolies, prohibition of competition, fixed prices by governmental decree, and prohibition of the free movement of goods across political borders, all are measures of government privilege and protection that must be abolished. The principle of "no special privilege" must be acknowledged as the fundamental principle of the liberal society.

All regional and national divisions should only be regarded as convenient divisions in the administration of safety and security of individuals by governments. If this attitude were held, it would be easily recognized that all limitations on trade are disadvantageous to all concerned. The functions of the state must be limited to securing the protection of life and property, a limitation which would eliminate the problem of boundaries. If the functions of the state are thus limited and no privileges can be attained through control over the apparatus of the state, it becomes a matter of utter indif-

[6] *Ibid.,* p. 30.

ference whether the state extends over a large or small territory and which state affords the individual's security of life and property. In a liberal society individuals all over the world could cooperate, and economic causes for conflict would no longer exist.

If the individual were freed from constant government interference and tutelage, he would go where the conditions of life would be most favorable for him. He would work and produce at a place offering the most suitable conditions for production. Thus individuals would migrate continually from places where the natural conditions of production are less favorable to places where they are more favorable. It is true, migration of individuals of various nationalities would create national minority problems. But these problems would be limited to cases of individual discrimination. The state whose function would be restricted to safeguarding life and property could not conceivably grant privileges and favors like the state founded on interventionism and socialism and in which political decisions have an enormous significance in the life of the individual.

The nations of Europe have the following alternative: either to continue their policies of government interventionism and socialism with their inherent seeds of conflict and disunity, or to abolish all infringements upon the liberty of individuals and establish a liberal society. Whether or not the European nations will cooperate and live in peace depends on this very choice.

II

Monetary Reconstruction

R ESTORATION of international co-operation and division of labor requires sound monetary systems. The prevailing doctrine among economists of the nineteenth century asserted that the individual could not be coerced into accepting depreciated media of exchange at an arbitrary value decreed by government. The present world of economic disintegration, however, offers the comfortless picture of governments fixing prices and controlling foreign exchange operations to prevent transactions that would recognize the depreciation of paper currencies. The depreciation of money by central banks and national treasuries naturally causes faith in such currencies to wane. Governments then attempt to substitute coercion for waning faith, which contributes to the spread of government controls over other aspects of individual action. The inevitable final outcome is the disintegration of the world economy. As soon as the detrimental effects of the depreciation of national currencies and disintegration of the world economy become apparent, the advocates of such policies begin to recommend international cooperation of governments in the regulation of monetary systems. They assume that the undesirable effects of policies of depreciation can be avoided through concerted action on the part of all governments conducting such policies. Based on the very principles of economic disintegration, international agreements on monetary cooperation are concluded that deal with the inevitable effects of inflationary policies while the causes themselves are left unchanged. But monetary depreciation and clamor for monetary cooperation are merely different aspects of the same phenomenon.

The idea of sound money originates from the principle of *decency and justice* without which there can be no exchange economy based on voluntary exchange and division of labor. The modern ideology

of sound money was devised to force decency and justice upon reluctant governments and sovereigns practicing debasement of currencies and to protect the civil liberties of individuals from
destructive inroads on the part of governments. The idea of sound
money, like constitutional guarantees and bills of individual rights,
was the reaction of weary people against arbitrary rule of governments and sovereigns ruling to the detriment of the people. It was
derived from the experience of the American Continental Currency,
the paper money of the French Revolution, and the British Restriction period. The liberal philosophers and economists of this and
following periods carefully elaborated and perfected the ideology
of sound money.[1]

The principle of sound money is the liberty to choose the media
of exchange that individuals see fit and the defense of such liberty
from the rulers' propensity to debase the currency in order to facilitate policies of easy spending. Thus the sound-money idea is one of
the essential postulates of individual liberty and liberal policy.

Sound money means metallic money which can be tested with
scales and with acids. It needs no endorsement and no government
stamp upon it. It calls for no act of faith, and no compulsion for acceptance is required. Men everywhere accept it in exchange for
goods or services. The *gold standard* is a standard providing for
metallic money in the form of standard coins of a definite quantity
of gold as precisely determined by the laws of a country. It provides
that all token coins and kinds of paper money and other promissory
notes should be redeemed, upon presentation, in standard money.
The gold standard thus renders debasement of the currency by governments impossible and keeps the purchasing power of money independent of the wishes and ambitions of "monetary authorities."

Substitution of paper money for the gold standard and of fictitious
money rates for free market values brings about the effects described by Gresham's Law. That is to say, gold is hoarded or leaves
the country. Gold and redeemable currencies cease to circulate,
leaving the dishonored paper money in possession of the field. Gold
is hoarded or escapes from countries where governments and central banks are not honest, where they fail to keep their promises on
demand or at maturity. Gold demands that central banks keep their
demand liabilities within the limits of their gold reserves and that
governments balance their budgets and refrain from creating debts

[1] L. von Mises, *The Theory of Money and Credit,* Yale University Press, 1953, p. 414.

without considering their repayment. Only under these conditions can a flight of gold and good currency be avoided.[2]

The flight of gold from countries whose governments are depreciating their currencies is a major calamity to such countries because gold has maintained its position as the international or world standard. While paper money has replaced gold in the domestic markets through the operation of Gresham's Law, it has failed to eliminate gold in international transactions between governments and central banks. They rightly distrust each others' paper issues and promissory notes. Just as there is honor among thieves, so do they insist upon paying promptly and redeeming their paper currencies in gold on demand. Thus the impregnable position of gold as the world's standard of exchange is built on the very principles of monetary depreciation and waning faith in the various paper currencies. Gold will maintain its position as long as there is a world economy in which goods and services are exchanged and various "monetary authorities" practice inflation and depreciation.

Unsound monetary policy causes gold and gold currencies to leave the country. Foreigners withdraw their liquid funds and citizens endeavor to exchange their funds for gold and better currencies and send them away for safety. Governments and "monetary authorities" then attempt to counteract the detrimental effects of their own policies by imposing strict controls upon capital and foreign exchange transactions. But government controls and regulations according to principles of "national necessity" and "essentiality" are identical with disintegration of the international capital and money market. Monetary disintegration then leads to disintegration of world trade and thereby to the economic isolation of each country. Thus the international division of labor is destroyed and the well-being of nations is injured.

The most decisive instrument of destruction of the world economy is government control over the individual's foreign exchange transactions. It all starts when the government decrees that its domestic paper currency should have a certain value and that it is to be exchanged at a certain parity to gold or foreign exchange. If the government-decreed exchange rate corresponds to the purchasing power value of the currency, neither law nor decree is required to induce the individual to exchange at this parity. However, if the purchasing power of the domestic currency is lower than the parity decreed by the monetary authorities, undesirable effects ensue. If

2 B. M. Anderson, *Economics and the Public Welfare*, Van Nostrand, 1949, p. 421 *et seq.*

the individual is forced by the power of the court to exchange his money against foreign money (or vice versa) at a rate at which the individual is short-changed, he will discontinue his transactions with foreign countries to avoid foreign exchange losses. Or he will conduct his monetary transactions through illegal channels. That is to say, he will attempt to receive the full and true value for his media of exchange on what governments enjoy labeling "black markets." Of course, these effects are undesirable for the "monetary authorities." They counteract these "unpatriotic" attempts by expropriating all gold and foreign exchange held by individuals and creating monopolies owned by the state and run by civil servants to deal with gold and foreign exchange. "Now we can stabilize the national currency!" say the monetary planners—and they continue to depreciate it and wreck it.

Naturally, the government monopoly fails to solve the fundamental shortcoming of the regulation of money value. Forced sales of foreign exchange to the foreign exchange monopoly against an indemnity *below the market price* which reflects its true purchasing power, is identical with a special tax or duty on the sale of gold or foreign exchange to the monopoly. It is obvious that such a special duty on the sale of foreign exchange to the government monopoly tends to burden exporters and reduce the volume of their business. On the other hand, sale of foreign exchange to importers at a price below that of the market constitutes a lucrative transaction for importers. The spread between market price and the price fixed by the monetary authorities is identical with a subsidy to importers and encourages them in their business. The final result of this policy of foreign exchange regulation and control by monetary authorities is what is commonly called a shortage of foreign exchange. It is a special kind of shortage which we may properly call a "planned" or "socialist shortage" which inevitably arises when a government enforces a maximum price below the true market price.

The foreign exchange shortage provides the advocates of public control with a welcome excuse for other controls. Step by step, the demand for foreign exchange is reduced by foreign exchange officials allocating the dwindling foreign exchange supply. A multiplicity of import quotas is imposed, transfer of funds from one country to another is prohibited or regulated, foreign capital is blocked, numerous price controls are established, and other schemes of planning and government intervention are devised to counteract the inevitable effects of these policies. It is obvious that all these measures are measures of economic nationalism which is tantamount to

the disintegration of the world market and the international division
of labor.

The Return to Sound Money. The return to sound money policies
is of utmost importance. Without sound money there can be no
economic recovery, no prosperity, no economic cooperation, no international division of labor, no unification. Sound money is the cor-
nerstone of individual liberty. Sound money is metallic money. It
is the gold standard.

The furious opposition against the gold standard by the advocates
of central planning and government inflation results from its natural
attribute of not allowing free printing by the government printing
office. The gold standard forces governments to refrain from spending more than tax revenues or funds borrowed from the public. The
gold standard forces governments to balance their budgets and refrain from policies of credit expansion which create booms and inevitably lead to periods of depression.

The stabilization of a national currency is a simple matter.[3] All
that is required is for a government to abstain from any further increase in the quantity of its currency. That is to say, in order to
bring about stabilization, a government must do precisely nothing.
Inactivation of the government printing presses and monetary authorities will immediately stop the rise in foreign exchange and gold
prices. Within a short time the exchange rate of domestic money as
to foreign money and gold will settle at the purchasing power parity
of gold and the various kinds of foreign exchange. Of course, in
order to stop the printing presses, government must learn to balance
its budgets, and live on the tax revenue authorized by parliament.

As soon as the stabilization of the national currency has been
completed, the gold standard may return. In his book *The Theory
of Money and Credit* Ludwig von Mises describes the return to the
gold standard by an imaginary country called "Ruritania." The unit
of its domestic money is the "rur." Having described the stabilization of the "rur," L. von Mises proceeds as follows: [4] "While an
increase in the production of gold or an increase in the issuance of
dollars continues abroad, Ruritania now has a currency the quantity
of which is rigidly limited. Under these conditions there can no
longer prevail full correspondence between the movements of commodity prices on the Ruritanian markets and those on foreign mar-

[3] For an excellent presentation of the principles of sound money and the problems
of monetary reconstruction, see L. von Mises, *The Theory of Money and Credit*,
p. 413 *et seq.*

[4] *Ibid.*, p. 444 *et seq.*

kets. If prices in terms of gold or dollars are rising, those in terms of rurs will lag behind them or even drop. This means that the purchasing power parity is changing. A tendency will emerge towards an enhancement of the price of the rur as expressed in gold or dollars. When this trend becomes manifest, the propitious moment for the completion of the monetary reform has arrived. The exchange rate that prevails on the market at this juncture is to be promulgated as the new legal parity between the rur and either gold or the dollar. Unconditional convertibility at this legal rate of every paper rur against gold or dollars and vice versa is henceforward to be the fundamental principle.

"The reform thus consists of two measures," L. von Mises continues. "The first is to end inflation by setting an insurmountable barrier to any further increase in the supply of domestic money. The second is to prevent the relative deflation that the first measure will, after a certain time, bring about in terms of other currencies the supply of which is not rigidly limited in the same way. As soon as the second step has been taken, any amount of rurs can be converted into gold or dollars without any delay and any amount of gold or dollars. But its main concern is, at least in the initial stage of its functioning, how to provide the rurs necessary for the exchange of gold or foreign currency against rurs. To enable the agency to perform this task, it has to be entitled to issue additional rurs against a full—100 per cent—coverage by gold or foreign exchange bought from the public."

According to Mises, "it is politically expedient not to charge this agency with any responsibilities and duties other than those of buying and selling gold or foreign exchange according to the legal parity. Its task is to make this legal parity an effective real market rate, preventing, by unconditional redemption of rurs, a drop of their market price against legal parity, and, by unconditional buying of gold or foreign exchange, an enhancement of the price of rurs as against legal parity.

"At the very start of its operations the agency needs, as has been mentioned, a certain reserve of gold or foreign exchange. This reserve has to be lent to it either by the government or by the central bank, free of interest and never to be recalled. No business other than this preliminary loan must be negotiated between the government and any bank or institution dependent on the goverment on the one hand and the agency on the other hand. The total amount of rurs issued before the start of the new monetary regime must not be increased by any operations on the part of the govern-

ment; only the agency is free to issue additional new rurs, rigidly
complying in such issuance with the rule that each of these new rurs
must be fully covered by gold or foreign exchange paid in by the
public in exchange for them."

As to subsidiary coins, Mises recommends that "the government's
mint may go on to coin and to issue as many fractional or subsidiary
coins as seem to be needed by the public. In order to prevent the
government from misusing its monopoly of mintage for inflationary
ventures and flooding the market, under the pretext of catering to
peoples' demand for 'change,' with huge quantities of such tokens,
two provisions are imperative. To these fractional coins only a
strictly-limited legal-tender power should be given for payments to
any payee but the government. Against the government alone they
should have unlimited legal-tender power, and the government
moreover must be obliged to redeem in rurs, without any delay and
without any cost to the bearer, any amount presented, either by any
private individual, firm, or corporation or by the agency. Unlimited
legal-tender power must be reserved to the various denominations
of bank-notes of one rur and upwards, issued either before the reform or, if after the reform, against full coverage in gold or foreign
exchange.

"Apart from this exchange of fractional coins against legal-tender
rurs," Ludwig von Mises continues, "the agency deals exclusively
with the public and not with the government or any of the institutions dependent on it, especially not with the central bank. The
agency serves the public and deals exclusively with that part of the
public that wants to avail itself, of its own free accord, of the
agency's services. But no privileges are accorded to the agency. It
does not get a monopoly for dealing in gold or foreign exchange.
The market is perfectly free from any restriction. Everybody is free
to buy or sell gold or foreign exchange. There is no centralization of
such transactions. Nobody is forced to sell gold or foreign exchange
to the agency or buy gold or foreign exchange from it.

"When these measures are once achieved, Ruritania is either on
the gold-exchange standard or on the dollar-exchange standard. It
has stabilized its currency as against gold or the dollar. This is
enough for the beginning. There is no need for the moment to go
further. No longer threatened by a break-down of its currency, the
nation can calmly wait to see how monetary affairs in other countries will develop."

This stabilization and return to the gold standard, as outlined by
Ludwig von Mises, would at once solve the multiplicity of monetary

problems of Europe. If the individual in each European country is perfectly free from government restriction, if he is free to buy or sell gold or foreign exchange at their purchasing power parity, if the numerous exchange restrictions connected with the alleged gold and dollar shortages and "unfavorable balances of payments," which are merely other names and aspects of the same monetary phenomenon, are removed, indeed a great deal of contemporary disunity of European nations will be overcome and the monetary foundation for European cooperation will be laid. European cooperation is cooperation of individuals, not governments versus individuals. If the individuals are free to trade and hold gold or any kind of foreign currency they please, and the free market for gold and foreign exchange is re-established, individuals may and will cooperate. They will buy and sell gold and foreign exchange, they will lend and borrow them, use them for exports and imports and for traveling abroad. Once again Europe would become an integrated community of trade and prosperity, a community of peace and civilization.

III

A Free-Trade Area

EUROPEAN unification movements are in unanimous agreement that national economies with their numerous market divergencies should be unified, and that men, goods, and capital should be allowed to move as freely within the union as in each member economy. The two preceding sections of this book show that hope for such a union must be in vain as long as there is government intervention in economic life. There cannot be a union where there are welfare states with a multiplicity of restrictive or protective measures.

The several unification movements also agree that the government of a European union should afford protection for particular industries within the union from competition by producers outside the European area. As has been stated repeatedly in preceding sections, this hope must also be in vain because no agreement can conceivably be reached among the various member nations as to which industry shall be protected and who shall bear the sacrifice which such a protection logically imposes upon the others. While it is comparatively easy to persuade a nation that it should protect certain of "its" industries, it is virtually impossible to persuade different nationalities to bear sacrifices favoring certain producers of another nationality in the union.

There is but one way to unify Europe. Nations eager to unify must abandon their government welfare and socialist ideologies and return to policies of individual liberty and free trade. All restrictive and protective measures within the union, as well as toward the outside world, must be abandoned. Where only free trade and individual liberty exist, there are cooperation and union.

The theory of international trade forms one of the most complicated subject matters of economic theory. In this age of utter

300

disregard for economics the theory of international trade is rejected because it conflicts with the basic tenets of the ideology of government welfare and socialism.

Foreign trade or trade among nations, as it is commonly called, is trade among individuals separated by national boundaries. The motivating forces leading to foreign trade are identical with those leading to domestic trade: they are the increase of utility and value resulting from exchange. That is to say, the value of the good received is, or at least is expected to be, greater than the sacrifice made for obtaining it. It is obvious that there would be no exchange if both parties were not expecting to benefit from it. The same holds true in foreign trade. The value of imports is, or at least is expected to be, greater than that of the goods exported in exchange. Exports merely are sacrifices of value given in exchange.

Imports enable the individual to procure commodities which he and his fellow citizens are unable to produce themselves. Imports also enable him to obtain commodities which he and his fellow citizens cannot produce with the same facility. It is technologically feasible, for example, to produce bananas in greenhouses in Alaska. But the costs of such a production by far exceed the costs for obtaining bananas by means of international exchange. Imports also enable the individual and his fellow citizens to employ their natural abilities and their land and capital in those fields of production which offer the best chance for high returns.

The efficiency of every producer and instrument of production is increased if they specialize in the production of those goods for which natural abilities and conditions are most favorable. It is the essence of the division of labor that every participant produces what he is most suited to produce, either because of his natural abilities or external conditions determining and influencing production. The territorial division of production is merely an aspect of the general principle of the division of labor. Just as an individual earns highest returns by employing his inborn abilities in an occupation requiring his special skill, producers, in order to earn highest returns, must specialize in the production of those commodities for which the existing conditions such as climate, land, capital, and labor markets are most favorable.

The elemental fact of foreign trade, as well as domestic trade, is a discrepancy in the existing conditions of production. Commodities are exchanged in voluntary division of labor because the conditions of production differ as to climate, land, capital, and labor services. However, an important difference between domestic trade and foreign trade must here be mentioned. While the discrepancies in the domestic conditions of production tend to stay at a minimum because of the mobility of the factors of production, the discrepancies in the international conditions of production are of more serious nature because of the relatively greater immobility of production factors. Under existing conditions of government interventionism and socialism, capital and labor cannot migrate from countries with less favorable conditions of production to countries where conditions are more favorable. Thus discrepancies in the conditions of production are added by numerous institutional obstacles to the natural discrepancies such as climate and land. This knowledge gained by simple reasoning clearly reveals the relative importance of foreign trade as compared with domestic trade. It indicates that the volume of foreign trade should tend to grow with growing discrepancies in the international production conditions. If we compare this principle of economic theory with the actual state of affairs, we begin to realize the detrimental effects of "welfare" doctrines and policies on the international division of labor. The foreign trade of welfare and socialist nations often amounts to less than a trifle of domestic trade. The detrimental effects to the nations themselves are easily discerned.

The protectionists object to freedom of international trade because a country's conditions of production may be less favorable in many or most respects than the conditions in other countries. What happens to these countries, they ask, whose production conditions are so unfavorable that they cannot stand the competition of the more fortunate countries? What choice do they have but to restrict imports from countries with more favorable conditions? Government control and restriction of imports is said to be a vital necessity for countries producing under disadvantageous conditions. The fallacy of this protectionist notion becomes apparent immediately if we observe two individuals, one greatly gifted and industrious, the other one inferior in all his performances. The president of a corporation who began his career as an errand boy and who served his corporation through many years as clerk, accountant, foreman, salesman, treasurer, manager, etc., is probably more industrious and talented than his many fellow workers and competitors. And yet, when he reaches the presidency, he does not discharge a clerk, accountant, or manager because he, the president, is more talented in filling all these positions. Obviously it would be foolish for the president to waste his time doing a clerk's job even though he can do it more efficiently than his clerk can.

But this is precisely what the protectionists are recommending to our governments. Let us illustrate the fallacy of their advices in the following example dealing with two different countries: Let us assume that conditions are such that in the United States the production of an automobile and a family cruiser require the expenditure of 1000 working hours each and that in England an automobile requires 3000 hours and the family cruiser 2000 working hours. Now the protectionists maintain that because English production conditions are less favorable for both commodities, foreign trade would be harmful to England. This is a serious fallacy. If each country turns toward the production of that commodity for which conditions are most favorable seen *comparatively*, the division of labor achieves a higher productivity of labor in both countries. If American producers turn toward the production of cars exclusively and English businessmen toward the production of boats, both countries will benefit from this division of labor. Though America has superior facilities for the production of both commodities, it is expedient for American producers to produce only cars, and for English producers to produce only family cruisers. If there were no interchange, 1000 working hours in both American branches of production would yield one car and one boat respectively. The same working time in England would produce ½ of a car and ½ of a boat, the total of both countries thus being 1⅓ of a car and 1½ of a boat, or 2⅚ units. But if each country confines its production to that commodity in which it has the greatest comparative advantage, the total will be 2 cars produced in the United States and 1 boat produced in England, or 3 units altogether. While England benefits from this division of production inasmuch as she can obtain one American car at a sacrifice that is smaller than her own production costs, America benefits from this division of production inasmuch as it can obtain an English boat at a sacrifice of less than a car, which is more favorable than its own ratio of 1:1.

Let us compare the prices. Let us assume that the American cars and boats costs $3000. The price for the same car in England is the equivalent of $3600 and that of a boat $2400. Of course, the English wage rates must be considerably lower than the American rates because of the lower marginal productivity of English labor. Now if each country specializes in the production of that commodity for which it has the greatest comparative advantage, American producers will build cars and English producers will specialize in boats. The advantages of this division of production and labor are obvious.

But according to your premise, somebody may object, the condi-

tions of production for *both* commodities are more favorable in the
United States. That is correct. Our price illustration does not conflict with the assumption that only 1000 American working hours
are required for the construction of a boat, while it costs 2000 working hours in England. The lower marginal labor productivity in
England determines a low rate of wages. Prices are determined by
the demand and supply situation on the English market and expressed in terms of pounds sterling. *On the whole,* they equal
American prices in accordance with the principle of purchasing
power parity of the media of foreign exchange.

David Ricardo, who first expounded these advantages of foreign
trade known under the name of "Law of Comparative Cost," presented it in a simple analogy. He said: "Two men can both make
shoes and hats, and one is superior to the other in both employments; but in making hats he can only exceed his competitor by
one-fifth, or 20 per cent, and in making shoes he can excel him by
one-third, or 33⅓ per cent. Will it not be for the interest of both
that the superior man should employ himself exclusively in making
shoes, and the inferior man in making hats?" [1] We may add: if two
countries can both produce cars and boats, will it not be for the interest of both countries if both produce what they can produce
comparatively best?

The higher productivity of labor achieved under the division of
labor serves the interests of all participants. Collaboration of the
more talented, more efficient, and more industrious with the less
talented, less efficient, and less industrious benefits both. Why
should this fundamental principle of the division of labor lose its
validity when individuals are separated by political boundaries?
Why should a border policeman make all the difference for the effects of human association and the consequences of the division of
labor? Of course, all such contentions are untenable and fallacious.

The law of comparative costs is based on one assumption: that
only commodities are freely mobile and that capital and labor are
hindered from crossing political borders by government restriction
and intervention. When only commodities are freely mobile, the
law of comparative costs applies. When capital and labor also enjoy
free mobility, they migrate to those places on the earth where natural
conditions of production are most favorable and where the productivity of labor is highest. People and capital tend to leave countries and places that are unsuited for production and settle at places
where higher incomes and returns are obtained. Industries produc-

[1] Ricardo, David, *Works* (ed. J. R. McCulloch), London, 1881, p. 77.

ing under costly and unfavorable conditions are abandoned, the least fruitful land is left untilled, and immobile factors of production are abandoned or employed in more extensive processes of production. Thus capital and labor are distributed according to the natural opportunities affording highest productivity.

If the European nations really desire unification and the advantages and benefits which such a unification affords, the following steps must be taken on the road to unity. First, all government favors and privileges must be unconditionally abolished; policies of interventionism and socialism must be abandoned; the numerous divergencies in the national structures of production must be allowed to be corrected and evened out by the forces of the market economy. Second, commodities, capital, and labor must be allowed to move as freely within the union as in each member state. In the absence of government restrictions imposed upon the individual by socialist and welfare governments, men and the mobile factors of production will migrate to those places within the union where the natural conditions for their employment are most favorable. Third, inasmuch as non-European governments would continue to impose restrictions upon the mobility of their own and European citizens and capital funds, the European governments must conduct unconditional policies of free trade with the outside world. European trade with foreign countries must be governed by the Law of Comparative Costs.

But someone may object that the communist economic bloc and other collectivist economies may disturb the market economies at will through transactions motivated by political considerations. Should a government not endeavor to protect the economy from malicious dumping of commodities by a communist government which is attempting to create political difficulties Many excellent economists are inclined to answer this question in the affirmative.[2]

We must reject their inference and advice on grounds of the following consideration. The powers of protection given to government can be used so abusively as to far outweigh any success it may have in combating a minor evil. It opens the way for the whole camp of protectionists to demand protection for their products from bothersome competition.

And who could truthfully make the statement, "This is malicious dumping." A communist economy lacks all means of calculation, inasmuch as the market economy with its determination of costs and

[2] E.g., Wilhelm Röpke, *International Ordnung-heute*, Zurich, 1954, p. 318 *et seq.*

prices has been abolished. It must be guided through comparison with the price structure of the world market.

Furthermore, we should bear in mind that sales below cost are always a heyday for consumers. The lower the commodity price, the higher is the standard of living. Communist dumping of commodities in the capitalist markets would enrich the latter at the expense of the former.

In the market economies only the specific industry exposed to foreign dumping would suffer and then only temporarily. Businessmen would have to readjust to the new condition. But this is their very entrepreneural function. They incessantly have to cope with readjustments and fluctuations. They know it infinitely better than politicians and policemen. Some industries, though "unprotected," undoubtedly cope with great risks and fluctuations even today. They would and could also manage the risk of dumping. This inference is all the more conclusive when we realize that the market economies constitute an interrelated world market which would absorb and evenly distribute all quantities offered. Thus the effects of communist attempts to disturb the national markets would be negligible and need not be feared.

IV

On Ideological and
Military Defense

W<small>E LIVE</small> in an age of conflict.
The accepted political and economic ideologies lead men to the use
of compulsion and violence in domestic as well as foreign relations.
Foremost is the ideal of the struggle for supremacy and of the survival of the fittest. The ideologies of socialism and communism do
homage to class struggle and to dictatorship of the class most powerful in number. The ideology of nationalism transfers the same struggle from "classes" to nations and states. The ideology of the interventionist welfare state justifies and advocates the national struggle
for the sake of certain domestic groups which it provides with special privileges and favors. It is obvious that such a world cannot
live in peace.

If nations would abandon the ideologies of struggle and war and
restrict their governments' functions to the protection of life and
property of individuals, conflict could not arise, for each individual
could live where he chooses, practice a profession he selects, and
associate with whomever he wishes. The states would have to refrain from all restrictions upon the liberty of the individual no matter what nationality, language, or religion. And capital and goods
should be allowed to move freely, unhampered by government decrees which grant favors and privileges to some and discriminate
against others. What reason and cause for national conflict could
there possibly be? The only reason for concern in such a society is
the danger arising from the existence of those nations and coalitions
of nations that continue to adhere to the ideologies of struggle and
conflict. That is to say, defense against foreign aggression is of vital
importance as long as other nations believe in communism, socialism,

307

nationalism, and the welfare state. As long as these ideologies inspire men to aggression, a liberal society must be prepared to meet and repel every attempt of aggression.

In our age Western Europe and other countries of the free world are directly threatened by a militant communist power, Soviet Russia. Communism moves with a giant's stride in its planned conquest of the world. At the end of World War II, communism ruled over only 200 million Russians. In 1945 and 1946, more than 100 million people in Eastern and Central Europe were added to the Soviet's sphere of power. At the end of 1949, about 600 million people in China were subjugated to communist rule. The communist bloc thus has grown from 200 to more than 900 million men—that is to say, from one-thirteenth to more than one-third of the world's population. In addition, large parts of the population of the countries in Western Europe and other parts of the free world are communistic and yearn for the day of communist "liberation" and conquest.

The most urgent task of the free nations in Europe, as well as in other parts of the world, is the cooperation in their efforts to counter an aggression by Soviet Russia. The free nations must be prepared to meet the enemy on two different battlefields—one ideological and the other military. If they should fail to hold their lines of defense through united efforts on both fields, they will ultimately succumb to the yoke of the totalitarian regime.

The *ideological* line of defense is the understanding and practice of the philosophy of individual liberty. It is the defense that is the sole responsibility of our intellectual leaders. Millions of people in all walks of life must be convinced that the social system of liberty is most beneficial for all. The people who, wittingly or unwittingly, choose between ideologies developed by a few philosophers and economists must learn to see the progressive improvement of economic and social conditions under the system of freedom and free enterprise. A free world united in honoring individual liberty will provide the communist world with ample demonstrations of the accomplishments and blessings of its civilization.

A European system of social organization that provides a steadily improving standard of living and safeguards its citizens' political and economic freedom will give the lie to the contentions of communist propaganda. It will radiate the message of individual liberty to millions of people behind the Iron Curtain; and each European broadcast and communication with the communist world will help to unmask the ideology of government omnipotence and dictatorship to be what it really is: a spurious ideology whose application means loss of liberty and poverty for the people. Millions behind the Iron Curtain and in Russia herself will begin to compare with their own the way of life of free Europe and begin to see the enormous accomplishments which liberty can bring about. A Europe that is healthy in its political and economic ideology not only would maintain its ideological position towards the communist area but could carry the ideological struggle in a counter-attack deep into Russia. Once the communist countries themselves have become the battlefield of the ideological conflict between tyranny and liberty, the external danger of communism will diminish.

The communist leaders are fully aware of the vital importance of the ideological struggle. There is hardly a field of government activity to which they devote as much effort, skill, and money as to communist propaganda. While the United States of America is aiding the poverty-stricken world with grants of foodstuffs and other materials, the communist governments are spending even larger amounts for their propaganda. While America is trying to fill the stomachs of starving people in underdeveloped areas, the communist leaders and agents are busily influencing their minds and converting them to the doctrines of communism. The political situation in all parts of the world is a fair indication of the relative effectiveness of these methods of international relation and communication.

The ideological counterattack by the defenders of individual liberty must be coordinated with European military preparedness against possible communist aggression. The communist leaders, becoming aware of the gradual disintegration of their ideological foundation through an infiltration of the ideology of liberty, may very well, in an act of desperation, order immediate military attack. Europe must be prepared for such an attack.

The *military* preparedness of Europe against communist invasion must at all times be adequate to repel the communist armies. The need for military preparedness is determined by the position of the hostile forces on the ideological battlefield. That is to say, the size and number of European armies must depend on the success or failure of the ideology of freedom in its penetration of the communist area. Military preparedness is merely a supplementary preparedness the extent of which must stand in reverse relationship to the strength of the ideological forces. When the ideas of liberty retreat because of our intellectual failure, we must build up our military forces to match our ideological shortcoming. We may observe the truth of this statement in the present ideological and military positions of the communist forces and those of the free world. In matters of propaganda and ideological warfare the forces of the free world have suffered repeated defeats and are definitely retreating. Consequently, we see the free nations arming and preparing themselves at heavy expense to meet the communist forces on the military battlefield. On the other hand, when the ideas of liberty advance and force communism into retreat, we may relax in our military preparedness and begin to disarm, always in proportion to the waning strength of the communist armies.

In a Europe of individual liberty, universal military service and conscription must be abandoned. Universal military service is the prototype of authoritative government and regimentation of the individual. It deprives a large part of the population of independent initiative and the right to independent decision. Central government agencies determine what the individual has to do. He becomes a number in a regiment which in turn has a number. His physical needs are taken care of by the collective, which does away with his freedom of vocation, residence, production, and consumption. Universal military service is the breeding cell for the ideology of government omnipotence and regimentation.

There can be no room for such an institution in a liberal Europe. European armies of volunteers who make the war craft their life's profession and vocation should form the defense forces of Europe. Armies of professional soldiers, comprising two to three million volunteers from Europe and other parts of the world, would be able to defend Europe very effectively. A capitalist Europe could provide its soldiers with always new and superior weapons. European routinized mass production in arms would by far excel that of the communist nations. European capitalism would always explore new methods of production, open up new industries, and put to use new technological inventions and methods. The enormous economic superiority of a liberal Europe would indeed make it invincible.

The European armies of professional soldiers and volunteers should be independent *national armies* subject to orders by their respective parliaments. No special arrangements of a defense community or military unification are needed—mutual defense agreements would suffice. No new supranational authority would have to be created, thus avoiding the many difficulties and sources of disagreements as to problems of contribution, leadership, stationing, training and educational programs, choice of language, etc. National armies would not require their governments to abandon independence of decision and sovereignty. And yet, national independence and sovereignty would not harm the true unification of

Europe, the unification through liberty, freedom of trade, and movement of men and capital.

Through mutual defense agreements the liberal nations would acquire security against aggression by non-liberal nations. The fighting power of allied armies has always been satisfactory in the past. Allied armies twice defeated a powerful German war machinery which was highly unified and centralized. It is our belief that there is no task which a unified army can fulfill that cannot be done as effectively or better by allied armies.

A liberal Europe would take care of its own defense. The system of free trade and individual liberty would provide Europe with enormous economic and military strength. Such a Europe would not have to plead continuously for American aid and its independence would not require an American guarantee. The North Atlantic Treaty Pact would lose its present tragic importance and signifiance or be wholly superfluous. Europe would very quickly regain its strength and old position which it maintained during its age of liberty and capitalism, for strength is inherent in liberty. He who is free need not fear.

V

The Gradual and Independent Realization of Freedom and Union by the European Nations

T<small>HE</small> liberal system of social organization is the only system that is capable of restoration. It may be defeated, subdued, and overthrown, but it rises again and again, always with the vigor of youth. The heart of man is filled with admiration and love for the times of liberty and for those men who founded or restored it. While all other systems of social organization, once abandoned or overthrown, can never be resurrected because of the indelible changes that have come over persons and conditions, the liberal state in the heart of mankind never dies. To erase the idea of liberty as an ideal and directing principle is impossible. Even dictators, eager to warm the hearts of their suffering nations for war and other collectivist purposes, pay lip service to the idea of liberty.

To restore the freedom of trade and movement of man and capital in Europe is an extremely difficult undertaking. But if the European nations really want to substitute peace for war and union for nationalism and conflict, there is no other way but to restore the freedom of the individual. It is true, restoration of the liberal system of society presently not only conflicts with the collectivist prejudices of the public, but also with the private interest of many individuals who in the past have gained, or are still gaining, protection and privileges from their government. The special favor groups, such as agriculture and labor, have become formidable pressure groups within our society. They are militantly organized and upon many occasions intimidate the legislature. Those members of legislature who dare to oppose them are subjected to the most infamous abuse, personal insults, and sometimes bodily danger. To take up the cause of liberty is no task for the timid. It is for the courageous and fearless, the generous spirit anxious for the advancement of mankind, the one who does not count personal costs.

To restore free trade in Europe and further the European division of labor is a task for each European legislature. No international agreement and no cooperation on the part of national governments are required. But it is necessary that governments withdraw from the economic sphere and abolish their numerous economic functions. First of all, no new privileges of any kind should be granted, and existing privileges should not be extended. For every such government regulation introduces some degree of international divergency through changes in domestic and foreign structures of production, which are afterwards difficult to readjust to the state of the international division of labor.

If we consider only the well-being of society, we must recommend that freedom of trade and the other freedoms of the individual be restored as quickly as possible. Restoration of unrestricted international competition would show its beneficial effects from the moment of inauguration. Those industries commonly exporting part of their production to other European countries would obviously be only favorably affected by this action. Many industries producing largely for local consumption and all distributive industries would be very little affected by foreign competition. The building industry and all service industries would have nothing to fear from freedom of trade.

Restoration of free importation of foreign goods, however, would hurt those industries that owe their existence to government regulations and privileges, or that are gaining from government intervention. Industries that have lived and prospered on government protection, i.e., restrictions on imports, production quotas, government licenses and subsidies, would no doubt suffer from free trade. To the extent that these industries would be unable to compete effectively with foreign industries working under more favorable conditions of production, they would have to contract or convert to more productive fields of activity in accordance with the state of international division of labor. During this period of conversion, unemployment of labor and capital will arise. On the other hand, the existing export industries will experience shortages of labor and capital.

The difficulties of conversion as far as labor is concerned will be kept at a minimum, provided the workers discharged are at liberty to engage in any trade they are prepared and trained to exercise. Therefore, they should be free to assume any trade or work they please. The present laws on apprenticeship, professional organizations and qualifications, examinations and other official requirements, all imposed to restrict competition and protect those holding jobs from the competition of newcomers, must immediately be repealed. Such a society would take the necessary but painful effects of recuperation in stride.

And yet we recommend that freedom of trade should be restored only by slow gradations. Though just those industries that enjoyed government protection and privileges to the detriment of society would suffer by a return to freedom of trade, the liberal philosophy requires us to give due consideration to every minority, indeed to each individual. The difficulties of conversion for labor and enterprise and the losses in specific and fixed capital which a readjustment would necessarily cause to their owners make it advisable, on grounds of equitable regard for the minority, that a period of warning should precede the readjustment, and that such readjustment should proceed in several stages. However, "equitable regard" does not mean that the return to free trade could not be achieved within a period of one decade.

Abolition of institutional barriers which prevent the free movement of workers among the free countries of Europe is another important task for the achievement of a free Europe. In the absence of migration barriers, workers would move from comparatively overpopulated areas to the comparatively underpopulated. A country is overpopulated if the capital invested per head of population is smaller and the consequent productivity of labor lower than in the country of comparison. That is to say, the wage rates are lower. On the other hand, a country is underpopulated if its wage rates are higher than those of another. The United States, for example, is comparatively underpopulated when compared with Germany where the wage rates are lower. But Germany is underpopulated when compared with Italy, Poland, or Russia. Consequently, under freedom of migration, the workers in the latter countries would be eager to migrate to Germany, while hardly a German would choose to migrate to these countries with lower wage rates.

But wage rates and standards of living are not the only factors that determine where people will choose to live and work. Language, religion, descent, and family ties each play an important role. Even in the complete absence of institutional migration barriers those factors tend to counteract the migration pressure caused by differences in wage rates and standards of living. This fact induces us to conclude that the European nations, on the way to freedom and union, could permit immediate freedom of migration without having to anticipate any great difficulties of readjustment. The flow of migrating workers from comparatively overpopulated countries, especially from Italy, to countries with higher wage rates, such as France and Germany, would probably proceed at first at a slow rate, accelerating as soon as linguistic, religious, and family ties with the new country are established. However, we feel moved to repeat that such an inter-European migration depends not only on the complete absence of national migration barriers but also upon the removal of many institutional barriers, such as the numerous government restrictions on professional and business competition and, above all, housing and rent controls. Governments must refrain from all economic intervention and discrimination based on language, creed, or nationality.

The return to freedom of trade and migration of men and capital is the responsibility of each nation. The European governments need not cooperate in this return to a free European society, nor conclude lengthy pacts and agreements on unification. As a matter of fact, it even seems advisable that they refrain from such cooperation and merely liquidate numerous economic and discriminatory functions on their own. Government cooperation would probably take the form of simultaneous and coincident action. But this would only render the process of readjustment less smooth than the independent abolition of government barriers. Furthermore, international agreements on the repeal of trade restrictions proceed from the erroneous notion that the country abolishing its barriers sacrifices welfare and prosperity for the benefit of foreign countries. This popular notion disregards the fact that a country which abolishes its barriers stands to gain by far the greatest benefit from the absence of trade barriers. Freedom of imports benefits the importing country which may buy goods it cannot produce at all, or not as cheaply, or not as well. Exports, which are merely payments for goods imported, are the purchase price for imports.

Another reason for each nation to abolish trade and migration barriers independently is the lesser likelihood of measures of retaliation if certain governments should continue to restrict free trade. Among contemporary governments there seems to be a common practice of attempting to compensate a foolishness committed by one country with foolishnesses of other countries. If one country erects a wall of restrictions by which it mainly hurts itself, we in turn begin to build an even higher one to hurt ourselves. This is nonsensical! If one country is bent on committing suicide, why should we? All we can do is demonstrate the advantages of freedom.

Freedom and union for the people of Europe solely depend upon their political and economic ideas. When this will be realized, we do not know. But we do know that the day will come, for the idea of liberty never dies in the heart of mankind.

Conclusion

Our interventionist age is an age of international conflict.

Governments motivated by socialist and interventionist ideas conduct policies of "welfare" and protection through tariffs, licenses, quotas, exchange controls, and many other welfare measures, all of which promote economic nationalism. Foreign trade becomes increasingly political. Changing political conditions and positions of powerful pressure groups in the national parliaments determine foreign trade and the opening or closing of foreign markets. But through intervention a government hurts not only the vital interests of its own people, but also those foreign nations that take part in the world cooperation and division of labor. Thus, international conflicts arise. Agricultural and industrial protectionism, for example, lead to restriction of imports which cause domestic prices to rise and depress world market prices. Since nearly all governments resort to such policies for the sake of domestic protection or retaliation against foreign policies of protection, world trade is in a state of perpetual readjustment and world relations become increasingly erratic and chaotic.

Mankind is yearning for international cooperation and peace. Men dream of a united Europe as an assurance of the preservation of Western civilization. Many efforts of unification are initiated by prominent statesmen and intellectual leaders and some gain public support. Governments adopt the suggestions and endeavor to realize them. Institutions are set up for the purpose of facilitating unification plans. But again and again the numerous discussions and top-level programs for unification prove fruitless and in vain. For some mysterious reason the obstacles to true unification seem insurmountable.

317

What is the reason for this failure? Why do the institutions set up for the purpose of unification fail so dismally in their objective? Why can the dream of European unification with its substantial public support not be realized? The answer is simple. Socialism and the welfare state irreconcilably conflict with the principle of unification. Where there are policies of government welfare, there can be no interstate unification. And where people wish to unite, there can be no government interference with the market economy. This is the crux of the problem of unification.

The principle of central planning and public welfare requires government to maintain wage rates by limiting the labor supply through immigration laws and other institutional restrictions. The principle of unification, however, assumes free mobility of labor that brings about equalization of labor productivity and wage rates.

The principle of central planning and public welfare requires government to raise costs of production for purposes of social welfare, security, and other social objectives. These measures depend for their effectiveness upon complementary trade and migration barriers. The principle of unification, however, requires government to abolish all barriers and refrain from raising costs of production so that the competitive position of domestic industries will not be endangered.

The principle of central planning and public welfare requires government to protect depressed industries from foreign competition. Unification, however, presumes absence of protective barriers.

The principle of central planning and public welfare requires government to expand credit, inflate the money supply, and control foreign exchange transactions. Unification, however, presumes stable and freely convertible currencies.

The principle of central planning and public welfare requires government to control capital investments and capital movements. Emigration and "flight" of capital are prohibited. Unification, however, presumes freedom of migration for capital.

It is obvious that the welfare state is incompatible with interstate unification, which requires the European nations to make a momentous decision. They must choose between government welfare and interstate unification. They cannot have both.

A realistic appraisal of Europe's problems and in particular the problem of unification cannot fail to fill us with deep pessimism. The majority of Europeans believe in socialism or the welfare state. And all European governments are committed to policies of interference with business. It is obvious that there can be no unification.

But communism is moving rapidly in its conquest of the world and its vanguards have reached the heart of Europe. The future of Western Europe is laid bare and the ways of life which are the heritage of Western man are at stake. Unification is a matter of vital necessity. "Unite or perish" is the watchword of Europe. Individual liberty or slavery is the choice.

Index

321

operation, 246
political unification of, 245
planning, 260
prices of, 242
quotas, 242
Schuman and, 235
social justice and, 246
socialization, 248
subsidies and, 243
tariffs and, 244
taxation, 262
transportation and, 244
wages and benefits, 243, 256
war and, 250
Collective bargaining, 127
Collectivism
    consumers and, 149
    control and, 150
    defense, 140, 276
    economic, 148, 149
    humanitarianism and, 146, 147
Colonies, British, 117
Common market, 239, 244, 259
Commonwealth
    competition, 121
    cooperation, 117, 120
    economic link of, 122
    freedom and, 121
    machinery of, 116
    preference, 120
    protectionism and, 121
    trade, 122
    see also, England
Communication
    control of, 36
    German, 187n
    socialism and, 59
Communism
    challenge of, 279, 308
    dumping commodities and, 305
    French, 104
    ideology of, 270
    Italian, 104
    market economy and, 30
    military preparedness against, 309
    Russian expansion and, 268
    socialism and, 101; see also, Social-
        ism
Comparative cost, Law of, 304

Competition
    American, 65
    Commonwealth, 121
    economic, 65
    European, 7, 49, 66, 71, 74, 121
    imperialism and, 79
    inter-European struggle for, 66
    war and, 81
Comte, August, 109, 112, 148
Conflict
    Coal and Steel Community, 252
    government, 285
    ideologies of, 30
    industrial federalism and, 110
    international, 149, 317
    solidarism and, 111
    see also, War
Congress
    Hague, 124, 126
    legislates depression (U. S.), 18
    Wagner Act and, 20
Conscription, 310
Constitution, Federal Union, 39
Consumption
    capital, 47
    collectivism and, 149
    production and, 242, 288
Contra-cyclical policies, 60
Control
    Australian, 10
    British, 9
    capital, 199
    central, 89
    Coal and Steel Community and,
        249, 264
    collectivism and, 150
    communication, 36
    currency, 199
    debtors, 206
    exchange, 9, 161, 207, 224, 294
    Federal Union and, 57
    gold, 19
    government, see, Government
    individuals and, 264
    industrial, 20
    intra-European payments and, 218
    lending, 206
    money, 36, 57
    national, 226, 264
    postal system, 57

64